THE NATIONAL TRUST

THE NEXT HUNDRED YEARS

THE
NATIONAL
TRUST
THE
NEXT
HUNDRED
YEARS

EDITOR · HOWARD NEWBY

THE NATIONAL TRUST

Supported by The National Grid Company plc

Phototypeset by Southern Positives and Negatives (SPAN), Lingfield, Surrey (9874)
Printed in Great Britain by BAS Printers Limited, Over Wallop, Hampshire
for National Trust Enterprises Ltd, 36 Queen Anne's Gate, London SW1H 9AS

Contents

Editor's Preface

I T HAS BEEN AN honour and a privilege to be invited to edit this book as part of the National Trust's celebration of its own centenary. From the beginning it has been my intention not to allow this volume to become self-congratulatory. While it has been only right and proper that the vision and efforts of the Trust over the last 100 years be duly acknowledged, I have encouraged the authors to look forward, in the belief that the Trust's best interests will be served by stimulating a constructive debate about the Trust's future direction, using the centenary as an excuse to take stock. The story of the Trust's past is already well-served by such books as Merlin Waterson's *The National Trust: The First Hundred Years* (1994). Moreover, the country house, often the irrational focus of attention on the Trust, is given relatively little space in this book, allowing the themes that will govern decision-making in the twenty-first century to dominate.

This approach has been enthusiastically endorsed by the senior officers of the Trust. However, I should make it abundantly clear that this book is very much the product of the authors and myself. I asked for, and was readily given, complete editorial independence by the Trust and therefore the strengths and weaknesses of whatever follows are my responsibility and mine alone.

I have encouraged the contributors to concentrate on those issues which, in their view, are of greatest importance within the topics they have been given. The book is not therefore a comprehensive assessment of the Trust's achievements over the last 100 years. Nor is it intended to be an encyclopaedic account of the many and varied challenges that lie ahead. Each chapter, in its own way, is a personal statement. The chapters have been written to stimulate debate rather than to close it. I have therefore edited them with a light touch, eliminating the more obvious overlaps presented by the first drafts and, where necessary, inserting the occasional cross-reference. However, the chapters can be read as stand-alone essays. I have not sought to impose a uniform editorial style, and if the result is a difference of tone and approach – or even the occasional contradictory viewpoint – then so be it. In this sense the book's value will be measured in the discussion it stimulates, rather than by any attempt to present an all-inclusive historical record.

It is my happy duty to conclude by offering my sincere thanks to those who have assisted in the book's production. I was persuaded to undertake this task by Lord Chorley, the Trust's current Chairman. Without in any way being intrusive he has assisted me considerably in defining the scope and structure of the book and in helping to recruit the top-quality contributions we have assembled. In the Trust's Head Office, Margaret Willes and Caroline Worledge have been indefatigable in relieving me of much of the burden of progress chasing. They have also organised the manuscript for publication and between them have been responsible for much of the editorial checking and the construction of the bibliography. Patricia Lankester, the Trust's Educational Officer, was kind enough to offer me an extensive briefing on the Trust's educational activities; and I have benefited enormously from the advice and input from Sir Angus Stirling, the Trust's Director-General.

It was hoped that Professor R.W.G. Carter of the University of Ulster at Coleraine would have contributed a chapter to this book; sadly he was taken ill with cancer and died suddenly in 1993.

Two other people, outside the Trust, also deserve my thanks. Frances Kelly, my literary agent for the last 20 years, not only assisted in the contractual negotiations, but provided her own helpful advice on how the book should be structured. Sarah Proctor, my secretary while I was at the Economic and Social Research Council, assisted at all stages of the editorial process with her customary efficiency.

*   *   *   *   *

The National Trust would like to express its appreciation of the generous assistance of the National Grid Co. plc with the publication of this book and with the associated Countryside Conference being held in Manchester.

The Contributors

Howard Newby is Vice-Chancellor of the University of Southampton. Formerly Professor of Sociology at the University of Essex, he served as Chairman of the Economic and Social Research Council from 1988–1994. His most recent books are *The Countryside in Question* and *Country Life*.

David Cannadine is Moore Collegiate Professor of History at Columbia University in New York. He is the author of many books including *The Decline and Fall of the British Aristocracy, G. M. Trevelyan: a Life in History* and *Aspects of Aristocracy: Grandeur and Decline in Modern Britain*.

Adrian Phillips is part-time Professor of Countryside and Environmental Planning in the department of city and regional planning, University of Wales, Cardiff. From 1981–92 he was Director-General of the Countryside Commission.

David R. Cope is Executive Director of the UK Centre for Economic and Environmental Development, an independent charitable research institute based in Cambridge.

Keith Clayton is Emeritus Professor of Environmental Sciences at the University of East Anglia, Norwich. He has recently written two reports published by the Countryside Commission, *Coastal Processes and Coastal Management* and *Climatic Change: implications for the English Countryside*.

Philip Lowe is Duke of Northumberland Professor of Rural Economy and Director of the Centre for Rural Economy at the University of Newcastle upon Tyne. His recent books include *Constructing the Countryside, European Integration and Environmental Policy* and *Regulating Agriculture*.

Peter Fowler is Professor of Archaeology at the University of Newcastle upon Tyne. Formerly Reader at the University of Bristol and Secretary to the Royal Commission on Historical Monuments (England), he serves on several National Trust committees. Recent books include *The Past in Contemporary Society: Then, Now* and (jointly) *Heritage and Tourism in 'The Global Village'*.

9

Gerald Cadogan is an archaeologist of Bronze Age Crete and Cyprus, and writes for the *Financial Times* on property, archaeology and heritage. He is author of *Palaces of Minoan Crete* and co-author of *The Aerial Atlas of Ancient Crete*.

Anna Pavord is the gardening correspondent of the *Independent* newspaper and associate editor of *Gardens Illustrated* magazine. Her most recent books are *Hidcote*, published by the National Trust, and *The Border Book*.

I

The First Hundred Years

DAVID CANNADINE

Introduction

The National Trust is the most important and successful voluntary society in modern Britain. There is no other conservation body remotely like it. Here are some indications of its importance and success. Its present membership is substantially above two million, which is more than the Conservative, Labour and Liberal Democratic parties combined. This means that *The National Trust Magazine* has a readership approximately equal to that of the *Daily Telegraph*, *The Times*, the *Guardian* and the *Independent* added together. As the owner of more than 590,000 acres (238,989 ha), the Trust's holdings are significantly greater than the Crown Estates, the Duchy of Cornwall, the Church Commissioners and British Coal, and they are surpassed only by the Forestry Commission and the Ministry of Defence. In addition, the Trust owns 550 miles (885 km) of coastline, 207 historic houses, 60 villages and hamlets, 8,000 paintings and a million books. No other body, private or public, philanthropic or profit-making, is so variously and so virtuously possessed. These are the results of its hundred-year history – a history that has already been twice written,[1] and which is being re-told three times in this centenary year.

Such commemoration at such a time is apt and appropriate. The National Trust has a history that needs to be better known. But while this institutional approach has great strengths, it also has inevitable weaknesses. The two histories which appeared before the Centenary were both written by employees of the Trust who had spent much of their professional lives in its service. Not surprisingly, their books were loyal, knowledgeable and well-meaning. But they were too pious and too claustrophobic in their outlook. Writing the history of the National Trust is one thing; placing the National Trust in historical perspective is another. This essay is a preliminary attempt to locate the Trust in the broader context of modern British history, in the hope of illuminating both subjects.[2] It is divided into four overlapping sections, which correspond to the different phases of the Trust's development and activity: the first, from its foundation in 1895 until 1920, when its main concern was with preserving open spaces; the second from 1914 until 1949, when it was primarily interested in proclaiming 'spiritual values'; the third from 1935 to 1970, when it was preoccupied with rescuing country houses; and the fourth, from 1965 to the present, when it has been more broadly committed to safeguarding the environment.

Preserving open spaces, 1895 to 1920

'Nine English traditions out of ten', an ageing academic observes in C. P. Snow's *The Masters*, 'date from the latter half of the nineteenth century.' Indeed, he could have been more precise and narrowed the period down to the years 1875 to 1900. Between those dates, many now-venerable British traditions were adjusted or invented, among them royal ceremonial, the old school tie, Sherlock Holmes, Gilbert and Sullivan, test match cricket, and bacon and eggs.[3] To these should be added a clutch of voluntary associations and publishing ventures, all of which have happily survived: the Society for the Protection of Ancient Buildings (1877); the *Dictionary of National Biography* (1885); the Royal Society for the Protection of Birds (1889); *Country Life* (1897); and the Survey of London and the *Victoria Histories of the Counties of England* (both 1900). As their names suggest, they were a diverse and distinguished group. But they also had much in common. For they were all concerned with recovering, preserving and celebrating various aspects of Britain's cultural and environmental heritage.[4] It is in this context that the foundation of the National Trust in 1895, and the first phase of its existence, need to be set and understood.

Despite the pomp and circumstance of Queen Victoria's Golden and Diamond Jubilees, late nineteenth-century Britain was in many ways an anxiety-ridden nation, and it was in response to such widespread feelings of uncertainty and concern that these cultural and preservationist initiatives were launched. In an era of agricultural depression, there was a well-grounded fear on the part of landowners and farmers that the countryside was being marginalised and depopulated.[5] At the same time the revelations of Charles Booth for London, and Seebohm Rowntree for York, described a lumpenproletariat impoverished and undernourished, and an easy prey to crime, vice and drink. And the faltering performance of the British economy, compared with the vigour of its German and American rivals, led to a pessimistic reappraisal of the Industrial Revolution. Instead of being seen as something which had made Britain pre-eminent as the workshop of the world, it was re-evaluated as a regrettable and disastrous phenomenon, which had brought – and was still bringing – human suffering and environmental degradation.[6] Britain may have been the heart of the world's greatest empire, but during the 1880s and 1890s, and on into the Edwardian era, there was growing concern among the educated classes that that heart was neither healthy nor sound.

This anxiety expressed itself in many different ways. Among the most important was a renewed interest in nature and history, which derived from the work of John Ruskin and William Morris.[7] Preservationists began to demand that ancient monuments and venerable buildings must be safeguarded from the builder and the speculator. Defenders of 'the landed interest' urged that the countryside should be given special treatment, and that agriculture must be protected from foreign competition. As the economic importance of the rural world diminished, its cultural importance significantly increased: witness Hardy's novels, Kipling's poems, Elgar's 1st Symphony and Lutyens's early, vernacular houses.[8] These modes of expression differed, but their message was essentially the same: the rural past was preferable to the urban present, and the contemporary English countryside was idyllic yet beleaguered. It was idyllic because, in contrast to the squalor and deprivation of the towns, it was the very embodiment of decency, Englishness, national character and national identity. But it was beleaguered because it was more than ever threatened by the forces of modernity – the last railway extensions, the first motor cars, and the ever-expanding urban frontier.

Then, as now, environmental politics was a broad church, encompassing as it did Conservative imperialists such as George Curzon and Alfred Milner, and radical socialists like Henry George. Somewhere between them came the liberal intelligentsia, many of whom played prominent parts in the foundation of the late nineteenth-century preservationist societies. Among its senior figures, such men as Henry Sidgwick and Leslie Stephen were obsessional walkers and moun-taineers, and believed passionately in the transcendent, quasi-religious qualities of nature.[9] Their views were shared by a younger generation which included C. F. G. Masterman, J. L. Hammond, Bertrand Russell – and G. M. Trevelyan and Hugh Dalton, of whom more later. Liberal politicians such as George Shaw-Lefevre and James Bryce were equally committed to the countryside: hence their extended campaign for public access to open spaces in England and Scotland, and their active involvement in the fledgling National Trust. And among the aristocracy, those who concerned themselves with the Trust in its early years tended to be renegade Whigs, such as the 1st Duke of Westminster and Lord Dufferin and Ava, or Liberal survivors like Lord Rosebery. Although it properly presented itself as a 'national' rather than as a partisan organisation, the tone of the Trust during this first phase of its history was closer to the left of the political spectrum than to the right.

As such, it merely reflected the outlook of the three founding figures – Canon Rawnsley, Sir Robert Hunter and Octavia Hill.[10] In their social origins, they were quintessentially middle class: Rawnsley had followed his father into the church; Hunter was the son of a businessman and trained as a solicitor; and Hill was descended from Robert Southwood Smith, one of the great early Victorian sanitary reformers. In public matters, they had little time for party divisions or Westminster wranglings. But Rawnsley was elected to the first Cumberland

County Council as an Independent Liberal; Hunter was described by Rawnsley as 'a sturdy Liberal from first to last'; and Hill's father had been a supporter of parliamentary reform and Corn Law repeal during the 1830s and 1840s.[11] Their conservationist priorities were similar but not identical. Rawnsley sought to preserve and protect the Lake District – where he had a parish for many years – in all its Wordsworthian purity. Hunter was an ardent supporter of the Commons Preservation Society (of which he was for a time the solicitor), and a champion of the rights of public access against assertive and over-bearing landlords. And Hill was the most famous housing reformer of her generation, who was appalled by the squalid conditions of slum life in London, and who saw open spaces as essential for the moral well-being of the working classes.[12]

Together, these three determined individuals set the tone and the policy of the National Trust during the first phase of its existence. They were decent, disinterested and high-minded, and they were sure they knew what was best for the country and for their social inferiors. They believed in self-help, hard work, individualism and voluntary endeavour. Their concept of the nation was English rather than British (not until 1931 was the National Trust for Scotland established), and with the exception of the Lake District, the properties they took over were more in the south than in the north. They were primarily concerned with preserving open spaces of outstanding natural beauty, which were threatened with development or spoliation. They were also interested in safeguarding buildings of historical importance, but this was lower on their list of priorities, and they were not especially concerned with country houses. The national heritage which they sought to preserve was natural rather than man-made, rural rather than urban. Like many of their contemporaries, they believed that the essence of Englishness was to be found in the fields and hedge-rows, not in the surburbs and slums.

On all these issues the founding triumvirate was largely in agreement. But in establishing the National Trust in the way they did, they left several questions unresolved, which have since become much debated. Was the Trust primarily concerned with preservation or with access? Rawnsley wanted to save the Lake District from trains and trippers; Hill sought to safeguard open spaces for the enjoyment of city dwellers. Was the Trust anti-landlord or pro-aristocrat? The Commons Preservation Society was by definition hostile to landowners asserting their property rights against the public. Hunter and Hill were both strongly of the same opinion. But like any late nineteenth-century voluntary society eager to establish its credentials, the Trust had sought, and secured, the patronage of some of the noblest names in the land. Was the Trust a paternal and oligarchic body, or was it a mass organisation? The founding figures had no doubt as to their answer. They ran the Trust as they saw fit, with help from friends and relatives – many of whom, during this initial period, were women. But if membership ever expanded significantly, there might come a time when this restricted way of doing things would no longer seem acceptable.

While Rawnsley, Hunter and Hill were in charge, these questions never sur-
faced. They were fully occupied in launching and establishing the Trust. The
earliest properties acquired were the cliff at Barmouth in Gwynedd and Barras
Head, Tintagel. In 1896, the Trust bought – for a mere £10! – its first historic
building, the fourteenth-century Clergy House at Alfriston in Sussex. Four
years later, £7,000 was raised to purchase a stretch of land at Brandelhow, on
the edge of Derwentwater, and soon after a further £12,000 was collected to
safeguard Gowbarrow, on Ullswater. In 1907, the Trust acquired its first
country house, Barrington Court in Somerset. But it was only able to do so
thanks to a legacy; the building was in a very dilapidated state, and for many
years thereafter, no funds were available for restoration work. It was this
acquisition which necessitated the passing of the first National Trust Act, which
empowered it to preserve 'land and tenements (including buildings) of beauty
or historic interest' for the benefit of the nation. The ordering of priorities is
again worth noting. The Act also introduced the concept that the Trust's property was 'inalienable': that it was to be held in perpetuity on behalf of the people
as a whole.[13]

The founding triumvirate were vigorous propagandists and effective fund-
raisers, but the National Trust remained a very small-scale organisation during
the first phase of its existence. That phase was effectively brought to a close with
their deaths: Octavia Hill in 1912, Sir Robert Hunter in the following year, and
Canon Rawnsley in 1920. By then, the Trust owned 13,200 acres, yielding an
annual income of £1,677, and had 713 members, whose subscriptions totalled
£532.[14] To put this in perspective, this meant that its entire holdings amounted
to little more than one reasonably sized landed estate, and that its total
membership was scarcely larger than that of the House of Commons. After 25
years, the National Trust had not established itself as an important element in
national life, national culture or national identity. It was neither the leading
conservationist body of the day, nor a serious influence on the public agenda of
the time. It lacked political connections at the very highest level. 'Of course it
might grow', Octavia Hill had shrewdly observed in 1896, 'but then it might
not.' Twenty years on, in the dark days of the First World War, that uncertainty
still remained.

Proclaiming 'spiritual values': 1914 to 1948

It did not remain for much longer. In the short term, the First World War was a
difficult time for the Trust, and its activities came to a virtual standstill. But in
the longer term, the War led to drastic changes in the context in which the Trust
operated – changes which proved greatly (and unexpectedly) to its advantage.
There was Bolshevism and Fascism abroad and, from 1918, mass democracy at
home. There was the Lloyd George Coalition, which was widely regarded as
unprincipled and corrupt. There were two Labour Governments, there was

serious industrial unrest during the 1920s, and serious unemployment during the 1930s. The demise of the Liberal Party and the break-up of the Liberal intelligentsia meant that conservationist endeavour would now be carried on by other political groupings. The 'revolution in landholding' after 1918 saw one quarter of the land put on the market, and meant that the traditional social structure of the shires was irrevocably weakened. And at the same time, the English countryside was subjected to the unprecedented blight of the motor car and the charabanc, the new surburban sprawl and ribbon development, semi-detached houses and seaside bungalows. [15]

In this dramaticaly altered political and environmental climate, the cult of Englishness and of rural decency became more appealing than ever before, and was now brought to the very centre of public affairs. One reason for this was that the dominant political figure for most of the inter-war period was the Conservative leader, and three times Prime Minister, Stanley Baldwin. Baldwin's politics were built around the avoidance of extremism, the cultivation of consensus, and hostility to Lloyd George, the press lords and corruption in public life. Although the son of a Worcestershire ironmaster, Baldwin was deeply attached to the English countryside, which he saw as the repository of everthing that was best about the English character. [16] One of Baldwin's greatest admirers was Lord Grey of Fallodon, who had been Liberal Foreign Secretary from 1905 to 1916, but who had fallen out with Lloyd George. Grey was a renowned country lover and bird watcher, and came to see Baldwin as the statesman who had delivered the nation from the 'Welsh wizard's' delinquencies. And the same was true of another of Baldwin's closest friends, Lord Halifax, who was Viceroy of India (1926–31) and Foreign Secretary (1938–40). Like Grey, Halifax was a highminded north-country landowner, who shared his belief in the close connection between rural life and 'spiritual values'.

Between them, these three men set the tone of English public life during the inter-war years, and under their moral and political leadership the cult of the countryside became more pronounced than ever before. There were renewed protests against urban encroachment and rural spoliation, such as *England and the Octopus* (1928) and *Britain and the Beast* (1937), the one written, the other edited, by the maverick conservationist Clough Williams-Ellis. The Council for the Preservation of Rural England was established in 1926, and there was a growing demand for National Parks to be set up. [17] In 1929, Longmans began to publish a series entitled 'English Heritage', with introductions by Stanley Baldwin, and in the following year Batsford launched another series called 'English Life'. Books with titles such as *The Landscape of England, England's Character, Heart of England*, and *The Beauty of England*, found ready markets. [18] In 1933–4, the BBC broadcast a series of talks on 'National Character', which were primarily concerned with celebrating rural England. And best-selling novelists such as Mary Webb and Francis Brett Young – both, incidentally, much admired by

Baldwin – waxed lyrical about the countryside, even as they lamented 'the passing of the squires'.[19]

These Baldwinite sentiments were fully shared by John Bailey, who had been connected with the National Trust from the beginning, and who became the dominant force in its affairs during the 1920s. His father was a Norwich solicitor and Norfolk landowner, and Bailey grew up with a passion for the countryside, strong religious convictions, and qualms of guilt about the wealth he would one day inherit. Like many of his generation, he was disturbed by 'the earthquake shock of the war', which meant that 'all established opinions' were now 'attacked or at least questioned'.[20] He was Chairman of the Trust from 1922 until his death in 1931, and during that time he recruited three important new men. The first was G. M. Trevelyan, Regius Professor of Modern History at Cambridge from 1929, and a personal friend of Baldwin, Halifax and Grey of Fallodon (whose biography he wrote), who was Chairman of the Estates Committee from 1928 to 1948.[21] The second was R. C. Norman (whose brother Montagu was Governor of the Bank of England), who was himself Chairman of the London County Council (1918–19) and of the BBC (1935–9), and who took charge of the Trust's Finance Committee from 1923 to 1935. The third was Oliver Brett, son of Reginald Brett, 2nd Viscount Esher, who had been something of an eminence grise in British establishment circles from the reign of Queen Victoria to the time of George V.

Like the founding triumvirate, Bailey, Trevelyan, Norman and Brett were exceptionally public-spirited men. But there were important differences. In the first place, they were much better connected with the highest echelons of public and political life: hence the appointment of Grey of Fallodon as a Vice-President of the Trust, and of both Stanley Baldwin and Ramsay Macdonald as Honorary Vice-Presidents. In the second place, they were non-partisan conservatives rather than non-partisan liberals: Bailey had stood unsuccessfully for Parliament in the 1890s; Norman had been Private Secretary to two Conservative ministers, George Wyndham and Lord Halsbury; Trevelyan gradually evolved from a pre-war Liberal into a Baldwinite Tory; and although Brett remained a lifelong Liberal, he hated Lloyd George and all his coalition stood for.[22] In the third place, they were, by birth or connection, from a higher social stratum than Rawnsley, Hunter and Hill. Norman and Bailey both married into titled families. Trevelyan was a member of the aristocracy of birth as well as the aristocracy of talent. Brett was heir to a peerage. To this quartet should be added the 2nd Marquess of Zetland who was the most well-connected, Conservative and patrician of them all. A grandee and north-country landowner, he was Chairman of the Trust from 1931 to 1945, and Secretary of State for India in the National Government from 1935 to 1940.

Led by these men, the National Trust became, along with the BBC, one of the main props to Baldwin's brand of emollient inter-war decency. It was the Prime Minister's rural nostalgia in action. Although it properly continued to present

17

itself as a 'national' rather than as a partisan organisation, the tone of the Trust during this second phase of its history was distinctly more to the right of the political spectrum than to the left. It was not just that the countryside must be preserved as the essential repository of 'spiritual values': it was also that those values were the necessary antidote to the 'base materialism' of the age – telephones, cinemas, Lloyd George, Lord Birkenhead, the *Daily Mail* and the *Daily Express*. It was these concerns which lay behind G. M. Trevelyan's two powerful pieces of propaganda on behalf of the Trust, *Must England's Beauty Perish?* (1926), and *The Calls and Claims of Natural Beauty* (1931). 'Modern inventions', the 'inexorable march of bricks and mortar', and the 'full development of motor traffic', were destroying the English countryside at an unprecedented rate. The National Trust was 'an ark of refuge, and a bulwark for the day of trouble'. And how necessary this was. 'Without vision', Trevelyan concluded, 'the people perish, and without natural beauty, the English people will perish in the spiritual sense.'[23]

These appeals met a ready response among the country-worshippers of inter-war England. As a result of its much higher profile, the Trust expanded at an unprecedented rate, greatly assisted by increasingly enthusiastic editorials in *The Times*, and by the willingness of Baldwin and Grey of Fallodon to lend their names to its efforts.[24] Some land came through benefactions: at Runnymede on the Thames in Surrey, at Sugar Loaf in Monmouthshire and at Dovedale in the Peak District. Some came through successful appeals: at Ashridge in Hertfordshire (for which £80,000 was raised), around Stonehenge (another £35,000), and in the Buttermere Valley. Lord Curzon bequeathed Tattershall and Bodiam castles to the Trust in 1926, and Ernest Cook presented Montacute in 1931. Nor was this the only evidence of expansion. Between 1920 and 1940, membership increased from 713 to 6,800, and subscription income from £532 to £5,772. Over the same period, the total acreage held by the Trust rose from 13,200 to 68,544 (5,342 to 27,739 ha), and its property income went up from £1,677 to £36,570. This represented progress far beyond the dreams of Rawnsley, Hunter and Hill. In *England Under Trust* (1937), John Dixon-Scott described a flourishing institution, confident of its mission, and enjoying widespread public support.

For Trevelyan and his generation, the Second World War spelt the end of civilisation and the death-knell of 'spiritual values'. But there was a significant growth in acreage if not in membership, and 1945 was not only a year of victory: it was also the Trust's fiftieth anniversary. As the senior survivor of the inter-war quintet, Trevelyan wielded his propagandist's pen once more, contributing an article to *Country Life* (in which he observed that 100,000 acres was 'a nice patrimony for a duke, but it is not much for a nation'), and writing the preface to James Lees-Milne's celebratory volume, *The National Trust: A Record of Fifty Years' Achievement* (1945). Trevelyan was also at the centre of the Trust's jubilee appeal, and donated to it the royalties from his *English Social History* – a book which was appropriately suffused with 'spiritual values' and rural nostalgia.[25] In addition, he persuaded Hugh Dalton – like Trevelyan a pre-1914 Liberal, but now Chancellor of the Exchequer in the post-war Labour Government – to match the public subscription pound for pound with a government grant, the first such gift the Trust had ever received. As a result, £120,000 was raised, and by 1950 membership had reached 23,403, and the Trust's holdings stood at 152,500 acres (61,715 ha).[26]

The retirement of Zetland as Chairman in 1945, the death of Stanley Baldwin in 1947 and the resignation of Trevelyan as Chairman of the Estates Committee in 1948, effectively brought this second phase of the National Trust's history to a close. It was a phase which may be described as élitist, paternal, and culturally and politically conservative. John Bailey believed that 'a class of cultivated intelligent people' was best able to decide what was good for everybody else, and in insisting that the Trust should put preservation before public access, he was holding fast to that conviction.[27] Whether the founding triumvirate would have expressed their unanimous agreement is a moot point. But during the inter-war years, this Baldwinite view of conservation enjoyed support on the liberal left as well as on the liberal right. Among senior figures in the Labour Party, those with patrician aspirations (Ramsay Macdonald and Hugh Dalton), and those with patrician ancestors (Noel-Buxton and Stafford Cripps), were frequently to be found expressing their public support. In 1935, Hugh Dalton had described the Trust as embodying 'practical socialism in action', and he reiterated this opinion in government eleven years later.[28] By then, however, the Trust's priorities had changed decisively and dramatically.

Rescuing country houses, 1935 to 1970

It is only in retrospect that the third phase in the Trust's history may be dated as having begun during the mid-1930s. Quite by chance, the very year that Hugh Dalton had written in praise of the Trust's 'practical socialism' saw the beginning of a new and very different policy, concerning the acceptance and preservation of country houses, which for a time would come to be – and would come to be seen – as its prime task and justification. To be sure, the Trust had always been interested in preserving buildings of historical interest and architectural importance. But they had been of varied size and use, and safeguarding places of outstanding natural beauty had always been its highest priority. It was pure coincidence that the National Trust and Death Duties had come into being within a year of each other. By the early 1930s, the Trust possessed only two country houses: Barrington Court, which was dilapidated and let, and Montacute, which had no furniture. And they were both unexpected acquisitions, the result of benefactions which the Trust had felt unable to refuse; there was no endowment in either case, and their acceptance did not reflect a coherent or concerted country house policy. There was none.

Such a policy tentatively emerged after Philip Kerr, 11th Marquess of Lothian, had addressed the Trust's annual meeting in 1934, and expressed his fears for the future of country houses in Britain. The matter was taken up by the Trust, which devised the Country Houses Scheme, and parliamentary legislation passed in 1937 and 1939 made it possible for owners to transfer their houses to the Trust, by gift or bequest, along with appropriate endowment for their upkeep. Provided there was adequate public access, there would be generous tax concessions on transfer, the Trust would maintain the house in perpetuity, and the former owners would be allowed to remain in occupation as tenants.[29] As a result, the Trust set up a Country Houses Committee, which was to be responsible for vetting potential donors and their properties. Its chairman was Oliver Brett, now 3rd Viscount Esher, and its secretary was the young James Lees-Milne, whose father was a Worcestershire squire. But there was little by way of immediate response. Inconclusive negotiations were begun with Lord Methuen (Corsham Court), Sir Henry Hoare (Stourhead), and Lord Sackville (Knole). But Sir Geoffrey Mander was the only owner to give his house (Wightwick Manor) to the Trust in 1937, and Lord Lothian was the first to bequeath his (Blickling) in the following year.[30]

This was a very small beginning: indeed, from July 1938 to March 1941, the Country Houses Committee did not meet. But the scheme was given an unexpected impetus by the Second World War. Most houses were requisitioned, and servants were called up. The aristocratic way of life seemed doomed. Evelyn Waugh wrote *Brideshead Revisited*. And the Labour Government of 1945–51 brought high taxes and socialist legislation which seemed to portend 'social revolution'.[31] In fact, it was Hugh Dalton, the Chancellor of the Exchequer, who in 1946 set up the National Land Fund, which was empowered to compensate the Treasury if it accepted land in lieu of Death Duty payments, and these provisions were subsequently extended to cover historic houses themselves, and also their contents. All this led to a massive increase in the number of houses conveyed to the Trust, some directly transferred by gift or bequest, others passed on by the Treasury. Between 1940 and 1949, there were 31 (including Blickling, Wallington and Knole); between 1950 and 1959, there were 34 (including Penrhyn Castle, St Michael's Mount and Waddesdon); and between 1960 and 1969, there were 13 (including Anglesey Abbey, Shugborough and Felbrigg). Within 30 years, the Trust had thus acquired 78 country houses from the old landed élite.

This new activity effectively eclipsed and superseded the Trust's inter-war championship of 'spiritual values'. But as with each phase of its history, there were broader forces at work which also influenced its changing policies. The men who had set the public agenda and dominated the Trust during the 1920s and 1930s had passed from the scene: Baldwin was very much out of fashion and out of favour, and Trevelyan would soon follow him. Dalton and Cripps, both members of the Labour Government, were arguably the last two politicians to believe in 'spiritual values' (indeed, Mrs Dalton sat on the Trust's Executive Committee). To be sure, love of the countryside remained strongly-felt: this was, after all, the era of *The Archers* and R. F. Delderfield. But the post-war world was one of Welfare State experimentation, and of unprecedented material improvement. In Britain as elsewhere, growth and modernisation were high on the political agenda. Neither Harold Macmillan ('you've never had it so good'), nor Harold Wilson ('white-hot technology'), were much concerned with 'spiritual values'. In the era of James Bond, the Profumo scandal, and the 'affluent' and 'permissive' societies, such sentiments were now at a discount.

In a sense, then, the unexpected success of the Country Houses Scheme gave the post-war National Trust a new purpose and justification, at a time when it very much needed one. And this cause was eagerly taken up by the new men in charge, who were as committed to safeguarding country houses as their predecessors had been to safeguarding the countryside. The 28th Earl of Crawford and 11th Earl of Balcarres, who was chairman from 1945 to 1965, knew about this 'national tragedy' first hand, having been obliged to abandon his house at Haigh, near Wigan.[32] Lord Esher, now the senior survivor, found no difficulty in adapting to these changed priorities. They were supported in their work and their views by the 6th Earl of Rosse, who chaired the Historic Buildings Committee from 1954 to 1969, by the 9th Earl de la Warr, who became chairman of the Estates Committee in succession to G. M. Trevelyan, and by the Duke of Wellington, Harold Nicolson and Vita Sackville-West.[33] In the long perspective of the Trust's history, this was aristocratic oligarchy at its apogee. Even Nicolson was a touch embarrassed by this blue-blooded excess:

> In the morning we had the Historic Buildings Committee of the National Trust. We have a new member, the Earl of Euston. You know I am always rather worried that this committee, which actually decides whether we take a house, is composed entirely of peers. Well, we are now to have a man called Mr John Smith. When his name was put up, Esher said, 'Well, it's a good thing to have a proletarian name on the Committee – anybody know the man?' 'Yes', said Lord Euston, 'he is my brother-in-law'.[34]

The fact that there were so many aristocrats involved with the Trust at a time when it was concerned with preserving so many aristocratic houses was hardly coincidence. What did these people think they were doing? Many of them were as public-spirited as their predecessors; but their social vision was much narrower, more exclusive. The Duke of Wellington was 'firm, precise, sneery and offensive'. Vita Sackville-West 'hated' the Beveridge Report, 'la populace' in general, and most aspects of the modern world. Harold Nicolson was a self-confessed snob, knew nothing about the lives of ordinary people, was equally ill at ease in the suburbs and the slums, and shared his wife's hatred of the lower orders.[35] Even more reactionary was their friend James Lees-Milne, whose dislikes included businessmen, politicians, and all members of the middle and lower classes. As Secretary to the Trust's Country Houses Committe, his mission was to preserve these 'secular shrines' from twentieth-century barbarism. As he candidly admitted, his priorities were the country houses, their traditional owners, and then the National Trust – in that order of importance.[36]

Notwithstanding their strong sense of public duty, it seems clear that these men sought to inflate the sectional interests of their class into the national interests of their country. It is pointless to speculate whether the founding triumvirate or the inter-war Baldwinites would have 'approved' of these changes in the Trust's policies: in the 1890s and 1900s, and even in the 1920s and 1930s, the prospect of country houses disappearing in large numbers was so remote that there is no way of knowing what they would have thought of it. Inevitably, and rightly, the Trust has adjusted its preservationist priorities and redefined the 'national heritage' in every generation. But there was a marked contrast between the anti-landlord feelings of Sir Robert Hunter and Octavia Hill, and the superior sense of class-ridden anxiety of the Lees-Milne generation. In 1881, the then Lord de la Warr was taken to court by the Commoners of Ashdown Forest, whose customary rights he was infringing.[37] Seventy years later, his successor was a pillar of the National Trust. Here was a measure of how much both the Trust and the aristocracy had changed. The earlier concerns which had animated the leading lights of the Trust – the well-being of the working classes, or the nation as a whole – were not shared by this new generation of patrician zealots and country-house addicts.

Despite the Trust's oft-repeated refusal to accept them, some of the earliest houses were inadequately endowed, and others became so as the costs of upkeep and restoration rose. Opening times were very restricted: sometimes only fifty days a year, and they were 'settled as far as possible to suit the donor's convenience'.[38] And initially the number of visitors was very small: even at the first opening of Blickling, it was scarcely a handful. For the Trust, the sudden acquisition of so many houses was a massive burden, which required substantial administrative restructuring. But as a proportion of the total country-house stock of the nation – variously estimated at between five hundred and five thousand – it was in fact relatively small. Indeed, with the exception of Blickling, Knole, Petworth and Hardwick, few of the nation's greatest houses came the Trust's way.[39] At different times, there were negotiations concerning Longleat, Harewood, Althorp, Holkham, Woburn and Arundel; but nothing came of them. Boughton, Chatsworth, Alnwick, Blenheim and Belvoir also remained in private hands. The very grandest aristocrats were usually able to hang on to their mansions (or demolish them). Most of the Trust's country houses came, predictably, from the poorer survivors of the old landed class.

The fact that many of these houses were endowed with land helps explain why the Trust's holdings more than doubled in this period, from 152,500 acres in 1950 to 328,502 in 1965. The growth in membership was even more sensational: from 23,403 to 157,581 during the same time. And after a slow post-war start, the number of visitors, both to beauty spots and to 'stately homes', increased beyond the wildest expectations. As a result, the 'preservation versus access' debate acquired a new intensity. Nor was this the only problem which arose during these years. Despite the sum raised at the Jubilee appeal, and the increase in income from members' subscriptions and visitors' entrance fees, the Trust's finances were far from secure, as expenditure on maintenance and administration consistently outstripped income.[40] In addition, Harold Wilson's Labour Government of 1964–70 was conspicuously less well disposed towards the Trust than that of Clement Attlee.[41] Moreover, the gap was inexorably widening between membership and management. In terms of its size, the Trust had become a mass organisation. In terms of its structure, it was a self-perpetuating, aristocratic oligarchy. Sooner or later, these problems were bound to come to the surface, and these contradictions would have to be resolved. In 1965, the 8th Earl of Antrim succeeded Lord Crawford as Chairman. These problems, and these contradictions, were very soon upon him.

Safeguarding the environment, 1965 to the present

The appointment of Lord Antrim, another hereditary peer who had previously been Chairman of the National Trust for Northern Ireland, was a vote for continuity over change. But the context in which the Trust was operating soon started to shift once more, as proliferating preservationist movements began to assume new forms and espouse new policies, and as the consciousness of conservationists was raised around the world to unprecedented altitudes.[42] Inspired by books such as Rachel Carson's *Silent Spring* (1962), disillusioned with the obsessive pursuit of economic growth, convinced that small was both better and beautiful, and anxious about world wildlife and the future of the rain forests, a new environmentalist movement came into being, concerned as much with animals as with the countryside, and with global rather than national issues. Hence the advent of radical conservationist politics, involving demonstrations, protest marches and other confrontationalist methods, as espoused by Greenpeace, the Friends of the Earth, the animal liberationist movement and the League Against Cruel Sports. Hence Prince Charles's much-publicised concerns with global warming, the ozone layer and organic farming. Hence the recognition by politicians the world over that they must at least pay lip service to the environmentalists' agenda. And hence the gradual greening of the British government, aptly symbolised by the appointment of Anthony Crosland as the first Secretary of State for the Environment in 1974.

At the same time, there was another development, more British than international, which centred around the increasing cult of the 'national heritage'. This phrase had been around for some time, and Canon Rawnsley had used the variant *A Nation's Heritage* as the title for his book surveying the Trust's prop-

23

erties in 1920. But during the 1970s and 1980s it became much more widely used in Britain. The preservation of such antique artifacts as the *Mary Rose* became a national obsession.[43] There was a great and formative furore over the sale of Mentmore in 1977: its loss led to the reform of the National Land Fund into the National Heritage Memorial Fund which was empowered to finance further preservationist ventures.[44] National Heritage acts were passed in 1980 and 1983. The cult of the countryside and of the country house reached epidemic proportions: witness the impact of the Victoria & Albert Museum's exhibition, The Destruction of the Country House, the sensational success of Mark Girouard's *Life in the English Country House*, and the great popularity of the television adaptation of *Brideshead Revisited*. Here was unbridled (and often uninformed) nostalgia: something very different from the sentiments which had lain behind the National Trust during the first three phases of its existence. In 1991, these developments in turn received their official recognition, when the Prime Minister appointed David Mellor the first ever Secretary of State for the National Heritage.

These diverse changes in the public mood, both in Britain and around the world, naturally carried important implications as far as the National Trust was concerned. Indeed, as early as the mid-1960s, there were signs that the Trust was becoming less interested in preserving country houses. As new legislation sought to limit further demolitions, as post-war austerity receded into the distance, and as the number of visitors to 'stately homes' increased inexorably year by year, country-house living underwent a modest revival, and the apocalyptic language of the 1940s and early 1950s became less widespread.[45] And for its part, the Trust became increasingly reluctant to accept any more houses unless they were lavishly endowed with cash, investments or land, and even then, only on condition that they would be opened to the public more frequently than previous agreements had allowed for. As a result, the number of country houses which were transferred to the Trust was markedly less in the 1960s than it had been in the previous decades, and it has continued to decline still further since then: to thirteen in the 1970s, and eleven in the 1980s. In the foreseeable future, there seems no likelihood that this downward trend will be – or should be – reversed.

Meanwhile, the Trust was gradually moving towards new preservationist interests and also, in some cases, back to its earlier conservationist concerns. In 1963, it was decided to extend its protection to industrial monuments, including machinery, buildings, canals and railways. Here was a very significant change: for the whole of its previous existence, the Trust had embodied the widespread view that the Industrial Revolution had been an unmitigated disaster.[46] Now it was beginning to deem its products worthy of conservation. There was also a renewed emphasis on the Trust's traditional role as the guardian of places of outstanding natural beauty. In 1965, it launched Enterprise Neptune, a much-publicised national appeal in England, Wales and Northern Ireland, initially for £2 million, for the safeguarding of the remaining 900 miles of unspoiled but threatened coastline. Within 25 years, £13.5 million had been raised, and more than 300 miles of coastline were acquired, much of it in Devon and Cornwall.[47] During the same period, the Trust's landholdings also went up dramatically: from 328,500 acres in 1965 to 569,500 in 1990 (132,939–230,468 ha).

As if to emphasise this return to earlier priorities, the appeal director appointed for Enterprise Neptune was Commander Conrad Rawnsley, the grandson of one of the original triumvirate. For reasons which remain a source of controversy, he was dismissed in 1966. His response was to mount a campaign against the Trust, accusing it of being undemocratic and inefficient. Along with his supporters, he alleged that it was too oligarchic and exclusive in its organisation, that it did not adequately represent the opinions of its much-enlarged membership, that Enterprise Nepture had been badly bungled, that there was insufficient public access to many of its country houses, and that their former owners had been treated too deferentially. The result was an acrimonious public debate, which coincided with rumours that the Labour Goverment wished to set up an official investigation into the Trust's affairs.[48] To quell the controversy, and to forestall the inquisition, Lord Antrim set up a broad-ranging inquiry in August 1967, chaired by an outsider, Sir Henry Benson, a South African-born accountant with wide experience in business and government, to examine the Trust's finances, management, organisation and responsibilities. His committee reported within two years, and recommended sweeping reforms, most of which were immediately accepted.[49]

As a result, the Trust was transformed from an amateurish oligarchy into a responsible business enterprise. Budgetary control became more stringent, and much of the administration was devolved on to regional committees. The Historic Buildings Committee and the Estates Committee were merged into a new Properties Committee, and the post of Director-General was created to supervise the day-to-day running of the Trust's affairs. And the patrician oligarchs were replaced by people drawn from very different backgrounds. Lord Antrim, who had himself presided over these momentous changes, was the last aristocratic chairman. In 1977, he was succeeded by Lord Gibson, a life peer with interests in finance, publishing and the arts, who had himself been a member of the Benson committee of inquiry. Gibson was followed from 1986 to 1991 by Dame Jennifer Jenkins, the first woman to occupy such a prominent position in the Trust's affairs since Octavia Hill herself. In addition, she was the wife of Roy Jenkins, formerly Labour Home Secretary and Chancellor of the Exchequer, and now leader of the SDP, and she had considerable experience of business and conservation. Her successor, Lord Chorley, was a hereditary peer, but in the mould of Gibson rather than Crawford. His father had been a professor and lawyer, and a member of the Trust's Executive Committee for 45 years; he himself had moved between the worlds of accountancy, academe, business and government.

In addition, the Benson Committee urged that the Trust must become more commercially oriented, and more responsive to, and appreciative of, its membership. Accordingly, a series of new initiatives was launched: National Trust shops were established in big towns and cities; National Trust publications were produced on country houses and country matters; and a North American fund-raising subsidiary was set up, called the Royal Oak Foundation. There was also a concerted drive to increase members, partly to give the Trust a firmer basis of popular support, and partly to raise essential extra funding. As a result, membership grew from 157,581 in 1965 to 539,285 ten years later. In May 1981, membership reached one million, and by October 1990, it had doubled again. On 31 December 1993, it stood at 2,189,386. This was a sensational – almost exponential – increase, and the Trust's campaign must rank as the most successful recruitment drive ever undertaken in Britain in peace time. The fact that much of it occurred during the years of Mrs Thatcher's pre-eminence is a coincidence deserving further investigation. As is the fact that more people now carry National Trust cards than regularly worship as members of the Church of England.

In the changed and broadened context of the Trust's recent activities, the preservation of country houses no longer bulks as large as it did between 1940 and 1965. To be sure, there have been some important recent acquisitions: Dunster Castle, Erddig and Kingston Lacy by bequest; Belton, Calke Abbey and Kedleston with the assistance of the National Heritage Memorial Fund.[50] And as the exhibition devoted to the 'Treasure Houses of Britain', staged in Washington DC in 1985–6 made plain, there are still those in the Trust to whom stately homes are sacred objects. But such views carry less weight than they did, and since it now often costs tens of millions of pounds to restore and endow a country house, it seems likely that the declining rate of transfers will continue. Hence James Lees-Milne's recent lament that 'the acquisition of country houses has had its day'. 'It is', he sadly concludes, 'no use battling against the Zeitgeist.'[51] But this also means that the houses which the Trust does possess are now being treated less deferentially and more historically. Since the brilliant and pioneering restoration of Erddig by Gordon Hall, Elizabeth Beazley and Merlin Waterson, more attention has been given in other country houses to life below stairs as well as above, and to getting away from the rather formulaic interior decorations – 'sprigged cotton style' – of the John Fowler era. All this is much to be welcomed.[52]

In the Britain of the 1990s, the conservationists are simultaneously more divided and more determined than ever before. The methods and priorities of the environmentalist pressure groups and of the heritage lobby are significantly different. But together they constitute an unprecedentedly numerous and vociferous movement. And because of the Trust's changed constitution, the spectacularly enlarged membership can now exert a significant influence on its affairs in ways that would have been unimaginable (and unacceptable) to the founding triumvirate and their successors. At the annual general meeting held in 1933, Lady Corry raised the matter of cruel sports being permitted on Trust land. The chairman, Lord Zetland, ruled her out of order.[53]. In recent years, the same issue has been the subject of heated debate at the Trust's annual general meetings, of a ballot among all members, and of widespread media coverage. It continues to be a controversial and divisive matter. Whether it will be possible, in the future, for the Trust to retain the support of both the heritage lobby and the environmentalist pressure groups, only time will tell.[54] Either way, those in charge of the National Trust no longer have the power to define the 'national heritage' that their predecessors possessed in the earlier years.

Conclusion

This is a very brief survey of a very broad subject, and as such it is inevitably an over-simplified account. But there are several themes which are worth drawing out by way of conclusion. The first is the cumulative impact on the holdings and the structure of the Trust of the changes in preservationist priorities that have been outlined here. In each generation, the Trust has conserved not only similar, but also very different things, and since virtually all the lands and the artifacts are inalienable, this means that over the years, the range of its responsibilities has become increasingly diverse, and there is every reason to suppose that it will become more so in the years ahead. At the same time, the bureacracy required to cope with this expanding and proliferating enterprise has become correspondingly more extensive and elaborate. Whether the Trust will be able to continue growing in this rather Topsy-like way, and whether the appropriate administrative structure exists for it or could be devised for it, are matters which are bound to be increasingly debated in the future.

A further conclusion is that throughout the Trust's existence, those in charge of it have defined and redefined what is meant by the 'national heritage'. Successive generations evolved different definitions: liberal-intellectual; Baldwinite Tory; country-house reactionary; and environmentalist-eclectic. But they were neither arrived at, nor implemented, in a ruthlessly partisan way. In 1913, the liberal-intellectuals appointed the 1st Lord Plymouth, a former Conservative cabinet minister, as chairman in succession to Sir Robert Hunter. During the inter-war years, there was support for the Trust from certain sections of the Labour Party. In the post-war period, Lord Esher, a lifelong Liberal, worked successfully with a Catholic reactionary like James Lees-Milne. And since the 1970s, the Trust has sought to negotiate its way between the more extreme views of the heritage and the environmentalist lobbies. These balances, carefully and consciously struck and re-struck in each generation, help to explain why the Trust has always attracted support throughout the country as a whole. At no stage in its history has it been so partisan that it could not plausibly claim to be national.

Nevertheless, it is also clear that for many of its dominant figures, the National Trust was indeed the pursuit of politics by other means. To be sure, it has always presented itself as a non-political organisation, and its leading figures have rarely been fierce partisans in the conventional sense. But throughout most of its history, there has been a general presumption that the few know what is best for the many, an unspoken assumption that reflected the essentially oligarchic nature of the organisation. Moreover, the particular preservationist policies adopted in each generation have invariably been politically charged. For Sir Robert Hunter and Octavia Hill, the desire to preserve open spaces inevitably brought them into conflict with landlords. For G. M. Trevelyan, conservation of the countryside was a Liberal activity before the First World War, but became Conservative afterwards. For James Lees-Milne, the purpose of the Trust was to safeguard country houses and their occupants against the levelling social tendencies of the time. These men were not party political activists on the hustings, but they did not take up politically neutral positions. Then, as now, the definition and preservation of the 'national heritage' are activities which inescapably carry political messages.

During the most recent phase of the Trust's history, the politicisation of conservation has become significantly more pronounced. But it has been a development more noticeable outside the Trust than within. The heritage lobby and the environmentalists are highly organised groups, with their own de-mands, divisions and debates. The Trust, by contrast, seems to have been less single-minded about its own conservationist agenda since the 1970s than it was in earlier generations. This may partly be explained by the reform of its oligarchic leadership, by the increased influence of its mass membership, and by the sheer range of responsibilities which, thanks to its history, it is now obliged to shoulder. For whatever reason, the environmental eclecticism which has characterised the Trust in recent decades has been the least definite and decisive phase in its history. At a time when conservation has become more popular but more contentious than ever before, it may have been a wise decision for the Trust to try to stay above the battle. In any case, if past experience is a reliable guide, it is highly unlikely that this current phase will endure long beyond this centenary year. Indeed, it may well be that, unknown to its management and its members, a new era in the Trust's history is already beginning.

Notes

1 R. Fedden, *The Continuing Purpose: A History of the National Trust, Its Aims and Work*, 1968; J. Gaze, *Figures in a Landscape: A History of the National Trust*, 1988.

2 For other accounts which take a broader perspective, see: R. Hewison, *The Heritage Industry: Britain in a Climate of Decline*, 1987, pp.51–72; T. C. Smout, 'The Highlands and the Roots of Green Consciousness, 1750–1990', *Proceedings of the British Academy*, lxxvi, 1991, pp.237–63; P. Mandler, 'Politics and the English Landscape Since the First World War', *Huntington Library Quarterly*, lv, 1992, pp.459–76.

3 C. P. Snow, *The Masters*, 1951, p.349; D. Cannadine, 'The Context, Performance and

Meaning of Ritual: The British Monarchy and the "Invention of Tradition", c1820–1977', in E. Hobsbawm and T. Ranger (eds), *The Invention of Tradition*, 1983, pp.108–38; D. Cannadine, 'Gilbert and Sullivan: The Making and Un-Making of a British "Tradition"', in R. Porter (ed.), *Myths of the English*, 1992, pp.12–32.

4 D. Watkin, *The Rise of Architectural History*, 1980, pp.94–5.

5 D. Cannadine, *The Decline and Fall of the British Aristocracy*, 1990, pp.447–55.

6 D. Cannadine, 'The Present and the Past in the British Industrial Revolution, 1880–1980), *Past and Present*, no.103, 1984, pp.133–9.

7 M. J. Wiener, *English Culture and the Decline of the Industrial Spirit, 1850–1980*, 1981, pp.37–40, 46–63; J. Marsh, *Back to the Land: The Pastoral Impulse in England From 1880 to 1914*, 1982, passim.

8 R. Williams, *The Country and the City*, 1973, p.248; G. Cavaliero, *The Rural Tradition in the English Novel, 1900–1939*, 1977, pp.1–13; A. Howkins, 'The Discovery of Rural England', in R. Colls and P. Dodd (eds), *Englishness: Politics and Culture*, 1986, pp.62–88.

9 A. Offer, *Property and Politics, 1870–1914: Landownership, Law, Ideology and Urban Development in England*, 1981, pp.328–49.

10 G. Murphy, *Founders of the National Trust*, 1987, is the only group biography.

11 Murphy, *Founders of the National Trust*, p.98; Canon Rawnsley, 'A National Benefactor – Sir Robert Hunter', *Cornhill Magazine*, new series, xxxvi, 1914, p.239.

12 H. D. Rawnsley, 'The National Trust', *Cornhill Magazine*, new series, ii (1897), pp.245–9; E. Rawnsley, *Canon Rawnsley: An Account of His Life*, 1923, pp.107–16, 220–29; E. P. Thompson, *Customs in Common*, 1991, pp.121–6; Lord Eversley, *Commons, Forests and Footpaths*, 1910, passim; Marsh, *Back to the Land*, pp.39–59; O. Hill, *Our Common Land*, 1877, pp.1–17, 105–51, 175–206; O. Hill, 'Natural Beauty as a National Asset', *Nineteenth Century*, lviii, 1905, pp.935–41; E. M. Bell, *Octavia Hill: Pioneer of the National Trust and Housing Reform*, 1956, pp.98–108, 125–33, 144–72.

13 *The Times*, 28 June 1906, 30 November 1907; Hewison, *Heritage Industry*, p.57. Thus, although the Trust is not a public body, it does possess a unique, legally privileged position. It abrogates one of the fundamental tenets of property rights in a free market economy – namely, alienability. This means that the benefits accruing to the Trust through its properties cannot be realised by any individual group. Its legislative position remains unique.

14 H. D. Rawnsley, *A Nation's Heritage*, 1920, gives a descriptive account of the Trust's holdings immediately after the First World War.

15 J. Lowerson, 'Battles for the Countryside', in F. Gloversmith (ed.), *Class, Culture and Social Change: A New View of the 1930s*, 1980, pp.258–80.

16 Wiener, *English Culture*, pp.100–110; J. R. Vincent (ed.), *The Crawford Papers*, 1984, pp.2–3, 521,541.

17 J. Sheial, *Rural Conservation in Inter-War Britain*, 1981, passim; D. N. Jeans, 'Planning and the Myth of the English Countryside in the Inter-War Period', *Rural History*, i, 1990, pp.249–64.

18 Wiener, *English Culture*, pp.72–7; A. Potts, '"Constable Country" Between the Wars', in R. Samuel (ed.), *Patriotism: The Making and Un-making of British National Identity*, 3 vols, 1989, vol. iii, p.160–86.

19 Cavaliero, *Rural Tradition*, pp.133–46; D. Cannadine, 'Politics, Propaganda and Art: The Case of Two "Worcestershire Lads"', *Midland History*, iv, 1977–8, pp.97–103.

20 J. Bailey, *A Question of Taste*, 1926, p.1. See also J. Bailey, *Some Political Ideas and Persons*, 1921, passim.

21 D. Cannadine, *G. M. Trevelyan: A Life in History*, 1992, pp.151–67.

22 S. Bailey (ed.), *John Bailey, 1864–1931: Letters and Diaries*, 1935, pp.12–13, 39; O. Brett, *A Defence of Liberty*, 1920, pp.34, 38, 43, 46–7.

23 G. M. Trevelyan, *Must England's Beauty Perish?*, 1926, pp.9, 14, 18–20; G. M. Trevelyan, *The Calls and Claims of Natural Beauty*, 1931, reprinted in *An Autobiography and Other Essays*, 1949, pp.101, 106.

24 *The Times*, 12 June 1923, 24 August 1925, 4 September 1930, 28 February 1935.

25 Cannadine, *Trevelyan*, pp.167–77; G. M. Trevelyan, 'Fifty Years of the National Trust', *Country Life*, 12 January 1945, pp.62–4.

26 *The Times*, 30 July 1945, 2 July 1946, 30 October 1946, 19 December 1946, 17 November 1947, 12 November 1949.

27 Bailey, *Bailey*, p.69.

28 H. Newby, *Country Life: A Social History of Rural England*, 1987, pp.174–9; Weiner, *English Culture*, pp.118–26; H. Dalton, *Practical Socialism for Britain*, 1935, p.292; B. Pimlott, *Hugh Dalton*, 1985, pp.455–6.

29 J. R. M. Butler, *Lord Lothian*, 1960, pp.144–58; M. Drury, 'The Early Years of the Country Houses Scheme', *The National Trust Magazine*, autumn 1987, pp.31–4; *The Times*, 11 January 1939, 1 March 1939, 18 May 1939.

30 J. Lees-Milne, *People and Places: Country House Donors and the National Trust*, 1992, pp.1–18.

31 Cannadine, *Decline and Fall*, pp.626–33, 639–45.

32 *The Times*, 13 October 1951, 20 September 1952, 11 October 1952, 13 November 1953.

33 See Nicolson's articles on the Trust in *The Spectator*, 16 June 1944, 15 August 1947, 2 July 1948, 18 November 1949.

34 N. Nicolson (ed.), *Vita and Harold: The Letters of V. Sackville-West and Harold Nicolson, 1910–1962*, 1992, p.405.

35 D. Cannadine, *Aspects of Aristocracy: Grandeur and Decline in Modern Britain*, 1994, pp.231–7.

36 J. Lees-Milne, *Another Self*, 1970, pp.53–4, 95–7, 120–1, J. Lees-Milne, *Ancestral Voices*, 1975, pp.170, 185, 187, 214, 225; J. Lees-Milne, *Prophesying Peace*, 1977, pp.85, 105, 109, 176, 209; J. Lees-Milne, *Caves of Ice*, 1983, pp.36, 53, 167, 172; J. Lees-Milne, *Midway on the Waves*, 1985, pp.23, 39, 117, 199.

37 Eversley, *Commons, Forests and Footpaths*, pp.115–17.

38 *The National Trust and the Preservation of Country Houses*, 1947, p.3.

39 St. John Gore, 'Foreword' to G. Jackson-Stops (ed.), *National Trust Studies*, 1980, p.6.

40 *The Times*, 16 October 1948, 15 September 1953, 20 October 1954, 25 May 1956, 11 April 1957, 11 October 1958.

41 R. H. S. Crossman, *The Diaries of a Cabinet Minister*, vol. i, *Minister of Housing, 1964–66*, 1975, pp.205, 345, 540–1.

42 Newby, *Country Life*, pp.229–37; K. V. Thomas, *Man and the Natural World: Changing Attitudes in England, 1500–1800*, 1983, pp.13–16, 300–3.

43 P. Wright, *On Living in an Old Country: The National Past in Contemporary Britain*, 1985, pp.162–9.

44 Cannadine, *Decline and Fall*, p.653; A. Jones, *Britain's Heritage: the Creation of the National Heritage Memorial Fund*, 1985, passim.

45 Cannadine, *Decline and Fall*, pp.650–2; *The Times*, 20 September 1962.

46 *The Times*, 15 October 1963.

47 *The Times*, 15 October 1960, 12 October 1964, 11 November 1964, 21 April 1970.

48 *The Times*, 28 November 1966, 19 January 1967, 13 February 1967, 23 March 1967, 5 May 1967, 2 November 1967; R. H. S. Crossman, *The Diaries of a Cabinet Minister*, vol. ii, *Lord President of the Council and Leader of the House of Commons, 1966–68*, 1976, p.458.

49 *The Times*, 17 January 1969, 7 October 1969; National Trust, *Report by the Council's Advisory Committee on the Trust's Constitution, Organisation and Responsibilities*, 1969, passim; Lord Benson, *Accounting for Life*, 1989, pp.147–9.

50 Cannadine, *Decline and Fall*, pp.653–5.

51 G. Jackson-Stops (ed.), *The Treasure Houses of Britain: Five Hundred Years of Private Patron-*

age and Collecting, 1984, passim; D. Cannadine, *The Pleasures of the Past*, 1989, pp.256–71; Lees-Milne, *People and Places*, pp.219–21; *The Times*, 23 October 1992.
52 M. Waterson, *The Servants' Hall: A Domestic History of Erddig*, 1980, pp.206–28; J. Cornforth, 'John Fowler', in G. Jackson-Stops (ed.), *National Trust Studies*, 1978, pp.39–49; *The Times*, 19 June 1988.
53 *The Times*, 18 July 1933.
54 *The Times*, 18 December 1982, 29 and 31 October 1988, 23 June 1989, 18 March 1992.

II

Conservation

ADRIAN PHILLIPS

THE ORIGINS OF THE National Trust's concern with the conservation of nature and natural beauty go right back to its foundation in 1895: its first property was $4\frac{1}{2}$ acres of land on the Welsh coast. In looking at the development of the increasingly complex issues of conservation, a selective approach has to be adopted, inevitably leaving some questions unasked. However, a clear pattern emerges: from the outset, the Trust aimed to protect beautiful places through their acquisition. It learnt, perhaps too slowly, about the importance of their management. It is now far better placed to fulfil its duty towards the extraordinary rich and varied estate which it owns. But it faces novel tasks as it shoulders broader environmental responsibilities and enters its second century.

Preservation, protection and conservation

In his history of the Trust, John Gaze takes Wordsworth – his 'Patron Saint' – as the starting point.[1] He invokes the poet's memorable phrase in his *Guide to the Lakes* (1810): 'persons of pure taste deem the district . . . a sort of national property in which every man has a right and interest who has an eye to perceive and a heart to enjoy'. Others have quoted this to show the inspiration behind the British National Park movement. The Lake District, and its greatest advocate, are thus the common origins of voluntary and official efforts to protect the beauty of the countryside.

We have come to think of the National Trust as a land-owning body which has only lately raised its head above the parapet to concern itself with broader environmental issues, like agricultural legislation or planning policy – and then only because of their implications for its estate. However, in its first leaflet, the Trust declared that it was:

> not only a holder of natural scenery and ancient buildings, but it also
> does what it can to promote local interest in the preservation of any

worthy historical object or natural beauty. . . . It helps when necessary to stimulate and promote legislation on matters cognate to its aims and intentions.[2]

Indeed, in the early days it exercised this campaigning role in such diverse matters as the condition of Stonehenge (*plus ça change* . . .), the railway up Snowdon and the spread of telegraph poles. It was an advocate of a National Park in the Lake District as early as 1904. Later, however, as the burdens of its estate became pressing, the Trust took a more cautious view of its role in influencing public policy, which will be examined later.

The 1907 Act gives a clear idea of the conservation values that the Trust's early supporters wanted to pursue. As well as being concerned with buildings of historic interest, the Act also speaks of 'the permanent preservation (so far as practicable) of [the] natural aspect, features, animal and plant life' of land. Language and concepts change over time, and few today would feel comfortable with 'permanent preservation'. Yet the wording of the Trust's purposes – in particular the phrase 'natural aspect, features, animal and plant life' – could be translated into late twentieth-century eco-jargon as the conservation of habitats and species. It signals that the Trust's early leaders saw their job as more than protection of historic buildings and open spaces. Indeed, John Gaze identifies open space protection and what he rather quaintly terms 'nature conservancy'[3] as two quite distinct strands in the Trust's early work.

And, having acquired a small part of Wicken Fen in 1899, the Trust can certainly claim to have been in the nature conservation business from its formative years. Blakeney Point (1912), Scolt Head (1923) and the Farne Islands (1925) were among several important sites acquired before 1940 (by which time it owned 42 nature reserves). Pending the post-war establishment of the Nature Conservancy and the subsequent expansion in the work of the County Naturalists' Trusts (made possible by the support given by the Nature Conservancy under Max Nicholson), the Trust was the leading manager of Britain's nature reserves. Moreover, links with the nature conservation movement were strong. The Entomological, Linnean and Selborne societies made nominations to the Trust's Council from its founding. The Society for the Promotion of Nature Reserves (now the Royal Society for Nature Conservation) acted as a 'ginger group' upon the Trust. In 1922 it too joined the Council and three years later proposed to the Trust, unsuccessfully, that they set up a joint committee to co-ordinate their efforts in regard to nature reserves.

In general, though, the Trust saw nature reserves as a less important aspect of its work than saving threatened landscapes from encroachment. This was before an effective planning system was in place, and there were strong feelings about the impact of suburban sprawl upon a hitherto deeply rural countryside. In evidence to the Addison Committee on National Parks in 1929, the Trust's chairman (John Bailey) and its secretary (S. H. Hamer) spoke passionately about those threats:

> the State has hitherto taken no steps to preserve the beauty of the most exceptional features of the English [sic] landscape. Quarrying destroys famous hills; garish bungalows, housing a few people, ruin many square miles of those English downs which have no parallel elsewhere; factories and gas works and sewage stations are carelessly allowed to be placed where there is no particular reason to place them and many very particular reasons for not doing so; promiscuous advertising disfigures our fields and roadsides and even disgraces some of the most historic and beautiful spots in the country. The State looks on all of this, and . . . does nothing at present to prevent it.[4]

Bailey and Hamer argued for planning and National Parks. But their only reference to nature conservation was a few words to the effect that 'reserves of fauna and flora would probably be required'. It is hardly surprising, then, that the Trust's acquisition policy in the inter-war years was driven by a concern with areas of beautiful countryside threatened by undesirable development, while its practice in acquiring sites of nature conservation value has been described as 'somewhat haphazard'.[5]

With the privilege of hindsight, the Trust appears to have been rather slow to recognise the nature conservation value of many of its open space properties – including places of such importance for fauna and flora as the Kent and Surrey Downs and the mountains of the Lakes and Snowdonia. Perhaps the small size of its central staff and the dependence on local voluntary committees to run sites was partly to blame. However, in taking a fairly limited view about the place of wildlife in the countryside, the Trust reflected the prevailing attitude of the times. It was generally assumed that protection against building effectively maintained the *status quo* for scenery and nature. The complex relationship between land management and conservation of fauna and flora was only beginning to be understood. The appeal of nature reserves was more for protection for scientific study and the control of shooting, than as places for sensitive habitat management.

The Trust began feeling its way towards the better management of its reserves and open space properties in 1938, when it set up an Advisory Committee on Natural History and published important advice on *The Management of National Trust Properties*.[6] According to John Harvey (the Trust's present Chief Adviser on Nature Conservation), the hand of Sir Arthur Tansley, the father of modern ecology and the Trust's Honorary Adviser from 1937, may be detected here: certainly the discussion on the need for active management makes instructive reading. The report's author is severely critical of the 'misconception' that 'preservation consists in the absence of any interference whatever, that it is in fact passive and not active'. 'Too often', he complains, 'it is thought that [preservation] can be accomplished by merely leaving an area alone. Nothing is further from the truth.' The idea that downlands needed grazing or that certain woodlands required coppicing was not an easy one to put across at the time, especially on open space properties that were not classified as nature reserves. It represented a break from the implicit view that the Trust's job was merely to preserve and retain open space for the benefit of city dwellers. Yet, as Tansley observed on another occasion, 'all reserves must be managed as "habitat reserves". If they are not, they are of no use scientifically, and their scenic nature is altered and often destroyed.'[7]

Learning – too slowly – about management

The contribution made by the Trust over the period 1945–75 in securing for the nation many of the finest stretches of countryside and coast has been recounted in detail by two central figures in its post-war history, Robin Fedden and John Gaze. They show that the Trust set for itself the aim of being an enlightened landlord, and it was successful in protecting much of the visual quality of the fine landscapes that came into its care. But while there is justifiable pride in this achievement, we can now see that the Trust's understanding of the management needs of its open space and agricultural estate did not keep pace with its expanding responsibilities.

For example, the advice that was given to local committees on the conservation of fauna and flora in 1948 was largely a reissue of that first published in 1938 (see above). This may not be surprising, given the far-sighted nature of the guidance, but it does come as a shock to find it being reissued yet again – with only some very modest updating and editing – in December 1966. True, the Trust had access in the early post-war period to the advice of Tansley and a former Director of Kew, Edward Salisbury; and the Trust's Nature Reserves sub-committee did much useful work. Even so, this slender ten pages of published advice was issued four years after Rachel Carson's *Silent Spring* had shaken complacency about the place of chemicals in the environment. Also the Nature Conservancy had been around for seventeen years, with an impressive record of scientific research (though some would question the quality of its nature reserve management at that time). Yet the published message going out from the Trust's headquarter still came from far-off days of ecological innocence.

It is bad luck for the Trust that it has been pursued to the present day for management failings that were made in this period and which have since been recognised and corrected. Moreover, there is an element of being wise after the event in some of the criticisms. Scientific research in the ecological and archaeological fields, for example, has revealed the richness of the Trust's estates in ways which were not evident 20 or 30 years ago when the destructive (or neglectful) management practices were taking place. Also, some of the critics overlooked the legal and other constraints under which the Trust often has to labour. For example, shooting leases may be held over acquired land; tenants have rights, they are not always easy to control and the Trust has obligations towards them; common land (of which the Trust is an important owner) is particularly difficult to manage; and there are always limits on funds and staff. Even so, some of the criticisms must be briefly re-visited, if only to show how much progress has been made since the mid-1970s, when the Trust began to respond to the concerns.

At Wicken Fen, for example, a plan was drafted for scrub clearance in 1936 after Tansley had pointed out the need to control invasive vegetation to protect the sedge fen. However, nothing was done for many years, inviting Oliver Rackham's recent comment that the Trust had 'nearly ruined' the reserve.[8] Rackham is no less scathing in his review of the Trust's past stewardship of Hatfield Forest: 'to judge by its own publications, the Trust was only vaguely aware of what it had acquired'.[9] He contrasts the high standards of scholarship, research and attention to detail applied to the management of the Trust's historic houses with its support, in the late 1950s, for damaging replanting schemes funded by the Forestry Commission in Hatfield Forest – although he overlooks the pressures put upon the Trust by the Commission at the time.

A more wide-ranging review of the Trust's stewardship of wildlife was undertaken by Clive Chatters and Rick Minter on behalf of the British Association of Nature Conservationists in 1985.[10] They claimed that some areas of high nature conservation value in the Trust's care had been 'destroyed or seriously degraded.' Though, as John Harvey notes, some of the evidence for detrimental change is 'anecdotal', there are sufficient concrete examples in the article to demonstrate the awkward truth that there had been significant erosion of the ecological interest of a range of habitats on Trust land: woodlands, downlands, heathlands, moorland areas and historic parklands, as well as on the agricultural estate.

A reasonable conclusion is that the Trust was, for quite a long period, not devoting the care to its nature reserves and open spaces that their nature conservation value merited, and which Tansley and others had called for. Also, on land that it farmed, or in its woodlands, many of its practices (encouraged by grants, such as those from the Forestry Commission) were not greatly superior in conservation terms to those being applied to such sad effect elsewhere on farmed and forested land. Moreover, as work in the 1970s was to show, serious environmental damage was being done to popular beauty spots by visitors because of poor or non-existent management.

The pressures for change

The real test of an organisation's effectiveness is not that it never makes mistakes but that it recognises and learns from them. Though initially slowly, the Trust has listened to critics of the management of its open spaces, reserves and farmland, and has made big changes in its practices and policies. How did this come about?

The National Trust is a large, powerful body, but it is subject to pressures from public opinion generally, outside experts, statutory bodies, its membership, Council members, and of course from some of its own staff at every level. All these forces were brought to bear from the mid-1960s onwards, and helped to guide the Trust into a new perception of its responsibilities. Most, if not all, of those who worked from outside to bring about change did so while still admiring the Trust's achievements. Those who worked from within were committed to securing the highest standards in the Trust's stewardship of its estate; no doubt they were on occasion happy to read the outsiders' criticisms which were useful ammunition for the in-house campaign.

The pressures for reform first became evident through the Countryside in 1970 movement, launched with a major conference in May 1963 to coincide with National Nature Week. This did much to awaken public interest in the destruction being done to the countryside and the loss of habitats and species, and broke new ground by showing 'the way to a more positive approach to countryside planning'.[12] The second conference in 1965 led to the 1968 Countryside Act, which set up the Countryside Commission and made the protection and enjoyment of the countryside an official responsibility. The final conference in 1970 came just two years before the Stockholm Conference put environmental issues on the world agenda. The whole Countryside in 1970 movement had helped to focus concern and knowledge about what was happening to the countryside. Every organisation involved was challenged to think anew about its role. In particular, it was clear that a 'preservationist' approach to the countryside had become outdated and had to be replaced by ecologically based management.

Despite the splendid success of Enterprise Neptune, launched in 1965, did the Trust move fast enough in the 1960s to keep abreast of the new thinking? Clearly John Gaze did not think so. Implicitly he recognised that leadership in conservation land management had slipped away to the County Trusts and the Nature Conservancy Council, both of which were critical of the Trust's lack of management – or at least the lack of ecologically sensitive management – on its fast growing estate.

Initially the Trust responded to the growing interest in nature conservation by making arrangements for other bodies with specialised knowledge, such as the NCC, the County Trusts and the RSPB to manage sites of known nature conservation value.[13] There were financial attractions in so doing, but this approach was more a tactic of abdication than the shouldering of responsibility. Aware of this, in the late 1960s the Trust began to adopt what John Gaze called a 'new professionalism' in the management of its land and the fulfilment of its conservation duties. He credits the new Chief Agent, Ivan Hills, appointed in 1969 – coincidentally European Conservation Year – with helping to bring about change, assisted by the climate of greater openness in the Trust following the Benson report.

The Trust began to show a greater willingness 'to learn and profit from the ideas of others',[14] and to adopt a 'more ecumenical' approach to other voluntary bodies in the nature conservation movement.[15] A good example was the approach to the British Ecological Society in 1976 for advice on the assessment and management of wildlife interest on the Trust's lands, a development which Chatters and Minter consider a watershed. It also set out to rebuild bridges with goverment agencies, not only the well-established NCC but also the new Countryside Commission.

Landscape protection and enjoyment rather than nature conservation were the remit of the Commision. However, it, too, pressed the Trust to draw up management schemes on the properties it helped it to buy, and sought the maximum public access compatible with protecting the quality of the site. It also encouraged the Trust to adopt the techniques of visitor management and interpretation to cope with the growing number of visitors to its more popular sites and the environmental impact they caused. In 1972, it joined the Trust in looking at the management of Box Hill, Tarn Hows, Ivinghoe Beacon, Frensham Common and Kynance Cove, and how to restore habitat degraded by too many uncontrolled feet. It published the results of these experiments.[16] In 1974, to promote the new practice of countryside interpretation, it invited experts from the United States National Park Service to help prepare an interpretive plan for the Trust's Tatton Park; a similar exercise took place at Clumber Park.[17]

Encouragement from outside was the more effective because the Trust made further important staff changes during the 1970s. John Workman, a respected forester on the Trust's staff, was appointed Adviser on Woodlands and Conservation; Gaze replaced Hills in 1975; and, in 1977 the Trust appointed its first full-time Conservation Adviser, Jim Helmsley. All these signalled a new, more sensitive approach to management of the Trust's countryside estate.

Putting conservation at the centre

The full extent of the National Trust's nature conservation responsibilities was brought home in the publication in 1977 of the NCC's *Nature Conservation Review*, which showed that the Trust was by far the largest private owner of Sites of Special Scientific Interest, with 342 sites. (There are now 432 such properties in England and Wales, and 5 in Northern Ireland, covering well over 163,090 acres [66,000 ha] in all.) Perhaps for the first time, there was wide recognition in the Trust that nature conservation interests were spread right across the open spaces and farmland in its care, not only in a few defined reserves. With this base line of information to hand, the Trust could now put into effect its new commitment to ecologically sensitive management. In 1979, Trust's Council formally acknowledged the Trust's interest in nature conservation, and a biological team was set up to survey the conservation value of its holdings and advise on management.

A year later, the Trust published a statement of intent which importantly linked two ideas: the extent of the Trust's nature conservation responsibilities and the need for positive management. In 1981, the Properties Committee received a new policy paper on Nature Conservation which recorded progress and noted that the Trust now had the capacity to manage its own land much more effectively, following the recruitment of more land agents and wardens on many of the Trust's open spaces (the latter partly through the assistance of the Countryside Commission). With increasing membership and income, the Trust now felt confident enough to declare that, while it would not be reducing its links with bodies like the County Trusts and the RSPB, it would not in future expect to hand over land to them.

The 1980s saw a deepening and widening of the Trust's understanding of its unique role as custodians of much of the nation's nature and natural beauty. Five aspects in particular confirm the extent to which the Trust's attitudes and practice in respect of conservation have developed, matured and moved to the centre of its work – although they also revealed some important gaps that remain to be filled.

First, acquisition policy was reviewed in 1985. The present formulation makes clear that 'the property must be of national importance because it is outstanding for its natural beauty or historic interest'. At first sight this appears to overlook the nature conservation value of the property, but there is an illuminating commentary in a 1989 Properties Committee paper on Nature Conservation: 'the criteria presently governing acquisition emphasise the primary importance of landscape merit, whilst recognising other interests. Experience suggests that many acquisitions made on landscape grounds also have considerable nature conservation interest; indeed most of the land designated SSSI on Trust properties was acquired for landscape reasons. The converse is also likely to be true, since natural beauty is often determined by landform and the pattern of vegetation.'[18] Quite so, and one might have gone further and suggested that the attempt to distinguish between natural beauty, nature conservation value and historic interest in our man-made countryside is sometimes unhelpful: in practice, the three interests so often occur at the same place that in buying land of natural beauty the Trust will inevitably acquire much land of outstanding nature conservation interest.

Next, ecologically sensitive management has made great strides in recent years. As John Harvey has put it, 'The need for management is now accepted throughout the Trust'.[19] The 1985 and 1989 papers to the Properties Committee record important developments in policy and practice: for example the adoption of new management guidelines for broadleaved woodlands, the drive to encourage the preparation of property managment plans and the importance attached to scientific survey as a basis of management. Projects to re-establish heathland at Middlebere (Purbeck), downland restoration at Melbury and pollarding at Hatfield and Holnicote are all cited as examples of a much more active management policy. Interestingly, these papers record one aim of management on Trust properties as being to *demonstrate* good practice to other landowners.

A fuller account of the Trust's wider range of innovative policies for nature conservation was given in *ECOS* in 1988 – in reply to Chatters and Minter's critique – by Katherine Hearn, a nature conservation adviser to the Trust.[20] The author is rightly cautious that management should be based on good research and may need to be tested before it is implemented; time is needed to get it right. Even so, she reports numerous practical examples of current management initiatives which confirm the progress made in recent years.

Thirdly, the Trust has greatly improved its standards of visitor management and interpretation. It uses information (and sometimes lack of it) and car-parking capacity to influence visitor numbers in sensitive areas of countryside. It employs a wide variety of techniques, from waymarked trails to the development of tourism strategies with the tourist industry, to match visitor numbers to environmental carrying capacity. It has made a major investment in repairing eroded paths, and is currently spending more than £150,000 p.a. on paths in the Lake District alone. The Trust has been skilful in bringing such policies into place at the same time as it has adopted a more user-friendly approach to visitors in general. Even so, the Trust's Director-General fulfilled a useful public service when, in 1990 he rang alarm bells about the impact of tourism on sensitive built and natural environments[21] and sparked a lively debate that culminated in the government's tourism and environment initiative a year later.

Next, the Trust has moved to work more closely with others in the voluntary and official sectors. It has cast off its rather aloof air towards other voluntary conservation bodies and has become an active partner in Wildlife Link and Countryside Link (now merged as one body). In recent years it has agreed a formal declaration of intent with English Nature. It has also made informal alliances with the Countryside Commission – for example, in successfully seeking to persuade Parliament to safeguard privatised water company land of conservation or recreation value, or in trying, with so far rather less success, to persuade the government of the need to reform common land legislation or to adopt a strategy for the conservation of Britain's coastline. Differences of view occasionally surface with other conservation bodies, of course, but it has been shown that collaboration pays dividends, especially when the Trust's immense practical experience is harnessed to the lobbying skills of other organisations in the voluntary sector to pursue some broader aim.

That leads to the final point. The Trust has become more open in its expressions of concern about government and EC policies which threaten its ability to fulfil its role. Particularly under the Chairmanship of Dame Jennifer Jenkins (1986–91), it has spoken out on lax planning policies (especially during the time that former Trust Council member, Nicholas Ridley, was Secretary of State for the Environment), the 'creeping suburbanisation' of parts of the countryside, aspects of agricultural policy and the Government's plans for an expanded road-building programme. And, while presenting its concerns in the context of its responsibilities as owner and manager, the Trust has, as we have seen, been ready to join forces with others who adopt a more overtly campaigning style.

The early years of the next century

As part of the centenary activities, the Director-General set up a Countryside Review Group in 1992 to develop a 'contemporary interpretation' of the Trust's role in the countryside and the policy and management guidance needed to achieve this. This is a welcome and timely initiative: welcome, because it demonstrates the Trust's capacity for healthy self-enquiry; and timely because the challenges facing the Trust on the conservation front have never been greater.

These challenges, which are developed further in later chapters, will have a major impact on the Trust's ability to discharge its conservation role. As well as all the internal ones of resources and organisation, four issues in particular seem likely to dominate the Trust's thinking about its countryside properties in the foreseeable future.

Agriculture

Dealing with surpluses will remain at the centre of European and national agricultural policy. There will be a continuing debate about the balance between reducing output per acre, or reducing acres of output, and around the proper role of diversification. This will present a very different kind of challenge on the lowland agricultural properties (many of which were originally secured as endowments for the historic houses to which they were attached), and on the upland farms, mainly in the Lake District, where farming has been seen as the way to maintain the landscape.

In the former, the challenge to the Trust will be to apply the highest standards of environmentally sensitive management on farmland: Trust ownership should be synonymous with the successful integration of environmental care and productive farming (though the limitations imposed by tenancy agreements may constrain or delay progress). Countryside Stewardship, Environmentally Sensitive Area (ESA) payments, set-aside, etc., offer the Trust innovative funding through which it can protect, or re-create conservation interest on farmland.

In the upland estate, the challenge is more fundamendal. Though there are good and bad years, the long-term trend is towards upland farming becoming more economically marginal. Environmental support through ESAs may help, but the pressure is on the hundred or so Trust tenant farmers in the Lake District. We return to this issue at the end of the essay, but it is becoming increasingly clear that the Trust, like many other bodies, cannot much longer postpone the need to face up to some awkward questions about the future of hill farming and the landscape it has created.

Leisure and tourism

The spirit that moved the founders – a belief in beautiful places being available to all as a national birthright – is as relevant in 1995 as it was in 1895. However, the practical implications are of a wholly different order. The Trust will be challenged as never before to find ways to reconcile its duty to protect, and its duty to provide the public with access to, our finest coast and countryside.

Perhaps the biggest single task is that of maintaining the landscape fabric under the pressure of boots (and sometimes hooves and bicycle wheels). The techniques for combating erosion of paths are generally known, from pitching to boardwalks. But the *scale* of the work which needs to be done is formidable. In the Lake District and Snowdonia, Trust appeals have recently been mounted to raise funds for the management of these over-loved landscapes. There is no prospect of relief as the work that needs to be done stretches away into the indefinite future. The Trust can surely argue that, in maintaining access to nationally important landscapes for which it cannot – by and large – charge, it should be entitled to look to more generous, long-term financial support from the government, not only as at present through the Countryside Commission but also from the National Park authorities.

Threats from outside

Land that is held inalienably by the Trust is protected from the direct impact of development as securely as any land in Britain. But it is still under threat. There is the impact of neighbouring development, with its noise, visual disturbance and so forth. Such development can also affect wildlife on Trust properties, as when ecological 'corridors' or 'reservoirs' that adjoin the site are lost. Its properties may also be assailed from above – by low-flying aircraft, for example – and from below – such as falling water-tables. On a larger scale, all the Trust's countryside work is put at risk by pollution, even climate change, and some by the prospect of sea level rise. The Trust must therefore be active in the planning system and collaborate with conservation partners at local, national and even international levels to address broader environmental issues.

Sustainability

The emergence of this concept, for all its present woolliness, provides a unifying framework within which the Trust could respond to the foregoing and other challenges. Sustainability requires that decision-making adopt inter-generational and international perspectives; it incorporates the idea that human demands upon the environment should not always be met, and must sometimes be constrained, in the interests of the environment; it requires that economic and ecological considerations be brought together; it establishes the significance of the conservation of biodiversity; and it recognises the importance of ethical values in managing the environment. Sustainability has big implications for the Trust, both in the management of its estate and in the arguments it deploys in its dealings with others.

The common theme is that the National Trust cannot cope satisfactorily with these pressures, and respond to the challenge of sustainability, only by being reactive; it has to take a proactive stand. This has been recognised in setting up the Countryside Review Group, which is actively engaged in promoting a forward-looking debate. This includes the identification of key objectives for the conservation of the countryside, which will guide the Trust over the next one hundred years. As a contribution to this debate, one hopes to see the following issues being addressed:

1 Promote a unified view of conservation

The Trust has not always been well served by a tendency to value the country-side separately for its scenic, nature conservation and heritage qualities. It is easy to see why there are separate disciplines, government agencies and legislation for each of these, but the Trust does best when it takes a holistic view of the coast and countryside in its care.[22] Much of the history recounted in the earlier part of this chapter has been about how nature conservation was eclipsed by a limited view of the countryside as scenery, or treated as relevant only to certain parts of the Trust's land. Latterly, however, it has beeen brought much closer to the centre of land management practice (there are some similarities here with the Trust's management of archaeology, where much progress has also been made). For the future, the Trust needs to reinforce its commitment to two principles.

First, it should take an integrated view of what it aims to conserve in the countryside. In practice this means that nature conservation is not an incidental part of a policy driven by a concern with aesthetic considerations, but is to be thought of as an essential element in the concept of 'natural beauty' (as it is defined in National Parks and countryside legislation); this should come through in all aspects of its acquisition and management policy. But it also means that a balance must be kept: there will be occasions, for example, when the Trust will need to ask itself whether the nature conservation advantages of fencing moorland are not outweighed by the landscape impacts.

Secondly, it should recognise nature conservation as a concern across all its coast and countryside properties. The Trust could do more to emphasise that it does not regard nature conservation as something to be achieved through site

43

safeguards at specified locations, but as an aspect of all land management. It should involve reconstruction and re-creation as well as the protection of habitats and landscapes, and include its farmed estates as well as reserves and open spaces.

2 Further the commitment to management

The Trust is now wholly committed to active management to achieve conservation and to cope with visitor pressures on the countryside. However, the process needs to be taken further.

Management planning ensures that all the qualities of each site are identified, and that internal and outside expertise are used in deciding how the land should be managed. Properly done, management planning also secures the support and involvement of neighbouring landowners and public and voluntary bodies – it brings them 'on side'. *All* the Trust's countryside and coastal properties now need up-to-date, ecologically sensitive management plans – as, for example, is the case on all 125 RSPB reserves.

Management planning is not a one-off exercise, but a way in which managers can achieve a consistent approach towards agreed objectives. This is particularly important as the managers of Trust sites are moved from time to time. Plans should be formulated from baseline data (including photographic records). They should also introduce monitoring programmes so that managers can know the consequences of policies they adopt.

The priorities are these

- expand training in the preparation of management plans;
- give flexible guidance on the form of management plans;
- advise on how to incorporate environmental considerations into farm management and tenancy agreements (Sherborne estate's farm and environment plan could be a model);
- put in place monitoring programmes; and
- set up an information system on the status of management plans on all Trust properties.

3 Clarify the role of the National Trust as an advocate

As this essay shows, in the early days the Trust was an active campaigner for what we would now call environmental causes. This practice declined as the Trust became increasingly involved in the ownership and management of land. Not only was there little spare energy and time to engage in such activites, but to do so might have put in jeopardy the Trust's generally close relationship with the government. Also the Trust, it has been said, enjoyed a 'sort of hallowed status that the Church of England used to possess, in that opposition to the Trust would seem at once sacrilegious and unpatriotic'. And 'to preserve this status, the Trust uses its influence judiciously and assiduously avoids the image of a pressure group'.[23]

Leading spokesmen for the Trust continue to emphasise that the Trust's purpose is the permanent protection, through ownership and management, for the benefit of the nation, of lands or buildings of beauty or historic interest. But, as we have seen, it has in fact been increasingly prominent in recent years in debates on current environmental issues, such as those on agriculture, planning and roads. Though it is not difficult to reconcile these two positions, perhaps the time has come to clarify how, and why, the Trust engages in such advocacy, especially as there is understandably some concern within the Trust that it might drift into becoming a campaigning organisation.

Both as the largest landowner in Britain and because of its place as a national institution with a vast membership of concerned individuals, it is inconceivable that the Trust would remain silent when faced with government policies that directly affect its ability to ensure permanent protection of its estate. The entitlement to speak out on such matters is enshrined in the National Trust Acts, where it is given the primary purpose of 'promoting' its interests.

The ever-greater complexity of environmental issues, and the way that they bear on the day-to-day business of land management, means that the National Trust is going to find itself seeking to influence public policy across a wider range of issues. Energy policy, transport policy, marine pollution and Britain's attitude to global environmental problems are all examples of topics on which the Trust will need a view as the millennium approaches, even if these would have been thought inappropriate for its attention ten years ago. But always its advocacy will be most effective if it bases its arguments on its unique role as the premier steward of Britain's countryside and coastal heritage.

Moreover, the National Trust can develop a different kind of advocacy, that of 'advocate by example'. It already sets out to adopt the highest standards for itself; it might now begin to use this record as the foundation upon which to promote (tactfully, of course) the adoption of high standards by others. The Trust has much to learn (it is taking advice from the RSPB on bird habitat management in Wales, for example) as well as to teach, but in many areas it could now set out to present its conservation management as a template against which others, including its immediate neighbours, might measure their own performance. With such a vast area of coast and countryside in its possession, the Trust already holds a significant proportion of the finest British countryside and – providing it adopts, and adheres to, exemplary standards of management – it is well placed to demonstrate a range of management techniques relevant to many other landowners in the countryside.

4 Be innovative in the area of sustainability

If such a role is developed, it will become all the more important that the Trust applies to the management of its estate the very highest environmental standards. This means that the conservation of nature and natural beauty as traditionally understood is no longer sufficient: the National Trust should also be among the leaders in demonstrating sustainability. The appointment of the Trust's Environmental Audit Adviser is an indication that this is already the course upon which the Trust is embarked.

Examples of innovation for sustainability include the use of less polluting ways of moving visitors on National Trust properties, or of encouraging them to travel to these by walking, cycling or public transport. It should adopt clean technologies for waste management, energy efficiency and better water management. This has begun; for example, the Trust has installed a reed-bed treatment of sewage at Dudmaston, an anaerobic digester for animal manures at Styal and a dry compost toilet system at Ebworth, in the Cotswolds, alongside a nature reserve. Its initiative in support of organic farms, taken in response to a members' resolution, is welcome,[24] but there is a long way to go: at present only 5 of its 1,217 tenants farm organically. And it needs to employ environmental assessment and audit techniques at all levels in its operations.

Technical innovation is only one aspect of sustainability. In its capacity as a leader in the field, the Trust may want to consider how it could extend the involvement of local communities in its conservation work. Hitherto the Trust has tended to turn to its membership (eg Acorn Clubs for young volunteers), whilst engaging help through Employment Training and similar government-funded schemes, and, of course, through its employees and contract staff. But the Trust could do more to reach into the rural communities where it has a large presence, and seek to involve them more, for example in conservation projects on its land which bring benefits to the villages and small towns nearby. Whilst it is right that the Trust should show most concern about its relationship with its members and its tenants, there is a wider community role which is appropriate to a body seeking to set exemplary standards.

5 Encourage links between conservation and enjoyment

On occasion in the past, the Trust has been taken to task for its grudging attitude to visitors to its land, seeing them more as problems than assets.[25] It has been one of the major achievements of the Trust in recent years to become more open and user-friendly in its dealings with its members and the public generally. However, legitimate concerns about the impact of large numbers of visitors on sensitive properties may occasionally blind the Trust to the potential to promote its conservation cause through visitors.

For example, the Trust may want to review these areas

- the information that it gives visitors, so that they are encouraged to be more sensitive to global and local environmental problems – and the linkages between them;
- its role in the field of conservation education, since the land in the Trust's care is a vast, and often untapped, resource for this purpose; and
- the part played by its tenants (especially farmers) in contact with visitors, eg providing information and marketing rural crafts and products, particularly in areas away from the traditional holiday centres like the Lakes where this has already become well established.

6 Collaborate with others in conservation

We have noted the advances made by the Trust in recent years in working with others in the conservation movement. The scope for extending this through a policy of 'advocacy by example' is considerable. The Trust's land management experience is second to none. Perhaps it could do more to share this through publications, audio-visual material, training courses, even a consultancy arm – and do so profitably as well. Of course, the Trust does not exist primarily for the purpose of helping others, and a great deal of interchange already takes place between organisations at the local level. None the less, the National Trust might consider developing a strategy to share its practical management experience. This would be with other land-owning conservation bodies but also public authorities and, most importantly, the growing number of private landowners who wish to apply ecologically sensitive land-management practices.

At the local level, the Trust has become an active partner with others in conservation through England, Wales and Northern Ireland. These arrangements are often complex, requiring the Trust to collaborate with other conservation charities owning land, the statutory conservation organisations, local authorities, regulatory bodies, etc. An example of this is to be found in the Gower peninsula. In the future, the Trust will no doubt need to devote even more of its resources to such collaborative working at the local level.

7 Be more international

The National Trust is the world's most successful non-governmental conservation land-holding body. Its reputation in other countries is formidable. Its standing is often such that it brings credit to the UK's reputation for conservation generally. In Japan, for example, the *National Report on the Quality of the Environment 1990* acknowledges a debt to Britain's National Trust in setting up its National Environmental Fund, whilst that of 1991 records the progress made by the National Trust of Japan.[26] In over 20 other countries 'national trusts' have come into being, even in developing countries like Malaysia.

In practice there is little homogeneity between these similarly named bodies (many concentrate on saving historic buildings, some are closer to their governments than is our Trust, and none can hold a candle to the National Trust in terms of resources or membership), and the network of collaboration between them is loose and informal. None the less, the international family of National Trusts is something to build upon.

In an increasingly international world, where there is a great appetite for sharing practical solutions to conservation problems, the experience of the National Trust in Britain could be at premium. For example, at the IVth World Congress on National Parks and Protected Areas, in Caracas (1992), which was attended by a representative of the National Trust, the importance of the non-governmental sector in setting up and managing protected areas (and not only in rich countries) was an important new theme.

The Trust could do more to make its knowledge available at the international level. It might develop a clearing house of experience among similar bodies around the world. It could promote its skills through the Overseas Development Agency. It might explore the potential for an international coalition of National Trusts to promote the land trust idea. It would be welcome to play a bigger part in such international bodies as IUCN – The World Conservation Union. No one would suggest that this should involve a major diversion of the Trust's limited resources of time and money, but the exercise of more leadership in this field ought to attract its own funding – and it is arguably a moral obligation for a body of the Trust's international reputation to share its conservation experience more widely beyond these shores.

8 Carry through the changes in institutional culture

This essay has described a veritable revolution in the culture of the Trust over the past ten years or so. The process, however, has further to go. Training at all levels in conservation management skills, exchange of experience amongst practitioners in the Trust and with outsiders, reaffirmation from the Trust's leadership on the importance of ecologically sensitive management, and policy changes of the kind suggested above will all help to bed conservation values still more firmly into the Trust's way of thinking and working.

There has been a view that the strong role exerted by land agents in the Trust has held back the adoption of conservation schemes. Whatever the truth in the past, it is testament to the Trust's land agents' professionalism and adaptability that many of them have been leaders in bringing about the changes of recent years. However, as the Trust itself recognises, it needs to bring people into senior posts in the regions with a wider range of professional backgrounds. The employment of more staff at this level, who are trained in the environmental and conservation field but who are also skilled managers, would help to deepen the cultural changes which have already occurred.

9 Review funding priorities

The Trust long ago recognised that management costs money, and that the more intensive management which is now required can be expensive. It has declared that it is attaching more importance to its countryside work.[28] The test of its commitment to change, therefore, is its willingness to re-examine the allocation of resources.

Open spaces are disadvantaged in that they do not, usually, generate much income, and visitors cannot so easily be charged as they are for entering houses. Moreover, the agricultural estate, which once supplied some 20 per cent of the National Trust's income, now provides barely 7 per cent. Therefore, those who wish to see a higher priority for the management of the Trust's countryside properties will have to marshal other arguments, especially as money spent on nature conservation and countryside work is, in many cases, money not available for its equally important work in the conservation of historic houses.

The numbers of visitors ought to be a powerful consideration. Around 20 million annually visit the Lake District. They do not all go on Trust land, of course, but the numbers that do probably exceed those visiting the most popular of Trust houses by a factor of ten or more – and every visitor to the Lakes, and many who go to the coast, are at least passive 'consumers' of the scenery that the Trust protects.

Another reason for investing in the management of countryside properties is that the resources that they contain are often irreplaceable. Whereas it is always possible to rebuild a house like Uppark as a complete replica of what was there before, a valued habitat, once lost, cannot be replaced.

In 1985 the Trust spent £36.2 m. on property maintenance generally, of which open spaces received £16.3 m. In 1992 the comparable figures were £76.2 m. and £25.7 m. Direct comparisons between expenditure on houses and countryside properties can be misleading, especially as the Trust's open space work is well suited to the employment of volunteers, assistance under government training schemes and grants from bodies like the Countryside Commission. None the less, although these figures confirm a sharp rise in expenditure on coast and countryside properties, they suggest that expenditure on other properties in the Trust's ownership has actually increased more rapidly. While all such figures should be interpreted with great care, does the trend do full justice to the national importance of the Trust's countryside estate?

10 Ask the long-term questions

All the foregoing ideas relate to the relatively short term but, when the Trust is celebrating its centenary, it is proper that it should consider conservation questions in the longer term. This is not an easy area since the Trust is quite properly reluctant to engage in crystal-ball gazing or theoretical work. None the less, the conservation scene is changing so fast that it needs the capacity to think long term if it is not to be caught out again as it was in the 1960s and '70s.

Consider these three questions, for example, the answers to which will directly affect the Trust's ability to manage conservation values on its property in the future.

When does subsidised upland farming become museum farming?

The Trust holds strongly to the view that, through support for traditional hill farming as a way of life, society can maintain the scenery of the Lake District, and elsewhere in the Welsh and English uplands; and this view also underpins its own approach as landlord in these areas. But looking to the long term, one must question how long the argument can be sustained. If hill farming can only survive through more and more amalgamations, and ever greater subsidy, what has become of 'the way of life', which is so highly valued? And if the landscape is being increasingly maintained in its traditional appearance through the efforts of Trust contractors or volunteers, what is the special role that farmers play?

Perhaps, therefore, the Trust should begin thinking about a new approach to land management that recognises that hill farming as we have known it will eventually disappear, and that well-meaning attempts to support it will ulti- mately collapse because they seek to prop up systems for which there is less and less social and economic justification. If so, thought needs to be given not so much as to how to maintain the existing landscape, but what kind of new landscapes we want in our uplands in future, which both reflect economic reality *and* meet the testing criteria of environmental sustainability. For example, one option might be the deliberate abandonment of farming in some valleys, allowing natural progression to take its course, thus creating a 'wilderness' area. The point is not that this is the right course to take, but that the Trust should not shrink from asking this kind of question.

What will climate change do to land use?

The Trust's adherence to the principle, embodied in its legislation, of 'permanent preservation' is not one which it is easy to reconcile with a physical environment that could be on the point of changing in unpredictable and unprecedented ways. For example, climate change can be expected to make it attractive to grow crops in some areas that are currently unsuitable for that purpose; it may change the economic prospects for forestry; and associated sea level rise could affect coastal properties. Although we do not know enough now about the course of climate change to make confident decisions on such matters, the most authoritative predictions suggest that such scenarios will challenge the Trust within the working lifetime of some of its present staff.

As with the case of upland farming, the Trust may need, therefore, to begin thinking more about a philosophy of managing change in the way in which it runs its countryside estate rather than of protection. This does *not* imply any weakening in its conservation commitment, but rather that creative conservation and dynamic policies for increasing biodiversity may need to replace, or augment, traditional defensive approaches.

What is the place of ethical issues in the Trust's management?

Debates in many conservation circles now often raise questions of ethics. These are of two kinds: a concern for the rights of species other than mankind; and an emerging belief that the environmental crisis facing the world calls for an urgent ethical commitment to underpin the new relationship with the earth, and fellow humanity. Both have implications for the Trust.

The Trust, like other conservation bodies, has hitherto taken the view that so-called cruelty issues, such as hunting, are quite distinct from conservation as generally understood. However, it is probable that questions about hunting and shooting, and the treatment of domestic animals on Trust farms, may be viewed differently in future, as a dimension of conservation. Certainly such issues will be debated more among Trust members. Whatever position the Trust may take on such matters, the apparently commonsense distinction previously made between cruelty on the one hand and conservation issues on the other will be harder to sustain.

The broader ethical issues which are enmeshed in the debate on sustainability are also explored in later chapters. But, at heart, these issues are about doing things now for generations to come, and having the vision to act for the broader public good. The Trust, with a hundred years' experience of acting for posterity, and on behalf of society as a whole, should be better placed than many to deal with them.

Notes

1 J. Gaze, *Figures in a Landscape: A History of the National Trust*, 1988.
2 Quoted in Philip Lowe and Jane Goyder, *Environmental Groups in Politics*, 1983, p.138.
3 J. Gaze, p.63.
4 *Report of the National Park Committee*, 1931, Cmd.3851, HMSO, p.53.
5 J. Harvey, 'Changing Attitudes to Nature Conservation: the National Trust', *Biological Journal of the Linnean Society*, vol. 32, 1937, pp.149–59.
6 *The Management of National Trust Properties*, the National Trust, 1938.
7 A. G. Tansley, *Our Heritage of Wild Nature: A Plea for Organised Nature Conservation*, 1946.
8 O. Rackham, 'Landscape and the Conservation of Meaning., *Proceedings of the Royal Society of Arts*, vol. cxxxix, no.5414, 1991, pp.903–15.
9 O. Rackham, *The Last Forest*, 1989, p.145.
10 C. Chatters and R. Minter, *Nature Conservation and the National Trust*, ECOS 7 (4), 1986, pp.25–32.
11 J. Harvey, p.156.
12 'The Countryside in 1970', Third Conference Proceedings, Royal Society of Arts, p.2.
13 'Nature Conservation' (Paper to the Properties Committee), the National Trust, 1981, p.2.
14 J. Gaze, p.246.

15 J. Harvey, p.153.
16 See Countryside Commission publications nos CCP 106 and 128.
17 Countryside Commission *Annual Report* 1975–6, and CCP 88 and 90.
18 'Nature Conservation: Second Review', the National Trust, 1989.
19 J. Harvey, p.157.
20 K. Hearn, *The National Trust and Nature Conservation: The Problems of the Next Decade, ECOS* 9 (1), 1988, pp.11–16.
21 A. Stirling, 'Too many Visitors?', address to ICOMOS Conference, 1990.
22 See, for example, Merlin Waterson, 'The Whole Picture', *National Trust Magazine*, 1993.
23 Philip Lowe and Jane Goyder, p.144.
24 'The National Trust to Launch Organic Farming Development Fund', National Trust press release, July 1993.
25 Philip Lowe and Jane Goyder, pp.148–9.
26 Both publications are available from the Environment Agency in Tokyo
27 See, for example, the 'Three Estates Study' in *Countryside Commission News*, May 1984.
28 A. Stirling, address to National Trust Land Agents Conference, April 1993.

III

Sustainable Development and the Trust

DAVID R. COPE

Forecasting the future

'Anyone who attempts to predict the history of the next ten years is a rash man, and if he attempt to make his forecast for a century he is very properly regarded as so foolhardy as not to be worth listening to at all.' So wrote Charles Galton Darwin, the grandson of the Darwin of *Origin of the Species* in his book *The Next Million Years*, published in 1953.[1]

Having to ignore such caution, this chapter is scattered with what may be called 'reasonable assumptions'. Most are essentially based on continuation of current trends, which betrays a value judgement that the next hundred years will be a period of incremental rather than the dramatic change which some of the more apocalyptic environmental forecasts have suggested.[2]

Sustainability and sustainable development

During the 1990s, there has been a mushrooming in the use of the neologisms 'sustainability' and 'sustainable development', or similar terms.[3] The phrase 'sustainable growth respecting the environment' found its way into the 1992 Maastricht Treaty, as one of its principal objectives, while, in January 1994, the UK government produced a 'Sustainable Development Strategy', the latest in a series of explorations which began in 1989, when it identified 'sustainable development' as the overarching principle of its entire environmental policy.[4] Not to be outdone, so have all the other main political parties. Local government and private enterprises have also staked their claim as leading agents in the cause.

This remarkable diffusion immediately raises questions about the concept. Is it of such fundamental significance that it transcends otherwise deep divides on what is politically desirable or economically feasible and, as a *zeitwort*, provides a unifying goal of unprecedented clarity and universality of application? Conversely, is it so anodyne as to be otiose and destined rapidly to become an ephemeral cliché?[5]

For some, the very vagueness and all-encompassing sweep of sustainability and sustainable development are a virtue – facilitating debate among those with widely divergent viewpoints. For the purposes of this discussion, however, such imprecision is unacceptable; it provides no basis to justify the concept as the keystone of future policy for an organisation such as the National Trust, let alone as the foundation of long-term government policy.

The most frequently quoted interpretation of 'sustainable development' is that presented by the UN-sponsored World Commission on Environment and Development (WCED), which, in its 1987 report, observed that:

> humanity has the ability make development sustainable – to ensure that
> it meets the needs of the present without compromising the ability of
> future generations to meet their own needs.[6]

The WCED definition makes explicit the *intergenerational* dimension of sustainable development. This dimension provides the link between theory and practice for an action-oriented organisation such as the National Trust. Indeed, going beyond this it may be asserted that the concept of a 'trust', organised as a body of freely associating citizens, is the most effective, perhaps the only, vehicle for achieving the goals of sustainable development.

Intergenerational responsibility and critical capital

A compelling recent interpretation of intergenerational responsibility is that 'this generation [should make] sure that it leaves the next generation a stock of capital no less than this generation has now'.[7] This capital stock comprises three components:

- *person-made capital* – both machines to produce goods, and facilities such as homes, roads, railways, etc.
- *human capital* –investment in knowledge, skills, good health, etc.
- *natural capital*[8] – the world's resources, both mineral and biological, including the atmosphere and oceans

Much of the current debate is about the extent to which these three main components are substitutable, so that a reduction in one may be compensated for by an increase in another – in particular, through the transformation of natural capital into one or other of the other two forms. There is a concern that depletion of the natural capital of ecosystems may threaten overall survivability if, by exploitation or inadvertent damage, stocks fall below threshold levels. Such elements are often referred to as 'critical natural capital'.[9] The relation of sustainable development to the protection of critical natural capital must therefore be a major theme of any discussion.

In 1994, the prevailing opinion is that humanity does not face serious imminent problems from the depletion of mineral resources. Far greater concern attaches to some biological stocks, above all the oceans' marine life and tropical land ecosystems. In the past few years, however, at least in the advanced economies, those aspects of the environment which are regarded as embraced by concepts of 'criticality' have increasingly been extended beyond physical survivability alone.

The particular relevance of this to the Trust can be seen in the comments of Pearce and his colleagues that 'some ecological assets would seem to be essential to human well-being even if they are not essential to human survival – the experience of space and amenity, for example'.[10] The UK's citizens place a particularly high value on the quality of our countryside, second only to our traditions of freedom of speech.[11] It may therefore be reasonable to accord it the status of 'critical natural capital'. The Trust, in this context, may be regarded as a major guardian of the critical natural capital of the nation.

Economics and environment

The third essential element of sustainable development, and the one which is most subject to misinterpretation, is its insistence on the centrality of economics in environmental policymaking. This does not mean that it requires all aspects of environmental quality to be expressed in monetary terms.[12] Sustainable development thinking powerfully asserts that not giving due recognition to environmental assets imposes considerable costs on individuals and societies. It has been one of the most significant impacts of sustainable development thinking to date to move the recognition of these costs to centre stage.[13] It also powerfully emphasises that, for a whole raft of historical, legal and technical reasons, the costs of failing to give adequate recognition to protection of environmental assets have built up over time, so that in no sense do the current dispositions of local, national or international economies fully reflect them.

There is also a tremendous force of inertia in the economic system and therefore a great deal of correction required to the processes of production, distribution and consumption to ensure that they do more fully incorporate economic consideration of environmental protection. The key problem is that the costs of environmental neglect are frequently difficult to identify and dispersed or delayed over time in their incidence. On the other hand, the prices needed to be paid to correct past neglect and to guard against future occurrences are often readily identifiable, fall on a comparatively small number of 'players' (who often have considerable economic and political muscle) and tend to need to be paid here and now. Fundamental economic conflicts are immanent in the pursuit of sustainable development.

Sustainable development theory and the Trust's history

The twin themes of intergenerational responsibility and critical (natural) capital discussed above are essentially the very underpinnings of the Trust's founding philosophy set out a century ago. The Memorandum of Association, drawn up on 12 December 1894, states:

3. The objects for which the Trust is established are –
(1) To promote the permanent preservation, for the benefit of the Nation, of lands and tenements (including buildings) of beauty or historic interest; and as regards lands, to preserve (so far as is practicable) their natural aspect, features and animal and plant life.

Paragraphs 3.6 to 3.10 variously refer to 'care', 'management' and maintenance of lands and properties in the Trust's ownership.

The wording of paragraph 3.1 was incorporated into the 1907 National Trust Act which gave the Trust its legal powers to hold land inalienably. While it is impossible to penetrate the minds of the founders of the Trust, surely 'permanent preservation, for the benefit of the Nation' was an expression of intergenerational responsibility.[14] The compilers of the Memorandum of Association probably subscribed to Edmund Burke's identification of the 'State' as the present manifestation of the endurance of future generations, so 'benefit of the Nation' was benefit extending into an indeterminate future.[15] The Trust's founders clearly did not believe, however, that the 'State' on its own had either the ability or inclination adequately to protect this benefit – hence the need for their initiative. While the rationale for the preservation is 'beauty or historic interest', it is significant that the generally existing disposition of land as well as its animal and plant life are also identified as worthy of preservation.

There is, of course, the qualifying clause of 'practicability'. This term, which also featured in the UK's pioneering pollution control procedures introduced by the Alkali Act of 1874, which referred to 'best practicable means', is self-evidently open to discretionary interpretation. It carries the connotation of some form of 'trade-off' between the identified goal and other requirements, which in the field of pollution control have always been understood, if not specifically spelt out, as 'financial implications'.[16] Its use in the Trust's founding remit implies that, not suprisingly, the total stock of 'natural aspect, features and animal and plant life' which might become parts of the Trust's landholdings was not seen as being at an irreducible minimum. The Trust's founders seem to have been prepared to accept some transformations of the natural capital that might fall under their care into the other forms of capital.

The term 'management' in various paragraphs also suggests that the Trust's founders conceived it as an *active* agency and not one which would freeze the existing characteristics of its holdings. 'Preservation' was, for them, very much an act of dynamic engagement and a vision of greater goals. Indeed, there is considerable evidence that Octavia Hill, in particular, saw the promotion of opportunities for active recreation by the inhabitants of the burgeoning industrial cities of the late nineteenth century, as a major, if not the principal, aim of the Trust and that this would involve development in various forms to meet this desirable demand. Management for recreation features in several of the Memorandum's paragraphs. The Trust's founders could not have anticipated how the growth in leisure time and of the means of access to the British countryside would so rapidly turn what they saw as a wholly reconcilable duality of aims into a major dilemma.[17]

But what of the third theme in the discussion of sustainable development above – the centrality of economics and the reflection of environmental costs in the prices of goods and services? The Trust's founders were certainly well aware that achievement of their goals would require significant financial resources. Paragraph 12 of the Memorandum of Association provides for the Trust:

> to make charges (of such moderate amount as may, in the judgement of
> the Trust, be necessary for the due preservation and maintenance of the
> property of the Trust) for admission to any land or building of the Trust.

The Trust's founders clearly believed that those who 'consumed' the Trust's environmental goods should contribute to their endurance, though they perhaps underestimated that it would require only 'moderate amounts' adequately to do this.

Intergenerational responsibility

It is quite easy to accept, at least in principle, the notion of intergenerational responsibility. It is particularly strongly articulated through the family, through mechanisms such as the formal educational process and through social inclinations such as the desire (sometimes apparently frustrated) of one generation to see its successors willingly clothe themselves in the mantle of what it considers the best of its own cultural and material endowment.

How far into the future does this responsibility or cultural inclination extend?[18] Consideration of this ethical point rapidly assumes a complexity incompatible with this essay. Unsurprisingly, there is a range of viewpoints. There are those who argue that current generations have *no* obligations to whoever comes after them, through to those who see an obligation extending to the 'indefinite unborn'. In the latter case, conceptual problems usually arise because of the uncertainty about what those who (might) inhabit the further future will actually value. Consideration of sustainable development certainly encourages an inclination towards the longer term perspective. One of the most cogent definitions talks of 'non-declining utility . . . for millennia into the future'.[19]

There are few formal policies which encompass such a far-reaching sweep of responsibility. Moreover, the experience of history has imbued western democracies with a deep-seated suspicion of grand goals which are proclaimed as working themselves out over periods such as centuries or millennia. Tyrannies, whether of the left or right, have all too frequently resorted to such imagery to justify dubious present actions.[20] More prosaically, however, some consequences of modern technology *have* forced consideration of longer term responsibilities, extending well beyond even a millennium, particularly the management of radioactive wastes.[21] It would be ironic if, out of a technology which is an anathema to many who profess a concern for the environment, a set of principles were to emerge to steer that very concern.

In generational terms, a century is well within the expected life span of those born only a few years from now. Indeed, a fortunate few of my youngest contemporaries may expect to check these words in a hundred years' time. This means that we may, perhaps, dispense with too convoluted an exploration of the mind-knotting question of the boundaries of intergenerational responsibility and consider, instead, some of its practical implications.

In response to the emphasis on the longer term which 'sustainable development thinking' has encouraged, some enterprises have, for example, sought to include 'representatives of the younger generation' on advisory panels or similar. The Cambridge social philosopher Peter Laslett[22] turns this thinking on its head and argues that it is those in the 'Third Age' – 'the crown of life . . . when there is sufficient freedom from family obligations, economic, social or political compulsion' – who have both a particular duty to, but also an acute appreciation of, the requirements of futurity. His interpretation emphasises actual experience of living rather than simply future life expectancy.

In one way, this is mightily convenient, since it is a demographic certainty that the proportion of the UK's population in this phase of their life will increase, at least in the nearer half of our century-long perspective. (This age group is also, of course, highly significant for Trust membership.) Most discussion of demographic change in western societies in the future concentrates on the negative consequences of the ageing of the population and there are certainly some major dilemmas in store from the growth of the 'Fourth Age' (of senility and dependency), but Laslett's perspective suggests some compensating processes will also emerge.

There is, therefore, perhaps no generational contest over who is the 'most future-oriented' – rather what Laslett has termed a 'conversation between the generations'.[23] For the Trust, one of the implications of this debate, to which it has responded willingly and positively, has been its education programme, which has expanded considerably in recent years, while the voluntary activity on which the Trust depends may well be boosted by willing 'Third Agers'.

The concept of 'trust'

The legal concept of a 'trust' is a well-established vehicle for the management of assets on behalf of a person or entity which has a claim to interest in them in the future. The National Trust fulfils this role, for posterity, in the management of the assets under its care. As Laslett notes,[22] this goes beyond the passive management of the assets and involves some limitation of 'the rights of living people in order to protect the rights of future people'. The parallel with a conventional trust is again explicit. A common motivation for the creation of a trust is a conviction that those to whom the assets in trust belong are, in some way (through immaturity of age or perception, in particular), incapable themselves of managing them and, possibly, at risk of squandering them in some respect.

This was most eloquently stated (if with a certain gender insensitivity) by G. M. Trevelyan at the time of the fiftieth anniversary of the Trust when he declaimed the following obligation on the British citizen:

> . . . unless he now will be at pains to make rules for the preservation of natural beauty, unless he consciously protects it at the partial expense of some of his other greedy activities, he will cut off his own spiritual supplies, and leave his descendants a helpless prey forever to the base materialism of mean and vulgar sights.[24]

It is likely that Trevelyan's 'partial expense of some of his other greedy activities' will weigh more and more heavily in the deliberations of the Trust on its policies and in the management of its landholdings. This will require a synoptic rationale which will both justify potentially contentious decisions and guide the management and acquisitions policy of the Trust. Sustainable development provides that rationale.

Sustainable development in practice

In examining what sustainable development means for the practical operations of the Trust and how these might evolve in the future, it is useful to distinguish between those aspects which relate to the Trust as an enterprise, similar to those relevant to enterprises of any form, and those which derive from its unique functions. Some matters, such as whether the Trust should promote renewable energy provision on its landholdings, straddle both aspects. There is obviously a specially powerful moral imperative on an organisation with such a central environmental remit as the Trust's, to give particular attention to the environmental consequences of its routine operations.

Through an income and expenditure of over £138 million in 1993–4; through being the largest private landowner in the country (over 590,000 acres [239,000 ha] about the size of Northamptonshire); through owning over 1,000 farms, over 20,000 buildings (including 60 villages and hamlets); through running 200 shops; through catering (both literally – 4 million cups of tea being served in 1990 – and metaphorically) for over 10 million visitors a year to paying properties (and an unknown larger number if free access properties are included); through employing over 2,700 staff; through a major publications programme; and finally through administering its membership of over 2.2 million, the Trust obviously has a significant impact on the environment simply by virtue of its own operations.

Because of its unique functions, the Trust's environmental 'footprint' probably extends over a wider range of environmental concerns than any other enterprise in the country. Its tenanted and managed farms involve it in all the issues associated with farming activities. Landholding also embraces matters such as forestry and water resource management, while it must also be mindful of the concerns about bio-diversity – another facet of natural capital. The maintenance of its buildings, gardens and general landholdings means it is a significant consumer of goods. Buildings need heating and lighting, the former not just for staff and visitor comfort but also in some cases to conserve the fabric and contents, giving the Trust a key interest in energy efficiency. Administration of a widely scattered land resource inevitably requires access – meaning road transport, overwhelmingly. The Trust is a retailer, with an annual turnover of about £19 million. Matters such as the sourcing of retail supplies and packaging are therefore germane. The inevitable throughput of at least some of the 4 million cups of tea gives it an involvement in sewage matters, to the point that the National Rivers Authority, responsible for waste water quality, has had cause to fix a quizzical eye on some Trust properties. Administering the functions and the enormous membership means that the Trust has all the environmental characteristics associated with a major office function – paper, energy, and so on. Furthermore, the footprint extends across the length and breadth of England, Wales and Northern Ireland, in both urban and rural settings.

Along with many conventional private enterprises, towards the end of the 1980s, the Trust realised that to manage the potential environmental impacts of its operations, it first needed to establish their nature. It conducted an environmental 'audit' during 1990–2. This was a formidable challenge because of its wide-ranging nature, of which just a few illustrative examples are given above.

As the results of its audit came in, the Trust has moved on to the next phases of environmental management – the nomination of staff with specific responsibility for environmental assessment and monitoring, organised through its regions – and the implementation, through a prioritisation process, of actions to address the environmental issues that the audit identified.

In the near future, the Trust will most likely follow the path of other enterprises in developing its internal environmental management. The reporting, either in annual reports, or in specialist reports, of environmental performance is a growing practice. Many companies, particularly those which are offshoots of American parents, where the practice is a legal requirement, are increasingly producing site characterisation reports which detail the environmental consequences of activities at their sites. This is also a feature of the newly introduced European Union 'eco-management' scheme, which is at present on a voluntary basis. Few, if any, of such companies have as large a number of 'operational sites' as the Trust and it might be impractical to follow this model to the letter. Perhaps reporting on a regional basis offers an appropriate compromise between practicability and openness.

Having identified and characterised their environmental impacts and set up management systems, some enterprises are setting themselves targets for voluntary reductions in their environmental impacts, going beyond any legal requirements which may exist. This has been spurred in many cases by the discovery that the focus on such issues as waste minimisation and energy conservation has brought with it the bonus of significant cost savings, at least in the first stages of trying to meet targets. Similarly, the Trust is exploring ways in which it can voluntarily reduce its environmental footprint, for example by management of its water supplies, or by developing 'carbon sinks' to compensate for the emissions arising from its fossil fuel use.

Enterprises have also realised that they are but one link in a chain of supply which delivers goods and services to their final users. No individual enterprise can in isolation manage the complete set of environmental impacts associated with this chain. Some companies are therefore reaching out to their suppliers as one link of the chain, and to their customers as the other.

With the supplier link, adoption of this approach by the Trust is relatively simple and uncontroversial. A start has been made looking at materials sourcing. The customer link, sometimes encapsulated in concepts such as 'product stewardship', is, however, considerably more problematic because of the Trust's unique function. One must first define the Trust's 'product'.[25] In one sense, it is the direct stewardship of the lands, and their environmental characteristics, and the buildings and other artefacts in its care. The Trust delivers their continued existence. But, in another sense, its 'product' is also the delivery of satisfaction to those who 'consume' the assets in its direct stewardship – by visiting them, by the knowledge that they *may* visit them and, at the most esoteric level, from the knowledge that they are being conserved, even though the individual knowing this may never visit a particular site.

This raises some interesting questions. For example, could the Trust in some senses be said to have a stewardship responsibility for the environmental consequences arising from the direct pursuit of this satisfaction – above all for the emissions, congestion and so on, resulting from the overwhelming use of motor vehicles for access to achieve the 'consumption'? Recent policy reviews by the Trust have already taken such far-sighted interpretation of product stewardship into account.[26]

An information provision – awareness-raising function might be a first-level response – advising 'consumers' of alternative ways of accessing their 'consumption', where these exist. This is to an extent already practised. The suggestion has been made that the Trust might attempt some 'zero net impact' initiatives: for example, planting trees at a rate which in some way matches the growth of carbon dioxide emissions resulting from increasing numbers of visitors, or reducing its own internal energy consumption as a compensation for the overall energy increases occurring because of increased consumption of its product. Might the Trust even operate a variable car-parking charges scheme, depending on how far visitors had driven to visit a site, as a form of miniature 'environmental taxation'? Currently, such an idea would seem fanciful and impossible to implement. But, if road tolling systems, with electronic monitoring and billing, were introduced, then the technical and informational obstacles might be removed at a stroke.

Of course, it can equally be argued that such thinking pushes the concept of product stewardship beyond its reasonable limits. There are certainly 'opportunity substitution' considerations to be taken into account. If the Trust properties did not exist, then maybe their 'consumers' would seek an equal amount of motorised leisure consumption by travelling the same distance on other leisure pursuits. Any attempt to raise a levy like that discussed above would almost certainly push some 'consumers' to seek these substitutes, which might not be subject to full environmental cost pricing. It could also be argued that the Trust uniquely compensates by delivering environmental 'benefits' which neutralise any environmental 'negatives' that arise – in particular its stewardship of aesthetic environmental quality. It is a challenge, however, beyond environmental economics at present, and probably for ever, to measure how much, of what type of, landscape quality compensates for a tonne of nitrogen dioxide emissions!

It is to this stewardship function of the Trust that we must now turn to examine the second, particular, element of the Trust's relationship to sustainable development. This is its role in relation to our country's stock of critical natural capital, in particular its aesthetic capital.

Here, again, we find that the Trust has been ahead of the field, operating according to sustainable development principles, without using its terminology (which many might feel is highly desirable for universal observance). In particular, its Enterprise Neptune initiative, begun in 1965, is clearly addressing what is indisputably part of the country's critical capital – its coastal zone. By 1995, this had secured 550 miles (885 km) – nearly the distance between London and Aberdeen – of coastline, with coastal landholdings totalling over 113,000 acres (46,000 ha). Some 186 miles (300 km) of this coastline was, in fact, already owned through the accessions of the Trust from its inception to 1965. Indicatively, the first property the Trust acquired, Dinas Oleu in Wales, was coastal land. Chapter IV considers coastal issues and Enterprise Neptune in detail.

The UK's coastal zone nominates itself more powerfully than virtually any other of the country's natural features as critical natural capital and it certainly 'involves many parts of our national psyche'.[27] This is not just because of its great visual quality, or the recreational opportunities it provides. Its eco-systems, at the coastline itself, to seaward and to landward, are among the most distinctive and fragile of any. This extends to those parts, particularly the coastal wetlands, whose visual qualities are perhaps more subtle than dramatic.[28]

When it comes to systematically establishing our nation's critical natural capital, some interesting questions arise. The first is whether it is appropriate to do this at the national level.[29] Many of the official designations which exist to help guide environmental policies have identified key national or even inter-national 'jewels' – the National Parks, Areas of Outstanding Natural Beauty, Heritage Coasts, Sites of Special Scientific Interest, Environmentally Sensitive Areas, 'Ramsar' sites (internationally significant wetland areas), World Herit-age Sites (such as the Giant's Causeway), and so on.[30] There is an increasing recognition, however, that 'the whole countryside, not just the outstanding parts, needs to be considered within policies for sustainability'.[31] There are some obvious parallels here with the Trust's policy on acquisition of the built cultural heritage; it has sought to embrace the 'ordinary', in the sense of the 'representative', as well as the spectacular.

Public acceptability, as well as more 'rational' inventories of the full richness of national natural capital diversity, requires consideration here. The in-habitants of north-west England, for example, might not take too kindly to suggestions that a particular part of 'their' natural heritage was sub-critical because there were ample 'supplies' in East Anglia.

One of the consequences of the focus of attention on natural capital that sustainable development thinking has engendered is the accumulation of various sets of data which identify and categorise elements of natural capital. Thus, English Nature has produced for England its Natural Areas scheme, as a rational basis for its own responsibilities on a regional basis, using ecosystem characteristics to identify 76 'natural areas'.[32] Adding the landscape dimension, the Countryside Commission has been piloting its New Map of England in the south-west and hopes to have a national classification by the end of 1995.[33] The Countryside Survey, 1990, published in 1993,[34] has combined sample site surveys with satellite-mapped land cover information to provide a comprehen-sive, highly detailed 'ecological census' of Britain. There is therefore no shortage of information on which to base the Trust's future management strategies for its existing holdings, or to determine future acquisition policies for environmental purposes.

Catering for the regional dimension – providing adequate representation of critical natural capital of as wide a range as feasible, within regions – as well as reflecting the innate natural diversity of the country's environmental resources, may also contribute to some of the other Trust concerns. If there is representation of the fullest possible range of assets liable to 'consumption' by visitors, then presumably there may be less inclination by visitors to travel longer distances to 'consume' environmental assets not present in their region. Clearly there is a limit to this possibility – there are few mountains or seacliffs in East Anglia, for example – and there will always be an understandable desire to 'consume' some characteristics that are unique to single locations, such as particular views, or cultural artefacts.

The Trust and sustainable development in the wider context

No single body, even one as large as the Trust (in terms both of its activities and its membership), can advance sustainable development in isolation. It requires integration of awareness and action from the global to the individual. It embraces concern with broad ecosystems that span continents to concern with the life sustained by a single leaf. It reaches the mainsprings of every human activity.

Our national sustainable development strategy places a strong emphasis on voluntary action, with government largely playing a co-ordinating, supportive role. Enterprises, local authorities, voluntary groups (of which the Trust is a very special example),[35] families and individuals are all identified as having complementary responsibilities. Some have criticised this position, favouring a more pro-active role for government. But, at a time when there is great concern about other dimensions of political life (though these all interact with environmental policy), Pearce is almost certainly right to say that 'translated into realisable political action, sustainable development is more about changes of emphasis than a wholesale restructuring of decision-making'.[36] The government's strategy is currently subject to independent scrutiny by a committee of the House of Lords. Their report should be available around the time this book is published but it is to the future, probably the not too distant future, that we must leave a definitive judgement on the current government position.

The government has proposed three, relatively modest, new mechanisms for taking forward its strategy. The first is a 'Government Panel on Sustainable Development' composed of five leading advisers, which has quarterly meetings to advise on 'strategic issues'.[37] The Trust will, no doubt, have access to the ear of members in the usual ways. An important message which should be conveyed, judging from the Panel's deliberations to date, is the theme which has run through this chapter – that sustainability embraces much more than a concern with issues of global span and indeed that the effective addressing of even these issues requires myriads of actions at a micro-scale. The seeds of sustainable development lie in the English hedgerow or Irish dry-stone wall as much as in the stratosphere.

The second government mechanism is a 'National Round Table for Sustainable Development', which may later be complemented by an associated network of regional or other sub-national initiatives. This is loosely modelled on a highly successful Canadian initiative, started in 1989. It meets quarterly and there are inevitable fears that it may prove little more than a 'talk shop'. Its membership is intended to reflect all the main interests concerned with, and with the power to influence, national environmental circumstances. The National Trust, however, is not formally represented on the Round Table, an unfortunate omission because no represented organisation has anything like as strong a claim to identify with, and routinely have to address, the intergenerational dimension discussed above, which is such a central concern of sustainable development.

Were the Trust to have been involved, this would almost inevitably have rekindled the continually smouldering internal debate about the extent to which the Trust should have clear policies on the entire environmental context of its operations and indeed on national environmental policy overall, as well as on specific direct impacts on its portfolio of lands and buildings. As Lowe and Goyder note,[38] the Trust's founders certainly envisaged it having such a role. Subsequently (and necessarily) the Trust became more 'introverted'. Sustainable development thinking, however, virtually mandates a synoptic, panoptic perspective. This could well be one of the more challenging and exciting features of the Trust's second century.

Trust participation would also probably place new fuel on the other smouldering fire – the relation between the Trust's governing structure and its membership. If the Canadian model is an indicator, success comes first from establishing a consensus in the round table mechanism (no small challenge in itself) and then proselytising the consensual conclusions within the participants' organisations. Obviously the Trust can take messages outwards to its members through its well-established channels of communication but it is a reasonable guess that (at least some of) the membership would expect reciprocal communication, followed by response.

The final, and most inchoate, mechanism introduced by the government is a 'citizens' environment initiative', called 'Going for Green'. The aim of this is to reach beyond existing local voluntary group initiative to the population as a whole, in families and as individuals, 'to encourage the growth of interest in the issues of sustainable development, and particularly in the things people can do in their own lives'.[39] Again, most probably mainly at the regional and local levels, there could be a key role for the Trust here.

One cannot but have a sense that, laudable though they may be, the trinity described above (and how the three elements will interrelate has still to be established) are certainly not sufficient to address the issues outlined in this chapter. To paraphrase the Chinese saying, however, a journey of a hundred years begins with three small steps.

Perhaps the route to sustainable development can be strolled. Some foresee a forced march. The journey from St Alban's Head to Durdle Door in Dorset springs to my mind – up and down, as the headlands rise and fall, sometimes raising doubts as to why one started, particularly in a strong headwind. At times, thoughts of the goal dominate (a car, ironically, in the car-park!) but always, along the way, there is a plethora of interest and, at the end, a sense that one is better, much better, for having made the attempt.

Coda

The final remarks are addressed specifically to any readers of this text in 100 years' time. Your existence, your expectations and your judgement on the way our responsibilities to you have been discharged have occupied my thoughts in the months of gestation of this chapter. If sustainable development is indeed, in the words of our current Minister for the Environment, 'growing in ways for which future generations will thank us'[40] then there is one forecast that transcends my assumptions throughout this chapter. It is a certainty. This is that you will have as many, if not more, grounds for being grateful to the National Trust for its activities in its second century as I have for those in its first.

Notes

1 Readers may wonder how Darwin reconciled this observation with the title of his book. He claimed that while forecasting details was an impossibility, it was valid to discuss what he termed 'average history'. His conclusions, based on a Malthusian interpretation of population/resource interactions, were distinctly pessimistic.

2 For example, the chapter makes the assumption that, at least over the next century, the most fundamental drive for the UK's population will be to improve its well-being. This does not necessarily imply an increase in consumption of physical resources, energy and so on, since these are merely means to the end of well-being, which can also increase in other ways. Nevertheless, it is likely that such consumption will increase, or at least not fall to any significant extent.

3 'Sustainability' and 'sustainable development' are not synonymous, though frequently so used. 'Sustainability' can be interpreted in purely ecological terms, relating solely to the biological environment as a whole, or to particular components (sometimes called 'environmental sustainability'). Allowing for natural variability, this is self-replicating and therefore self-sustaining. From this, it is a short step to concepts of 'sustainable yields' – the 'harvesting' of biological resources by humans within the limits of natural systems to replenish themselves. Human history is replete with examples of societies which have transgressed such limits, sometimes with disastrous consequences (Pezzey, 1992).

A particular characteristic of virtually all economies and certainly of contemporary ones is the use not only of renewable resources but of stocks of non-renewable mineral resources, particularly fossil fuels. As the earth's complement of these resources is fixed, and as they are usually degraded in their use, taking a long term view, an apparent paradox arises as to whether such economies are inherently unsustainable.

This chapter is about 'sustainable *development*', which is a special case of 'sustainability'. It clearly encompasses human purpose for human ends and implies some form of increase above an earlier level. An economic interpretation of 'sustainability' is maintenance of utility – the economist's somewhat breathtaking shorthand for the entire set of circumstances – goods, their means of provision, attitudes, relationships and so on – that together make up human well-being. From this, it is a short step to realise that 'sustainable development' implies some *increase*, over current levels, in this basket of desirables.

4 HM Government 1989; HM Government 1994.

5 The terms 'sustained', 'sustainable', etc. are frequently used in conventional political and economic discourse, in a way which is most definitely far too restricted an interpretation. This usage, explicitly or implicitly, refers to (indefinitely) continuing growth of an economy, in ways, and at a rate, which avoid the periodic booms and recessions (particularly the latter) of the past, especially the recent past. It lacks any acknowledgement of the critical role of environmental resources in underpinning economic growth. It is noteworthy that the British Prime Minister, speaking only a few days after attending the public launch of the UK's Sustainable Development Strategy, used the term 'sustained' with this narrow, restrictive, connotation. ('Mr Major insisted, "We now have the conditions for long-term sustainable growth."', *Financial Times*, 29 January 1994.)

6 To the limited extent it does concern itelf with definitional niceties, the 1994 government Sustainable Development Strategy implicitly adopts this definition. This is because this particular interpretation immediately raises the distinction between 'needs' and 'wants' and therefore the thorny question of how to (and the even more thorny question of who should) distinguish between the one and the other.

7 Pearce, *et al*, 1993.

8 The use of the term 'natural' in this section does not necessarily mean that the valued environments are totally unaffected by human hand, directly or indirectly. In the UK, virtually no part of its land surface has such 'wilderness' charactersistics – the countryside has been shaped by thousands of years of human economic activity, particularly agriculture and forestry. This poses particular dilemmas for its conservation, if sustainable development considerations suggest this be done, because this almost automatically mandates continuation of the activities which result in the present disposition of the landscape and its ecosystems. Economies inevitably change and the changes associated with agriculture are particularly significant, as the National Trust is only too well aware. The term 'environmental capital' is increasingly being used to refer to the results of the intimate interaction of purely natural and human-originating processes.

9 The protective function of the stratospheric ozone layer is probably the best example. The earth's natural (and therefore variable) heat balance is another, although it is doubtful that even the most extreme scenarios of human-induced global warming would actually threaten *overall* human survival, even though they would undoubtedly be traumatic.

10 Pearce *et al*, p.16. One has to be careful to note that subjective, often culturally related, factors may come into play here. Marjorie Nicolson's classic work, *Mountain Gloom and Mountain Glory* (1959), demonstrated that the Western esteem of wild, pristine environments (and the flora and fauna that inhabit them) is a comparatively recent phenomenon. Before, the dominant cultural preference was for the Arcadian (reflected, to an extent, in the landholdings of the National Trust) and the urban. Nevertheless, it is a virtual certainty that the high value placed on such environments will continue to be a dominant cultural feature in the UK, other western societies and increasingly, other societies, as the growth of vibrant National Trusts, primarily focussed on landscapes and ecosystems, in places such as Japan and Fiji illustrates well. It seems unlikely that such a powerful inclination could disappear in the short space of a century.

11 Dower, 1994.

12 Most, if not all, environmental economists who have discussed sustainable development thinking are well appraised of 'you cannot value a sunset' type arguments. They would, however, point out that implicitly we do value them. Many a stunning sunset completely

passes us by as we go about our daily business. Conversely, we may occasionally be prepared to travel considerable distances (paying significantly for doing so) to enjoy a particularly striking descent below the horizon. For a strident denunciation of ideas of economic valuation of the environment, see Adams, 1993.

13 Around this centrality revolve several associated considerations. One is the 'polluter pays principle' – not, as it is sometimes misinterpreted, a moralistic admonition but an economic principle which insists that those who produce or consume a good or service should have its environmental costs fully reflected in what they pay to produce or consume it. Sustainable development abhors all forms of subsidy and market distortion since these usually lead to the environment being undervalued in economic decision making.

Another consideration is the 'precautionary principle'. In response to the uncertainty which so frequently surrounds environmental issues, this asserts that caution should be exercised, particularly when dealing with situations involving critical natural capital. It is somewhat analogous to the concept of an insurance premium. Just as an individual makes a choice about which risks he or she will or will not insure against, so there is a debate about the extent to which precautionary action should be taken, and therefore costs incurred, potentially to protect environmental assets, even though the threat, given current knowledge, may not be fully substantiated.

It is some others of my 'reasonable assumptions' that closer to the nearer end of the century under examination than the farther, the centrality of economic valuation in environmental policymaking will become an unremarkable convention, with its limits *and* its potential well recognised; the notion that environmental costs should fall wholly on those who create them will be assiduously applied; and a consensus will have emerged on the extent to which due precaution should be taken in implementing environmental policies.

14 A sterling effort to set the thinking of the Trust's founders in the context of their own life experiences and the social and cultural influences on them is given in Gaze, 1988.
15 Laslett, 1991.
16 In the Clean Air Act of 1956.
17 Fedden (1974) chronicles how rapidly this dilemma emerged, with the Trust expressing concern about day tripping in 1902 and new road schemes soon after the First World War.
18 Laslett and Fishkin, 1992; Cope, 1993.
19 Pezzey, 1992.
20 Bock, 1970.
21 NRPB, 1991.
22 Laslett, 1991.
23 Laslett, 1972.
24 Lees-Milne, 1945.
25 Some of its products are straightforward and conventional – for example, it publishes guides and other books, but these are a very small component of its overall 'product'.
26 I am grateful to Rob Jarman, of the National Trust, Cirencester, for discussions on the Trust's explorations of these issues.
27 Rich, 1990.
28 English Nature, 1993b.
29 Cope, 1992.
30 Nor have these 'jewels' necessarily been selected on a totally rational, environmentally determined basis, as anyone familiar with the story of the non-National Park status of the New Forest will be aware.
31 Countryside Commission, 1993 and also 1991.
32 English Nature, 1936.

33 Countryside Commission, 1991.
34 Department of the Environment, 1993.
35 Lowe and Goyder, 1983.
36 Pearce, *et al*, 1993, p.10.
37 The Secretary of State for Scotland has also set up a national panel for Scotland.
38 Lowe and Goyder, 1983, p.138.
39 HM Government, 1994, p.236.
40 Gummer, 1993.

IV

The Coast

KEITH CLAYTON

W E LIVE ON A relatively small island with a long coastline and a strong maritime history. Perhaps this is why the one hundred years that this book springs from began on the coast at Barmouth, with the desire of the Trust's first donor to protect an open hillside and its coastal view; to allow wild nature to have its own way and 'to avoid the abomination of asphalt paths and cast-iron seats of serpent design'. A high coast, with its views dominated by the open sea, has always captured the imagination, and it is notable that headlands were particularly likely to come into Trust ownership in its first seventy years. Further, the despoliation of long lengths of coast by industry, bungalows and caravans sites became increasingly obvious between the wars and were reminders of the vulnerability of the coastal zone. Finally, the coast can be delineated on a map, and thus quantitative measures by length are feasible and can bring some precision to debates about what has been lost and what might still be saved.

The Trust has always had the coastal zone high on its list of priorities, but these were redefined with the decision in 1965 to launch Enterprise Neptune. This was dedicated to saving the remaining high-quality undeveloped coast from the threat of development; this persisted after 1945 despite strong planning legislation since it failed to distinguish between the coast and any other type of undeveloped land. Unlike the situation inland, where the Trust will never own more than a very small fraction of the total area (significant though that holding will be), the National Trust may already be the largest single owner of coastal frontage and will certainly dominate coastal land ownership by the end of the next century.

This chapter will examine briefly the reasons this dominance has come about, and the responsibilities for coastal management it will entail. However, it will also note the skew of Trust land to wild rocky coasts, mainly in western Britain, and discuss the desirability of shifting the balance towards other coastal environments worthy of preservation. As is widely understood, the next century promises to be a period of major environmental changes, and global warming will ensure that sea levels rise much faster over the next one hundred years than they have over the past century. Will this threaten low-lying coastal land in the Trust's ownership, and will the high rocky coasts be untouched by these higher sea levels? The coast has always been a dynamic and hazardous environment and whatever else may be required of the Trust's policies over the next hundred years, they are going to have to be sufficiently flexible and robust to cope with considerable changes along the coast. This will be achieved if policies are developed with a full understanding of coastal processes and of what is becoming known as Coastal Zone Management.

Problems of the coastal zone

Prior to the Industrial Revolution, almost all our coast was wholly natural and changed slowly through the effects of winds and waves, of tides and currents. Local catastrophes occurred, such as the tidal flooding caused by major storms, slower destruction as sand dunes moved inland, or a coastal port such as Dunwich was gradually eroded away. But most of the coast was uninhabited and even isolated farms looked for protected sites someway inland, facing away from the sea and the cruel winds that blew off it.

Social changes which roughly coincided with the Industrial Revolution changed all this. Sea bathing became popular and thus developed the seaside resort; the natural landscape became attractive rather than terrifying, encouraging tourism; retirement to a new location became common and many sought out suburban areas alongside the major coastal resorts. Industrialisation itself brought increasing trade and thus growing ports, adjacent coastal industries grew up using imported raw materials, and new industries requiring huge quantities of cooling water sought coastal locations, a process that has continued through to the dominance of coastal sites for nuclear power.

In many cases land for these developments was reclaimed from the sea or from coastal landscapes such as salt-marshes. Where developments were located on coasts that were eroding or liable to tidal flood, the coastline had to be stabilised, a demand enthusiastically met by the engineers using their newly acquired industrial skills. As we shall see, the stability secured has been temporary, rather than permanent, and there is now a search for more sustainable solutions to these coastal problems. However, the outcome for the Trust was the realisation that natural coast, untouched by modern man, was not only limited in extent, but rapidly disappearing as the various demands upon it expanded. By the mid-twentieth century, the need to secure the remaining unspoilt coast seemed urgent, and the Trust acted before it was too late by establishing Enterprise Neptune. Its target was 900 miles of coastline considered 'worth preserving'. Well over half this length has now been acquired.

However, as the Trust makes such good progress, the way in which our coastal zone has been managed (some would prefer 'mismanaged') is being challenged, and new approaches are emerging as old methods become dis-credited. The trigger has been the availability of public money – in this case for coastal defence against both erosion and tidal flood. The sums are not exces-sively large – at the most £100–£200 m each year – but the resulting concrete appears to the Treasury to be disappearing into a bottomless hole, for no sooner are defences completed than damage begins to occur; few measures last much longer than 30 or 40 years, while even fewer bring about the cessation of flooding or erosion claimed at their inception. In addition, these defences are increasingly extensive, carrying the penalty that local natural sources of sediment are eliminated, and concern is growing that they are both environ-mentally unsound and visually unfriendly.

The result is a current reappraisal of coastal management. The latest gov-ernment (Ministry of Agriculture, Fisheries & Food) publication proposes sustainable defences; these will entail increasingly careful cost-benefit assess-ment of schemes, relying on evacuation following flood warning as much as on ever-higher walls, limiting defence to urban frontages already defended, and increasingly choosing to 'do nothing', allowing nature to take its course. Alongside this, and encouraged by planning guidance issued by the Depart-ment of the Environment, there is the presumption that there should be no further development in areas at risk from cliff erosion or tidal (and river) flood. If this precludes replacement of property when it ends its useful life span, it will signal a move towards a truly sustainable coastal zone. Implicit within this new advice is the anticipated sea-level rise of about 2 ft (60 cm) in one hundred years' time. This will make the coast more mobile, and make any strategy that seeks to keep the coastline in the same place even more costly and increasingly prone to early failure.

As the major coastal landowner, the Trust will need to consider carefully these changes in policy and attitude, together with the impacts of rising sea level. Already parts of its coastline are defended, and even on rocky cliffed coasts local landslips have affected coastal paths and property. New sea defences have been built on Trust land, for example in the Lleyn peninsula. It is important that the Trust sets an example, by learning to live with natural change along the coast. To oppose coastal processes is no solution to coastal change. There is much talk these days of 'working with nature'; on the coast the Trust must be prepared to 'live with nature'.

Enterprise Neptune and coast 'worth preserving'

Although the catalyst for Enterprise Neptune was a simple piece of academic investigation, there seems to have been no subsequent academic appraisal of the scheme and the assumptions upon which it is based. The academic input was a survey of the entire coast, conducted on the ground and with the aid of aerial photographs by geographers from the University of Reading. Using the

1:25,000 ($2\frac{1}{2}$ in to 1 mile) map, they recorded land use in the entire coastal zone, including not only houses, but military constructions, active and abandoned, industrial uses, old and new, and temporary coastal homes such as caravans. The Trust took these maps and proceeded to classify the coast into three categories: Developed; Not for Acquisition; and Coast of Outstanding Natural Beauty. The middle category included not only coastline considered of too little value in landscape terms to be worthy of the Trust's interest, but also some areas regarded as already in 'safe hands'.

This simple message of a coast at risk with some 900 miles worth preserving has been the basis of the remarkably successful Enterprise Neptune. With the help of a re-launch in 1985 it has raised £18 m., and over £1 m. in the best years, allowing the acquisition of over 350 miles of coast to add to the 187 miles held in 1965 when Neptune began. The 500th mile was acquired in 1988, a length of Durham coastline of some symbolic significance because it had been despoiled by the tipping of colliery waste and was not deemed worthy of preservation in 1965. If the average acquisition rate of the last three decades is maintained, all 900 miles will be protected by the year 2030, little over one-third of the way through the Trust's next hundred years. By then the arithmetic of the 3,083 miles of the coast of England, Wales and Northern Ireland would be:

- Developed coast   1,100 miles (1,770 km)
- Undeveloped and in NT ownership   900 miles (1,450 km)
- Remainder of undeveloped coast   1,030 miles (1,660 km)

Acquisition has concentrated not just on the coastal strip, but has tried to bring into ownership the whole coastal zone, from the beach or cliff to the ridge that culminates the slope inland from the coast. This ensures protection of the whole coastal scene and of the whole view from any point. Thus the average area now acquired is 218 acres for every mile (60 hectares for each kilometre). This is an average depth from the coast of just over $\frac{1}{3}$ mile ($\frac{1}{2}$ km).

The current dominant interest of the National Trust, both in terms of ownership and recent acquisitions through Enterprise Neptune, is epitomised by open, cliffed coast, generally on the western side of Britain (where most of this coast lies). With some notable exceptions, such as Blakeney Point in Norfolk, which was acquired in 1924, and Orford Ness in Suffolk acquired in 1993, the Trust owns very little of the low coast of eastern England. It is interesting to note that the actively eroding coastal cliffs of glacial sediments in north Humberside, Norfolk and Suffolk are also not in Trust ownership; the single exception is Dunwich where the Heath (and with it the local cliff) was acquired in 1968. The Trust still owns no coast at all in nine counties, though only five of these have significant lengths (over 35 miles or 50 km) of coastline; these are Humberside, Lincolnshire, Hampshire, Clwyd and South Glamorgan.

Undeveloped coast 'not of high scenic value'

The coastal survey undertaken by the University of Reading for the National Trust included no value judgements. These were added by the Trust itself which understandably took the view that a rescue operation such as Neptune must concentrate on undeveloped coast of high scenic value.

Yet in selecting about half of the undeveloped coast for its attention, the Trust was setting aside over 1,000 miles (1,600 km) of coast which had not been despoiled by building. Much of this was the low coast of eastern England, and some was in the ownership of the RSPB, local naturalist trusts or the Nature Conservancy Council (now English Nature). Most was backed by farmland, and a considerable length was marred by sea defences against tidal flood, such as the shores of the Wash or the more open coast of Lincolnshire. The Trust list also excluded the rapidly eroding soft cliffs at Holderness in Yorkshire, and others in Norfolk and Suffolk.

Recently the Trust has reconsidered the status of this half of our undeveloped coast. Thus the opportunity was taken to acquire a large area of Orford Ness, one of the most important areas of coast shingle in Britain, from the Ministry of Defence. The southernmost length of the Ness has long been a National Nature reserve. The central and northern parts have been built on for military purposes, including the extraordinary 'Pagoda' buildings, as well as a building surviving from early work on radar. It has also suffered badly from the ill-considered extraction of shingle for the site's ambitious sea defences constructed by the Public Services Agency. Thus Orford Ness is by no means an undeveloped site, but it has been acquired and will gradually be restored, not to its original natural state, for that would not be rational, but to accept and utilise the historical significance of much that has gone on there in the name of defence of the realm.

In a similar way, some now-derelict partially industrialised coasts have been acquired for restoration and, where appropriate, preservation. These include the ancient metal-mining areas of the Hale peninsula in Cornwall and a section of the Durham coast near Easington. Nevertheless, this still excludes a huge length of rather ordinary, yet undeveloped, coastline in eastern England. The very fact that the Trust has not a single coastal holding in Lincolnshire epitomises the exclusion of these lengths of the coast from its active concern. As we shall see when we come to consider the projections for sea-level rise, there are good reasons why parts of these low coasts should be acquired and managed by the National Trust.

The nature of developed coasts and their value in landscape terms

Clearly there are many miles of developed coast that will not find themselves illustrating books designed to appeal to the tourist, such as the industrialised shores of some of our estuaries (whether the Thames or the Tees), the seaside villas and protective sea wall of Jaywick in Essex, or the bungalows of Canvey Island in Essex or Peacehaven in East Sussex. But the Trust does seem to have suffered from tunnel vision in its concentration on the undeveloped coast and there are landscapes within the developed coast which would be missed as much as many a windswept cliff in Devon or western Wales. Clough Williams-Ellis, in creating Portmeirion, was consciously seeking to create an Italianate village, cascading down the little valley to the sea. Many a Welsh or Cornish fishing village has achieved much the same effect through centuries of vernacular construction, rebuilding and modification, quite innocent of any plan to be artistic or consciously beautiful.

Less obviously worthy of the Trust's attention, yet surely deserving preservation when they are at risk, are some of Britain's seaside resorts and maritime buildings. The Lanes of Brighton, the few surviving Rows of Great Yarmouth (most have been victims of wartime destruction followed by the demands of modern vehicular access), and the Regency terraces of Hove are all part of the coastal scene. Fine buildings abound, from the Georgian elegance of Chatham dockyard to the Royal Pavilion at Brighton, or the 1930s modernity of the de la Warr pavilion at Bexhill. The aerial view of the Needles on the western end of the Isle of Wight is embellished and set in scale by the lighthouse.

Nor must the Victorian piers be forgotten, rapidly succumbing to decades of neglect and attack by salt and the undermining of their foundations as beaches are eroded away. At a rough count more than half Britain's stock of piers has been destroyed since the end of the Second World War, mostly in storms such as the surges of 1953 and 1978. Some pathetic stumps remain, as at Skegness, or the unsafe West Pier at Brighton. As recently as December 1993 the pier at Cromer was sliced through by a construction rig set loose by storms, though in this case the damage has been repaired. With the lifeboat station on the end and a traditional 'end of pier show' in the pavilion each summer, the pier at Cromer epitomises the case for preservation. When will the Trust acquire its first seaside pier?

Much of our most attractive coast is developed coast, and in time the Trust must surely come to terms with that and the fact that it is neither unchanging nor safe from deterioration. The replacement of open estuary moorings by huge marinas, the lack of maintenance of harbours too small for modern boats, the virtual abandonment of fishing ports like Lowestoft, rebuilding to accommodate fast-food takeaways or even more car-parking – all threaten the little seaside settlements dotted along some of our best coastlines. Modern planning legislation should take care of some of this, though the increasingly *laissez-faire* attitude to development control makes this an uncertain safeguard. The Trust must ensure that, where it has a foothold in a coastal village, it not only sets an example, but makes the necessary effort to educate those responsible for individual buildings and ensures that the local parish and district councils understand the importance of maintaining the overall quality and style that makes these little fishing villages so attractive.

Of course, purchase of built-up land, as of land threatened by development, is exceedingly expensive, so acquisition of critical buildings would have to be selective. But some key acquisitions and innovative management could show the way to district councils, which are both the planning authority and responsible for coastal defence along our upland coasts; they have as much interest in retaining the quality of their environment as any, for it is the basis of their tourist trade and thus of much of their prosperity. But above all we need to build on the hesitant steps towards different standards of planning control in the coastal zone, introduced to reduce the dangers of living near the coast, in order to achieve a new quality of design and control over redevelopment of built-up areas.

Managing the coast

The case for treating coastal development in a different way from development generally is implied by the establishment of Heritage Coasts by the Countryside Commission. Though managed differently from National Parks, these coastal zones are selected for their combination of scenic importance and tourist significance. Investment needs to be carefully directed and an awareness of the character and quality of the coastal environment developed amongst those responsible for it.

Compared with the 900 miles (1,450 km) of coast deemed worthy of National Trust ownership, almost the same length has been designated (usually by the Countryside Commission) as Heritage Coasts in England and Wales. The Trust owns about 40 per cent of the total length of Heritage Coasts, but with a wide range from 100 per cent on Lundy and 77 per cent for the Lizard, down to 23 per cent for North Yorkshire and what was 15 per cent on the Suffolk coast before the acquisition of Orford Ness in 1993. Again it is largely the rocky cliffed coasts where the figures exceed 40 per cent, though north Devon (Hartland) is only 28 per cent and for the fine, largely limestone, cliffs of south Pembrokeshire, only 24 per cent.

In future the coasts where the most careful and understanding management will be required will be the low coasts of sandy beaches, sand dunes and salt-marshes along the exposed coastlines of England and Wales and the estuaries. This is especially so because in the past estuaries and salt-marshes have suffered most from reclamation for agriculture and industry, and reclaimed land cannot adjust to sea-level change. Thus it will be necessary either to try to increase coastal protection in these areas (and thus manage them more intensively) or seek to return as much as possible to their natural state.

This introduction may be concluded by analysing the current National Trust holdings using eleven roughly equal lengths of coast (Table 1).

Table 1
National Trust ownership, cliffs, salt-marshes and embankments
(all percentages rounded; England & Wales based on JNCC data)

	LENGTH (MILES)	% OWNED BY NT	% CLIFFS OVER 20M	% SALT-MARSHES	% EMBANKED
Northern Ireland	335	13	8*	0*	†
Cumbria/Lancs	275	7	3	39	55
North Wales	317	9	12	8	6
Dyfed	283	22	48	7	3
S Wales, Somerset & N Devon	301	20	17	23	29
Cornwall	313	34	45	10	3
S Devon & Somerset	247	30	31	19	11
Hants, Isle of Wight & Sussex	240	9	13	18	29
Kent & Essex	256	5	4	58	70
Suffolk, Norfolk & Lincs	250	12	4	41	36
North Humberside to Berwick	287	11	15	4	36

*Data for Northern Ireland from *Atlas of Britain*, 1964
†No data available for Northern Ireland

As Table 1 shows, there is a very close (and statistically significant) correlation between the proportion of high cliffs (over 65 ft or 20 m), a close inverse correlation with the proportion of coast owned and the proportion of coast occupied by embankments against tidal flooding) and a less close inverse correlation (though still statistically significant) between the proportion of coast owned and the percentage of salt-marshes. This provides us with a precise starting point for looking at the challenges of management of the coastal environment over the next one hundred years and the appropriate response of the National Trust in both its acquisition and management policies.

The major problems for the Trust's coastal policies

Pressures for coastal development do not cease with ownership, and the larger the proportion of coast in inalienable ownership, the greater the pressures for development on the remaining coast, which may spill over onto Trust land. Some are relatively easy to resist: plans for housing and ugly agricultural buildings can be turned away; caravans and tents can be sited a little way from the coast itself; and public access threatening the vegetation of sand dunes, unstable cliffs and salt-marshes can be restricted. But gas and oil pipelines have to come ashore, ships must dock and industries requiring large volumes of cooling water may require a coastal site. Military use of the coast has always been significant, and its increasing technical complexity can increase its impact on the landscape. Renewable wind energy resources are greatest at coastal and adjacent inshore sites, and it will be hard to limit the spread of modern turbines as we try to move away from dependence upon fossil fuels.

The second management problem results from those natural processes which have built the coast, the waves and the tides. Coastal cliffs have been formed by marine erosion, and our beaches, sand dunes and salt-marshes have been built up by marine deposition. Indeed the two are connected, because the sand for our beaches and the mud for our salt-marshes come from cliffs, the only exception being those highland coasts where steep rivers can carry such sediment to the sea. In general, it is only by maintaining the natural processes of change at the coast that these landforms can continue to develop; cut off wave action and cliffs degrade, and salt-marshes and dunes cease to be replenished with the sediment they need. The coast is a mobile environment subjected to varying conditions of wave and tide as storms pound the coastline, moving back here, building out there. Change is the only natural way to accommodate the effects of wind and waves from different directions. The complexity of adjustment is such that natural wave-induced currents move sediment from eroding cliffs to broad beaches further down the coast, from headlands into bays, from beaches into sand dunes, from inter-tidal mudflats on to salt-marshes; this interdependence between erosion and accumulation is at the heart of the natural balance at the coast. Everywhere on our low and weak coasts fronting the lowlands of England, but increasingly even on rocky western coasts, the National Trust will have to learn to accommodate and live with these natural processes of change.

The third issue for the future stems from that third of the coast which, though undeveloped, was dismissed as 'not worthy of preservation', in 1965. Questions will increasingly be asked why any undeveloped coastline on two small islands is not worthy of preservation from development, and indeed from some of the worst attentions of our sea defence engineers. Such issues were raised by Malcolm Smith in the *Guardian* in February 1990 in a review of the achievement of Enterprise Neptune. Excluding the land held by other conservation bodies, that still leaves a lot of coast at risk from future development, including new sea defences. Can this further third remain largely outside the Trust's concern?

Finally, Trust management will have to continue to re-examine the one-third of the coast which early leaflets promoting Enterprise Neptune described as 'coastline ruined for ever'. In fact, as we have seen, some of the recent acquisitions of Enterprise Neptune fall into this category: the Durham coast scarred by mining and the dumping of colliery waste on the beaches, Orford Ness scarred by military activities, and parts of the Cornish coast with a legacy of mining and attendant pollution from waste dumps and acid mine water.

However, alongside such properties is the developed coast of current or potential visual quality, and it has already been argued that while this cannot be acquired on a large scale by the Trust, through critical acquisitions and education of owners and the planning authorities, the Trust has an important role to play in what is for many the most interesting part of the coastal scene. The Trust owns several historically significant lighthouses, opportune acquisitions at a time when modern navigation techniques have rendered them obsolete. But built-up sites have not been common in the acquisitions of Enterprise Neptune. Can this attitude survive the next century?

Coastal evolution and coastal management with a rising sea level

Low coasts

The sea has been close to its present level for over 5,000 years, but its level is not fixed. Quite apart from the twice-daily oscillations of the tide, a slow rise of sea level has been going on for some decades. The present rate varies a little around the British coast because some areas, like the Thames estuary, are sinking, whilst Scotland is rising, but the average rise is just under two millimetres a year. Over time this adds up – the rise has been about 6 in (15 cm) over the last century. The cause is the expansion of the oceans as they warm up after the cold climate of the 'Little Ice Age' of the seventeenth and eighteenth centuries, and this will increase with global warming as carbon dioxide from our heavy use of fossil fuels like coal and oil builds up in the atmosphere. To ocean expansion will be added more rapid melting of our mountain glaciers, so sea level is expected to rise two or three times as fast in the future, and by about 8 in (20 cm) by 2050. Problems of coastal flooding and erosion will worsen, calling for new remedial measures.

Flood defence of areas worthy of protection such as coastal towns and industry, or large areas of agricultural land such as the Fens or the Somerset Levels will pose no serious problems. Banks can be built higher to retain existing standards of flood defence and the additional expenditure will be fully justified. However, some smaller areas will become relatively expensive to protect, and since government intends to check the viability of schemes by comparisons of costs against benefits, we may expect that some will prove unviable. This will bring increasingly frequent floods and perhaps the intentional abandonment of existing defensive lines, allowing the tide to reach banks further inland, or the natural rise of the coast landward of the salt-marshes, dunes and beaches of the original unreclaimed coast.

Perhaps more serious will be the changes along those coasts currently protected from erosion. As the Royal Commission on Afforestation and Coastal Erosion pointed out in 1911, it is only possible to protect parts of the coast if other parts are left to erode to supply sediment to adjacent beaches. The same view was taken in the 1993 *Strategy for Flood and Coastal Defence in England and Wales* prepared by the MAFF: 'To attempt to protect every inch of coastline from change would not only be uneconomic but would work against the dynamic processes which determine that coastline and could have an adverse effect on defences elsewhere and on the natural environment.' Yet our ambitious coastal engineers have protected very high proportions of our eroding coastline and ignored this long-standing wise advice.

The result has been a catalogue of short-lived schemes that have accelerated sediment loss from beaches; threatened walls have been protected by ever larger groynes; and, most recently, giant Scandinavian boulders have been used to try to imitate the protection offered by the denuded beach, though failing to protect coastal recreation or amenity. In a similar way, some of the eroding salt-marshes left in front of flood banks protecting reclaimed farmland are becoming so narrow as to offer inadequate protection against wave attack.

The only possible solution in both these cases is to provide a greater width of beach or salt-marsh in front of the coastal defences. This can be achieved in two ways: by falling back (in a planned way or by simply ceasing to maintain the existing banks) where there is space to do so; or where this is not possible because of buildings, by building up the beach with natural sediment dredged from offshore. Such beach nourishment need be no more expensive than a traditional scheme based on stronger walls and larger groynes; it provides a far better recreational environment, and also has the virtue of reinforcing, rather than opposing, nature and the natural process of change along the coast.

Nevertheless, beach feeding is an interference with natural processes and, quite apart from the economic case which will tend to restrict its use to areas with existing wall and often with urban frontages, there is a strong case for letting nature take its course wherever this can reasonably be done. As discussed below, this will be easier if legislation is introduced allowing compensation to those farmers and house owners directly affected. But the National Trust should be prepared to allow a natural coast to survive or to redevelop, even where the immediate effects seem deleterious. It should realise that even if it does interfere and spend large sums of money, the likely effect is no more than postponement of the changes that nature will inevitably bring about. The history of coastal engineering shows that at most it wins two or three decades of stability, but by the end of that period the problems are increasingly intractable; indeed, after storm damage, most rebuilt coastal defences are set back by the very same amount that nature would have achieved year by year had things been left alone.

Thus there is currently much talk of planned retreat, and of 'working with nature', though some of this is rhetoric and an attempt to justify entirely conventional coastal defences in terms of the dynamics of sediment movement. The 1993 MAFF publication already referred to states that all coastal defence schemes should be sustainable – this is not defined, and taken literally it would probably stop all coastal defence work. It says nothing about 'managed retreat', simply requiring the 'do nothing' scenario to be subject to cost-benefit analysis. However, in introducing the report at Great Yarmouth in 1993, the Secretary of State said

'Managed retreat' I would define as a deliberate decision to set back the line of coastal defence, a decision which may or may not be accompanied by measures to enhance the environmental interest of the site in question. As such we would see it as one of a range of options for consideration in rural coastal areas. . . . Its advantages can include the creation of a foreshore which, by absorbing the energy of the sea, will form part of the new line of defence. It may also enable the creation or recreation of intertidal habitats. But I want to emphasise . . . that there is no central Government policy to impose 'managed retreat' in localities where it is inappropriate.

The National Trust, in conjunction with English Nature, has just undertaken the first British experiment in setting back a flood bank and returning reclaimed salt-marsh to the tides. This has been done for one field on Northey Island in the Blackwater estuary in Essex/Suffolk; although a modest experiment, it is exciting since it indicated how quickly the abandoned field was colonised by the appropriate salt-marsh plants as seeds were brought in on the tide. It demonstrates how readily reclaimed land can be successfully returned to its natural, tidal state. However, volunteers for managed retreat will be scarce along most of the English coast, though 'doing nothing' may be imposed by the failure of any other scheme to meet the increasingly tough cost-benefit criteria imposed by government. However, the Trust is in a strong position if it accepts the argument that the geomorphologically unstable natural condition of the coast is part of the heritage it seeks to preserve. There is actually a great opportunity for the Trust to adopt a strong ethic of leaving, and in many places returning, our low coasts to nature.

To leave coastal evolution to nature is not as dangerous as it seems; coasts usually adjust quite slowly because change involves moving large quantities of sediment by waves and currents. In any case, so far as a sustainable solution goes, there is nothing better able to cope with sea-level rise than a wholly natural coast. Beaches can adjust their shape and position, coastal dunes can store vast quantities of sand blown off the beach against a great storm, when it will buttress the beach against wave attack. And best of all, salt-marshes almost by definition will keep pace with any persistent rise in high tide, with the more frequent flooding quickly building up successive mud layers to keep them just below the level of the highest spring tides.

It is to be hoped that proposals for managed retreat will be encouraged by central government through some scheme of compensation for those whose land is in this way returned to the sea. At present large sums of public money are spent on sea defences, yet the contribution from those few individuals defended against erosion or flood is infinitesimally small. But where it is deemed inappropriate to spend public money in this way (because the value of property at risk is less than the cost of the defences required), there is currently no compensation for those denied protection.

Outside wholly rural areas, which in any case come bottom of the government's list of priorities for money to assist the construction of coastal defences, managed retreat may not be the most sensible solution; in these areas increased use of beach-feeding schemes is likely. This is a logical approach at seaside resorts where the wall in front of the promenade needs protection and a wide beach does that whilst also serving the needs of recreation. The logic of such schemes was demonstrated by the use of two large feeds from offshore at Bournemouth, and they are widely used abroad, as in the Netherlands and the USA.

Cliffed coasts

It is usually assumed that the rocky coasts of western England, where the bulk of the Trust's holdings lie, are free of the problems brought by sea-level rise. This is strictly true only for those lengths of 'plunging cliffs' where the cliffs descend into the sea at all states of the tide. These will change no more in future than they do at the moment, which is usually very slowly since the rocks are tough and the sea has nothing more than water and trapped air to aid it in quarrying away at the coast. But most of our rocky cliffs rise above a coastal platform with a gentle slope, cut in rock and covered at high tide. In places the foot of the cliff has a narrow beach of rounded boulders or shingle, with sand in the deeper inlets and bays.

Geomorphologists know less about the behaviour of these coastal platforms and the cliffs behind them than they should, but it is likely that they will begin to erode in a noticeable way, even where this is not currently the case. Of course, there are already areas of instability along our western coasts, and some of the land held by the Trust has been affected: for example, around Porth Neigwl on the south side of the Lleyn peninsula the cliffs of glacial till suffer from landslides where the till descends to the beach and can be eroded during storms. In places the coastal slopes have been stabilised (though only temporarily if beach erosion continues) by draining and/or the construction of revetments; elsewhere the coastal footpath has had to be relocated. The coastal road past Plas-yn-Rhiw was stabilised in 1968 (with much detailed discussion between the Trust and the County Council to secure a high quality of landscaping in the reinstatement), but was again threatened by another landslide in 1983. It was yet again stabilised by a combination of a basalt rock revetment and drainage of the slope under and below the road. Long-term stability along the Porth Neigwl coast is probably unattainable, but this does not prevent ambitious plans for coastal protection schemes being put forward.

In the 1980s there were ten other reports that National Trust land was being affected by landslipping, and at least three of these were coastal slides – on the north Cornish coast, on the southern side of the Isle of Wight and at the Giant's Causeway in Northern Ireland. In all these cases the Trust agreed to some drainage work to aid stabilisation, at least in the most critical areas. Although more extensive work has been resisted at some sites on landscape grounds, there is no indication that the Trust appreciates the value of these landslips as natural events, or their academic interest for the geomorphologist and the civil engineer. On some Heritage Coasts with cliffs, though not necessarily in areas of Trust ownership, action has been taken to try to stabilise dangerous cliffs to reduce the hazard for holidaymakers on the beach below. An example is the cliffed Glamorgan Heritage Coast, where some of the more spectacular efforts, such as blasting one length of cliff, have been of little value; education and warning signs would probably be a more appropriate management technique. It has to be appreciated that steep cliffs are created only by attack from the sea, and if this attack is stopped, the cliff will decay; if the cliffs are intentionally graded to a lower angle, in time marine erosion will restore them to their natural oversteepened and hazardous state.

Coastal platforms control the attack on the base of the cliffs behind them. Erosion occurs at high tide and when the sea surface is raised by storms, and even then the largest waves will break at the edge of the platform, expending their greatest forces before the cliff. Over time these coastal platforms are lowered – by the disintegration which accompanies twice-daily wetting and drying, by the abrasion of particles moved around by the sea, and by the not insignificant grazing effect of limpets and other animals which live in crevices on the rock and feed on the algae colonising and invading the rock surface. This slow lowering of the coastal platform has the effect of allowing greater wave energies to reach the cliff foot more often, and thus coastal platform lowering and cliff retreat go hand in hand; they are connected by the geometry of the coastal platform slope and the rate of surface reduction.

Sea-level rise will speed up this process and bring about increased cliff retreat and the formation of wider coastal platforms, though these can also suffer erosion at the seaward edge. Where cliff retreat already occurs and cliff falls or coastal landslides are the result, this will become more rapid and will spread to adjacent lengths of coast which at present appear to be stable. On tough rocks or in sheltered locations, the very slow rates of erosion today may increase so little that they remain imperceptible and of no practical concern. But it remains likely that troublesome erosion will become more common along these cliffed coasts, and pressure to take remedial action will increase.

Particular problems will occur as the upper, more gentle slopes above steep cliffs become reactivated. These cliff profiles are often known as 'slope over wall', the near-vertical rocky cliff leading upward to steep vegetated slopes, often on weathered and broken rock or glacial till (boulder clay) overlying the solid rock outcropping in the cliff. Excellent examples are found along the Yorkshire coast between Whitby and Scarborough, but it is also a very common coastal form in Devon and Cornwall. At present these upper slopes are fairly stable, though they may show signs of movement after heavy rain, especially in hollows where water converges and reduces the internal strength of the underlying soil.

With more rapid erosion of the steep cliffs below as sea-level rise takes effect, the base of these slopes will be undercut, and they will reactivate, leading to minor slips, small mudflows in wet hollows, and, in some places, much larger, deeper-seated landslides. This instability will extend over the whole slope with time, increasing the problems for livestock management since fences will be damaged by slope movements, especially just above the rocky cliff where they are most needed for safety. It will also make it difficult to maintain safe all-weather paths across these upper slopes; the only long-term solution may be to re-site the coastal path on the west of the coastal slope.

The long-term role of the National Trust as the major coastal landowner

The Trust will need to consider its policy if, as seems likely, instability of coastal cliffs and slopes becomes far more common. The isolated cases so far dealt with have perhaps seemed necessary interference with the natural instability of coastal slopes. But the action taken is short-term and only a partial remedy, not a cure. The problems are deep seated (in a literal sense too) and will return to trouble future generations of coastal managers. Thus the relatively minor and essentially local costs of drainage schemes, of rather tidier and remodelled slopes, of walls or revetments separating the cliff from the beach, must be viewed as the beginning of a process of coastal modification which can have no end. The Trust should be encouraged to take a long-term-view and to accept that coastal properties will always be at risk from modification by the sea, and that the preservation of a dynamic, slowly altering, yet relatively stable coastal cliff and slope is wholly consistent with its remit of preservation. The alternative would be to create a continually extending collection of coastal defences, expensive to maintain, and ineffective in any long-term view; or a collection of increasingly tidy, man-made under-drained slopes in place of the wild unpredictability of truly natural coastal slopes and cliffs.

The Crown Estate is responsible for most of the British foreshore (between the water marks of high and low ordinary tides) and for utilisation of the offshore zone; thus it is the Crown Estate which issues licences (in conjunction with the MAFF) for offshore marine dredging for aggregates. The National Trust is already the largest single coastal landowner and will be even more prominent by the end of the next one hundred years; it will therefore increasingly dominate the major actors on the coastal scene. These include the MAFF, responsible at a national level for our coastal policy, and the National Rivers Authority, which is the main agent for carrying out flood protection (sea defence) measures on the coast. Coasts liable to erosion, but not tidal flood because of their altitude, are the responsibility of the coastal district authorities. Any schemes proposed for the coast must be notified to those listed under statute: English Nature, the National Rivers Authority, the Countryside Commission and local landowners.

All have the opportunity to comment on schemes at a formative stage and to oversee them through whatever modifications may ensue. In addition, the public has a chance to comment on, or formally to object to, schemes – provided they see the press advertisement and act within the required period. However, the public cannot usually follow a scheme through its design stages, and even if their objection is upheld at enquiry, the revised scheme is not open for further public comment.

So far, few schemes appear to have been designed for National Trust frontages, or were built so long ago that current concerns about the length of coast subject to engineering works were not an issue. Increasingly, as the Trust acquires coastal properties in our lowland counties, such works will become more controversial. Currently proposals for the renewal and improvement of flood banks on the north Norfolk coast, part of which is in Trust ownership, are under discussion. Some of this work could cost £2 million for just a mile or two of bank protecting a nature (bird) reserve which has been created by keeping the sea off former salt-marsh. Is it justifiable that man-made habitats accorded international reserve status should then be protected artificially at ever-increasing cost? Perhaps suitable areas with grazing and small ponds and lakes should be developed on lowlands inland and the coastal zone left to natural salt-marsh and the associated birds and animals.

The Trust has recently acquired Copt Hall Farm which slopes down to an Essex estuary where grazing and rich arable fields reclaimed from former salt-marsh lie behind a flood bank. The grass is grazed by geese and other migrant birds and poses the Trust interesting management questions. In front of the bank the pitiful remnant of the unreclaimed salt-marsh is decaying, with enlarging creeks and pools and an ever-decreasing vegetation cover: many different methods have been put forward to remedy this marsh decay, which is widespread in Essex. These remedies stem from different assumptions about the underlying cause, but the basic reason must be interference by man, since the marsh has been growing in these estuaries and along the open coast for the 5,–6,000 years that sea level has been at its present position. Reclaiming a large part of the natural marsh and excluding the tide changes the balance of water movement and pattern of mud deposition. Tidal creeks adjusted to carrying the large volumes of water on and off a marsh find themselves beheaded and without the major part of their natural catchment. It is hardly surprising that the remaining marsh loses its natural stability.

At Copt Hall Farm the Trust will have to choose between retaining the traditional (for the last 150 years that is) pattern of farming and the winter attraction for geese and related grazing birds, or taking out the flood bank and returning to the natural slope of the land and the natural width of salt-marsh. A factor in the Trust's decision may well be the existence of a major RSPB site further up the same estuary. The RSPB manages its holdings with a single aim – at times pursued with a ruthless single-mindedness. The Trust has far wider aims, and as the RSPB maintains goose grazing further up the estuary, it may be easier for the Trust to return part of its land to a natural state; this would remove the long-term cost of maintaining the banks against a rising sea level when the outer remnant of salt-marsh offers less and less protection against erosion as time passes.

The purpose of land acquisition is central to management policies at the coast: the Trust seeks to maintain a reasonable natural diversity and tries so to manage tourist pressure that properties are not damaged by the very people who seek to enjoy them, not to run them solely as nature reserves. This is the task of English Nature, which will consequently find itself faced with some awkward and philosophically challenging choices as sea level rises. Even the Countryside Commission, whilst seeking to manage tourism in an acceptable way, must keep as its priority the enhancement of recreational access and use.

The broad remit of the Trust does not make choices easier. Ruthless single-mindedness will be abhorrent to some, but at least the goal is always clear, to maximise the resource in view. While other organisations with a single purpose can alter the landscape to achieve a particular aim – for example, the RSPB's policy on the north Norfolk coast – the Trust has to balance a whole series of sometimes conflicting considerations. Again, on the island of Ramsey the RSPB can prohibit access by geologists to one of the finest fossiliferous exposures of the Tremadoc series in the United Kingdom, simply because it does not want its bird colonies disturbed. It may even be that fuller consideration of these issues would in some cases modify the Trust's view of which bits of the undeveloped coasts are truly in safe hands.

V

The Countryside

PHILIP LOWE

C ONCERN FOR THE countryside is the emblem of the British environmental movement. Much of the most cherished countryside is owned by
the National Trust, which is one of the oldest environmental organisations in the country. This gives the Trust a unique role and special
responsibilities in countryside protection and management, but also a particular and changing relationship with the wider environmental movement. It
is from an understanding of how this relationship has evolved and its present
basis that we can begin to consider not only how the Trust might continue to
protect for public benefit its own extensive holdings but also to mobilise its
considerable expertise and great reserves of goodwill to help achieve a vibrant
countryside.

The Trust and the rural environmental movement
in retrospect

As one of the oldest environmental groups, the Trust was founded as part of
a general movement for the preservation of open space threatened by urban
expansion. The concept of the Trust arose specifically out of the work of the
Commons Preservation Society which, since 1865, had been conducting a battle
to save common lands. It was from recognition that the Society's inability to
acquire property was a drawback to its work that the proposal emerged to
create a special body to buy and hold land and buildings, to secure their
protection from development and for public enjoyment.[1] However, as Chapter
Two demonstrated, the balance of its efforts inevitably shifted, not only as it
began to acquire properties but also following its reconstitution in 1907 as a
statutory body by Act of Parliament. The Act charged the Trust with 'the
permanent preservation' of property 'for the benefit of the nation' and conferred
upon it the powers, not only to create bylaws for the regulation and protection of
its land and buildings, but also to declare them inalienable. This unique status
meant that the Trust could not divest itself of them, the intention being to

inspire confidence in donors and supporters that properties donated to the Trust would be preserved in perpetuity.

With the numbers of properties in its ownership having passed a hundred in the early 1920s, the Executive Committee of the Trust found that the care of these and acquisition of more presented as much work as the organisation could manage. It formally decided to limit its public intervention to matters which affected either what it already owned or expected to acquire. The broader campaigning role passed to other groups, especially the Council for the Preservation of Rural England, set up in 1926 with the Trust's backing.

Nevertheless, the eventual success of the preservation movement in its dealings with government after the Second World War had profound implications for the role of the National Trust. In particular, as legislation was passed to preserve buildings and landscape, government sought to use the existing machinery of the Trust rather than extend its own establishment. That gave the Trust unique legal and financial privileges and a working relationship with government not enjoyed by other private landowners or environmental organisations. This semi-official status had to be handled with delicacy and discretion on both sides, so as not to jeopardise the respect that the Trust enjoyed amongst potential donors and supporters as a worthy and essentially independent body. Its ability to maintain that particular balancing act provided the basis for the Trust's massive post-war growth. In twenty years after 1945, its estate trebled in size to 330,000 acres (133,546 ha), adding an average of 11,000 acres (4,452 ha) as well as five historic houses each year. The demands of upkeep and restoration put immense strains on the Trust's financial and organisational resources. Inevitably, it became ever more preoccupied with the management of its own estate. A general cautiousness, arising from a wish not to overcommit itself and from the considerable burden of responsibility it had to bear as a large landowner and as a statutory body, meshed with a more general conservatism in the Trust's outlook.

While such changes in outlook were perhaps inevitable in an organisation seeking to insert itself into the rural fabric, it had the unfortunate consequence of isolating the Trust from the broad currents of the access and conservation movements in the post-war period. It was ill at ease with the advent of mass participation in countryside recreation and the increasing professionalism and popularity of conservation.

With the spread of car ownership in the 1950s and '60s, the Trust grew concerned at the 'threat' posed to the beauty and attractions of its properties by the sheer pressure of visitors. The Trust's report for 1965 betrayed grudging bewilderment at its popularity: 'for the gregarious visitor the Trust can offer little and suffer fewer'. Undoubtedly, it faced a real dilemma. It firmly believed that preservation must be its first task and must take precedence over public recreation. The maxim coined by its chairman, John Bailey, in the 1920s was often repeated: 'Preservation may always permit of access, while without preservation access becomes for ever impossible' (quoted in Fedden 1968). A restatement of the same theme in the early 1970s was that its open spaces 'are held in trust for future generations and must not be sacrificed to short-term pressures' or transformed into 'popular playgrounds' (Fedden 1974). This lack of sympathy with the recreational needs of ordinary people was reflected in the attitude towards its growing membership. Distrustful of the possibility that increasing numbers might put it under pressure to alter its priorities, the Trust's leadership was emphatically against any positive steps to enlarge the membership. It also disdained publicity and was reluctant to appeal for funds.

Another set of issues that the Trust found it difficult to come to grips with in the post-war period was the growing professionalism and specialisation in the conservation world (see Chapter Two). Increasingly, the Trust's dedicated amateurism and the traditional approach to estate management of its regional staff were assailed by external professional groups in such fields as nature conservation, countryside management and archaeology, which were developing new techniques and setting more exacting standards of protection and management. The feeling often was that the Trust was not sufficiently energetic or imaginative in developing the opportunities which its wide range of possessions gave it. The response of the Trust tended to be a certain aloofness to what it regarded as the special pleading of sectional interests wanting 'to get their hands' on its property. Apart from forestry, where the Trust's agents were typically active, and in some cases excessively so, its approach to estate management might best be characterised as benign neglect. In a period of large-scale agricultural transformation, that was probably no bad thing. But in a context in which the public interest in the rural environment and land use was increasingly expressed through local planning authorities and statutory conservation agencies, the Trust risked appearing to be an anachronism. With the large majority of its properties now embraced by such protective planning designations as National Parks and Sites of Special Scientific Interest overseen by official bodies, this raised the question of whether Trust ownership merely to preserve was any longer necessary.

Finally, the Trust seemed quite out of touch with the new wave of environmentalism which began to emerge in the late 1960s and which threw up new groups and revivified many of the older conservation and amenity organisations. The new concerns of resource conservation, pollution and economic and population growth seemed distant from those of the Trust. The populism, radicalism and youthfulness of the new environmentalism also were a world apart from the Trust's way of operating. The environmental radicals of the time, if they gave any thought to the Trust, saw it as elitist and smug and contributing little to the environmental cause beyond protecting its precious 1 per cent of England, Wales and Northern Ireland.

The considerable changes in the organisation and management of the Trust since the early 1970s have blunted some of these criticisms, and have provided the basis for a new rapprochement between the Trust and the wider environmental movement. Undoubtedly, a key catalytic event in the modernisation of the Trust was the dispute which arose in 1966 over the conduct of the Enterprise Neptune campaign; this led the Trust to dismiss the campaign's director, Commander Rawnsley (a grandson of one of the Trust's founders). Rawnsley became the focal point for members of the Trust discontented with its policies. Their central criticism was that its constitution had failed to adapt to changing circumstances and they called for a more open and accountable organisation, one more responsive to popular interests.

Although the criticisms of Rawnsley's reform group were roundly defeated at a requisitioned Extraordinary General Meeting and in a subsequent poll of the members, the charges they had made and the publicity these attracted stung the leadership of the Trust. An advisory committee under the chairmanship of Sir Henry Benson was appointed to conduct a thorough appraisal of the Trust's work and organisation (Benson Committee 1968). Major changes followed. The Trust began to value and promote the expansion of its membership and closer contacts with ordinary members. The system of regional committees was established to decentralise the Trust's administration. At the same time, the managerial function of headquarters was strengthened and its professional staff enlarged.

These developments unleashed a massive growth. In the 25 years up to 1990, its membership grew more than thirteenfold to reach two million. Membership income rose rapidly – from less than one seventh of annual revenue to about a third in the 1980s – to become the Trust's biggest source of income. With three-quarters of Trust members being recruited at its properties, membership growth drew upon and in turn swelled visitor numbers, as the vast majority of members then made use of their right of free entry to Trust properties. Since the early 1980s the Trust has also begun to make significant profits from what members and visitors spend once inside properties, at shops, restaurants and tea-rooms. While the Trust regards its membership, above all, as a source of funds, it has also come to value them as a source of voluntary support in helping out at properties: in 1993, over 28,000 volunteers put in 1.63 million hours of work, carrying out many tasks that the Trust could not otherwise afford to do.

Of necessity the Trust has had to cope with the growing number of visitors in the way it manages its properties, and it has learnt to do so with considerable flair and skill. Its presentation of historic buildings led the way, but it has also become adept at caring for large numbers visiting its countryside properties while maintaining their physical fabric and 'sense of place', thereby developing considerable expertise in such fields as the repair and maintenance of footpaths, landscape screening of car-parks, environmental interpretation, guided walks and visitor management. In doing so, the Trust has responded to criticism of having been too preoccupied in the past with historic houses to the neglect of the open spaces in its possession.

A new rapprochement

The new emphasis on services to visitors, the large numbers to be accommodated and the Trust's growing professionalism converged in the 1980s on the issue of management, focussing on the quality and sensitivity of the care that the Trust showed in the management of the landscape and the buildings in its keeping and of the visitors they attracted (see Chapter Two). This has made the Trust attentive to the professional world of conservation, raising standards to the point that in many fields, particularly the conservation and presentation of historic houses, their furnishings and their grounds, it is the acknowledged pacesetter. In part, this new emphasis marks a shift for the Trust in the balance between acquiring new properties and maintaining its existing estate, in favour of the latter. But it also reflects a growing realisation within the Trust that inalienability implies not only ownership in perpetuity but also long-term care. Perhaps the most telling expression of this new outlook has been the decision of the Trust to take back some properties leased to conservation organisations in cases where it was felt that the Trust's resources and holistic approach might improve standards of management.

It is in the exemplary way in which it manages and presents its properties, rather than the fire brigade role of rescuing endangered sites, that the Trust now tends to base its claim for public support. As the present Director-General has put it:

> The Trust has accumulated formidable experience in the practical conservation of both nature and the wider landscape. It is through the appreciation of that experience, renewed and augmented as it must always be by learning, that the Trust is able to make an authoritative and often pioneering contribution to the protection of the environment. [2]

The Trust's claim to authority in this regard rests on its ownership of the crown jewels of British conservation. For example, it is the largest owner of National Park land, with 9 per cent of the total, which is over six times more than that owned by all the park authorities put together. The importance of the Trust in the fulfilment of the parks' objectives is enhanced by the fact that its holdings are concentrated in the heartland of the parks and in those parks subject to the greatest popular pressure – the Lake District, the Peak District, Dartmoor, Exmoor and Snowdonia.

Likewise, the Trust is one of the major owners of land of nature conservation interest in England, Wales and Northern Ireland. It owns about 9 per cent of the total area of SSSIs, well in excess of that owned by any of the official conservation bodies. Included in its holdings are good examples of communities of plants and animals now rare in the United Kingdom, including chalk and limestone grasslands, fens, sand dunes, montane vegetation and ancient woodlands. The Trust's holdings include about one-third of the uplands in England and Wales identified as being of national or international importance for the survival of particular species with a very restricted distribution, such as the Fen Violet, the Glanville Fritillary and the Little Tern.

Then again, the Trust's ownership of more than a quarter of the undeveloped coast encompasses most that is of significant scenic or conservation interest, including 40 per cent of designated Heritage Coasts. The Trust is also the largest landowner of archaeological sites (with over 40,000 – about 6 per cent of the national total), and the largest owner by far of vernacular buildings.

A consequence of this great treasury is that the achievement of official policy in the fields of scenic protection, historic preservation, nature conservation and countryside recreation depend critically on the Trust. Official bodies in the respective fields must operate with and through the Trust in much of their work. In turn, the Trust has been able to draw upon their expertise, specialist support and sources of grant aid.

In this partnership with statutory agencies, the Trust can draw on sources of authority which they cannot. One of these is the great variety and diversity of its properties. What might once have been regarded as a hopeless eclecticism is now undoubtedly a strength in the pursuit of a holistic approach to environmental management in an age of professional specialisms. In the words of a former Chairman of the Trust: 'no other body has such a range of conservation responsibilities . . . The Trust is in a position to manage this country's heritage in a comprehensive manner'[3].

Another of the Trust's advantages is the large reserve of goodwill it enjoys. Its influential support among the leading institutions of high culture is reflected in the quality of expertise it can command on a voluntary basis, as well as the services of the great and the good and of media celebrities to head up appeals and serve on committees. In addition, the Trust's mass membership attests to its wider popularity, as does the flow of donations that gives it one of the highest voluntary incomes of all British charities.

If anything, the Trust's moral authority has grown in recent years while that of government bodies and many other national institutions has waned. In the conservation field the authority of official agencies has been weakened as the permanency of statutory commitments and responsibilities has fallen into doubt. In a reversal of the process that took place in the 1950s and '60s, when the Trust seemed anachronistic beside the steady advance of statutory protection, the experience since the late 1970s of 'rolling back the state' has given it new importance by underlining the absolute commitment that inalienability entails. In a period which has seen government efforts to weaken rural planning constraints, the privatisation of Forestry Commission and Water Authority lands (many of them being of considerable amenity or conservation interest), pressures on the Nature Conservancy Council (now English Nature) and English Heritage to divest themselves of properties in their care, and the extensive reorganisation of statutory bodies, the Trust is right to stress that its 'great strength lies in its commitment to taking the long view'.[4]

In becoming 'public property',[5] the Trust has had to learn to be more open in its decision-making. This has involved efforts to be much more positive in informing members and the public of its thinking and action; to broaden the social base for recruitment to the Trust's council and committees; and to improve its capability to handle internal debate and external criticism about its priorities and decisions. As with the Rawnsley affair, some of these changes were stimulated by controversy – for example, over the Trust's agreement in 1981 to lease land at Bradenham in Buckinghamshire for the construction of a NATO command bunker. The net effect has been to open up the Trust more to the broader currents of the environmental movement.

On its part, there has also been growing recognition that it cannot manage its own properties as preserved enclaves in isolation from the wider environment. The fall out from Chernobyl still contaminates some of its Lakeland fells; nitrogen enrichment from aerial pollution threatens the integrity of its heaths; acid rain impoverishes its lakes and streams in North Wales and the vegetation on its extensive holdings in the Peak District; some of its rivers, lakes and wetlands are suffering from the lowering of groundwater tables and effects of agricultural pollution; and global climate change poses an uncertain threat to many habitats and coastal properties. In consequence, the Trust has become more actively involved in environmental debate and in seeking to influence policy and legislation in Britain and Europe.

Undoubtedly, the Trust has a very important role to play in this regard. It has the authority which most other environmental groups lack of being able to base its arguments on its own extensive practical experience. Its properties present the potential of a test bed for progressive environmental management, demonstrating the validity of practical solutions but also providing a standard from which to gauge the extent of a degradation occurring elsewhere.

The gulf between practice and theory is not the only one that the Trust could help to bridge. Another one is that between environmental protection and social and economic development. The fashionable term to signify the common pursuit of these objectives is sustainability. While it is not clear that they are easily reconcilable, in key fields the Trust's hard-won experience points the way. Its own outlook for many years was that certain special places of historic or aesthetic value must be rescued and set aside from the onslaught of progress. In practice, though, it has had to find levels of acceptable use that do not compromise their essential character but which generate sufficient resources to ensure their continued maintenance. In this sense, the Trust has long been in the vanguard of sustainable leisure, sustainable tourism, sustainable agriculture and sustainable forestry.

A commonly quoted definition of sustainability is that formulated by the Brundtland Commission as 'development that meets the needs of the present without compromising the ability of future generations to meet their own needs'. Inalienability clearly embodies this principle of protecting critical natural and cultural capital for the future. However, the issue of fairness to unborn generations cannot be considered in isolation from present needs, including the question of the very unequal distribution of access to resources within the present generation. This is especially so if arguments concerning the welfare of future societies imply restrictions that actually compound existing inequalities.

Rural preservation, responding to middle-class concerns, has often been insensitive to the needs and aspirations of the less well-off. Certainly, the Trust has neglected the hopes of its founders to improve the recreational opportunities of the urban poor. In rural areas, though, it is not divorced from the lives of working people, unlike most environmental groups. Here again, the Trust presents another potential bridge, with its vast middle-class membership and huge rural estate that includes many country people, tenant farmers, estate workers, foresters and wardens. The Trust has always taken seriously its responsibilities towards its staff and tenants. It is well placed to counter the negative impression among ordinary people living in rural areas of conservation and preservation, as controls imposed on their lives and livelihoods from outside for the benefit of the well-to-do; and to demonstrate instead how rural areas can benefit socially and economically from positive environmental management that is responsive to the wishes of rural people.

What does this all imply for the Trust's roles as a landowner, land manager and landlord?

The National Trust as landowner: towards a truly national Trust

With about 600,000 acres (242,811 ha), the Trust is the largest private landowner in England and Wales, owning more than $1\frac{1}{2}$ per cent of the land surface, including much of the finest scenery. For at least its first half century, its acquisitions were largely opportunist and were often unpredictable, diverse and sporadic. Gradually it evolved a set of criteria for accepting new property, recently summarised in the following terms:

- The property must be of national importance because of its natural beauty, historic interest or nature conservation value, or of local importance because of the protection it would afford to a property already held for preservation.
- The property must provide benefit to the nation, which will usually include public access.
- The property must be in danger of deterioration if it is not acquired by the Trust, or of inappropriate alteration or of development that would harm its character or environment.

- The property must be, and be expected to remain financially self-support-ing.[6]

The last of these criteria has not always been observed; and specific mention of nature conservation as an objective distinct from that of natural beauty represents a recent enlargement of the Trust's acknowledged purposes. By and large, though, the Trust has been the recipient of land and buildings judged by it to be of national importance from an aesthetic or historic point of view, facing some sort of threat, but also able to pay their way through endowments, rental income, admission charges or other forms of revenue. This has made the Trust highly dependent on willing donors of property or on local appeals. The result is a large and extensive land holding containing a great variety of landscapes: from the sunken green lanes and small field patterns in Devon and Cornwall; the bleak heather moors of Derbyshire; the rugged crags of the Lake District and Snowdonia; the rolling downland of Sussex and Berkshire; the sandy heathland of Surrey and Dorset; and the landscaped parks of great country houses such as Stourhead in Wiltshire.

Some landscapes and regions, though, are much more strongly represented than others. Half the Trust's land is in the uplands; 20 per cent is on the coast; and 9 per cent is woodland. Away from the coast, the Trust has a limited presence across much of the lowlands of the Midlands and eastern England, but it is well represented across southern England. In the uplands the Trust's hold-ings are concentrated in certain regions, particularly Cumbria, the southern Pennines and North Wales, and are few and far between in mid- and South Wales and the north-east of England.

This reflects a number of factors. One has been the Romantic predilection of the Trust's founders and its subsequent leaders for the wilder landscapes, epitomised above all in the scenery of Wordsworth's Lake District. Another factor has been the threats faced by the countryside. In broad terms, the Trust has responded to two major types of threat: the spread of urban development; and the decline in aristocratic landownership.

Through its own growing identification with rural landowners, the Trust did not perceive or failed to acknowledge the other major threat to rural landscapes of the twentieth century – the technological and productivity revolution in agriculture. Arguably, the resultant industrialisation of farming has more profoundly and more extensively transformed the countryside than the other two threats, eliminating a great deal of diversity, beauty and natural history, particularly of the lowlands. But it is an issue on which the Trust has seldom exercised its voice or its protective potential.

A further factor shaping the Trust's geographical development has been the changing social composition of the countryside, as Robin Fedden, the Trust's historian, has pointed out:

Danger most commonly follows the break-up of estates. Where great landlords are secure, there is less threat to the landscape pattern [and] the Trust has a limited contribution to make.[7]

The Trust and its supporters have thus been most active in areas such as Surrey, Cornwall and the Lake District where the fragmentation of land ownership has provided opportunities for acquisition but also threats of change. Indeed, in these areas the Trust has come to play the part of the great landlord. In addition, where land has been secured largely through local appeals, a certain amount of well-heeled NIMBYism has also been a significant factor, accounting, for example, for the extensive Trust ownership of the Surrey Heaths, the North Downs and the Chilterns. Thus, in a sense, the emergence of National Trust ownership marked the ebb of aristocratic control and the entrenchment of upper-middle-class groups in particularly attractive parts of the countryside. And these patterns, which were established early in the Trust's career, have, if anything, consolidated as it has grown.

It is only on the coast where the Trust, through Enterprise Neptune, has pursued a systematic strategy in the acquisition of open land. Not only has this resulted in a much more even geographical coverage of properties, but the Trust's coastal holdings encompass nearly all the coastal landscape types and the habitats within them, including: islands; leases of the seabed and foreshore; estuaries, salt-marshes and mudflats; sand and shingle beaches; cliffs and dunes and coastal hinterlands back from the coastline.

In contrast, the Trust possesses a limited range of lowland landscapes, even though it is these landscapes which have been most under pressure through agricultural intensification or the intrusion of development. A few are well represented on Trust land, notably heathland, oceanic oak wood, historic parklands and chalk grasslands. But there are other quite rare habitats which are not, such as raised mires, water meadows, hay meadows, unimproved grassland, chalk and limestone river systems, ancient lime and hazel woods and old orchards.

As the emphasis in the Trust's development moves away from the acquisition of properties, it is important that future additions to its estate should be even more carefully considered than in the past, with a much greater sense of strategy. The prevailing approach to the rounding off of the Trust's estate has been through accretions to existing holdings. While this has made a great deal of sense from the point of view of efficient estate management and the creation of coherent landscape units, it has served to perpetuate the imbalance in the Trust's geographical and habitat coverage.

The existing approach must yield diminishing returns. Can further significant additions to the Trust's 25 per cent of the Lake District be justified in terms of the range of conservation and amenity benefits that the Trust offers? Continued expansion in particular areas invites its own hubris, as the Trust has already experienced in the Lake District and in the south-west where some local residents have voiced their resentment of a too dominant part played by the Trust in determining the prospects for their communities. There is the paradox of the Trust creating huge estates in areas whose landscapes were not the product of lordly design but of the cumulative and collective actions of many generations of small-scale farmers, with the risk now that this process of evolution is either frozen or tightly trammelled.

On the other hand, can a truly *National* Trust be comfortable with the observation that 'the concentration of properties in the southern half of England accentuates the great divide between north and south which is reflected in so many institutions in British society'.[8]

This regional inequality in its ownership of historic houses has been compounded by a lack of interest in protecting open spaces close to densely populated areas. The consequence is a pattern of holdings in which the Trust offers limited recreational opportunities close to the major conurbations and certainly very little that is accessible to those without a car. Not only has this pattern greatly stimulated recreational motoring, with all its undesirable environmental consequences, but it is also out of keeping with the spirit of the Trust's founders who were committed to improving the recreational opportunities and access to the countryside of disadvantaged urban groups. The Trust has some way to go if indeed it is fully 'to recover its original social purpose'.[9]

In pursuing this mission, the Trust would have a lot to learn from the urban nature conservation movement in the creative management of open spaces and wildlife sites in cities. It could also be that the Trust has a role in rescuing from neglect some of the invaluable historic spaces in inner city areas such as Victorian pleasure grounds, botanic gardens and cemeteries.

The other major priority for Trust acquisition would be relict lowland habitats and historic agricultural landscapes. Not only are these under severe threat, but such acquisitions would extend the range of landscape types and redress the geographical imbalance in the Trust's estate.

The National Trust as land manager: the challenges ahead

For a long time the Trust believed that its central task was preservation, which would be achieved by bringing properties into its ownership. It was a late recruit to the post-war philosophy of conservation, of the need for active management to maintain the value of safeguarded sites and to accommodate and regulate the pressures upon them. Initially, it was pushed and prodded into action through having to cope with a growing volume of visitors and in response to the criticisms of conservation organisations. During the past twenty years the Trust has absorbed the conservation philosophy and has become an energetic practitioner of active management of the landscape. It is now one of the leading organisations in conservation land management and should begin to use its position and experience for demonstration and training purposes, to improve the skills and influence the practices of other land owners and managers, and for experimenting with ways to respond to major new challenges facing the rural environment.

The Trust's integrated approach to management encompasses nature conservation, archaeology, agriculture, forestry and public access and recreation. Increasingly, it can call upon detailed surveys of the natural history, archaeology, landscape and vernacular buildings on its holdings, and of the needs of its visitors. This information is fed into a management plan for each property. The preparation of such a plan provides a mechanism for resolving possible conflicts between the Trust's various objectives. It then acts as a framework for maintenance and investment programmes, guiding the work of the Trust's staff and volunteers. To raise the standards of its countryside management the Trust has also sought to improve the technical information and advice available to its land agents and wardens and the specialist training provided for both staff and volunteers.

The leading position it is adopting and the new challenges it faces means that it can no longer necessarily rely on conventional approaches or the experience of other organisations; it should be more experimental in developing novel approaches – for example, in regenerating woodland, restoring habitats, and reviving or replacing traditional practices such as coppicing or grazing. This calls for more monitoring of the impact of different management regimes. What makes the Trust's efforts of such interest is the scale of its ownership. It is becoming clear that the conservation of landscape and wildlife at, say, the level of an individual farm is profoundly affected by practices on surrounding land. Effective conservation therefore demands co-ordinated action at a higher level. Thus the Trust's ability to orchestrate management practices over extensive areas offers a unique opportunity to test and demonstrate the ideas emerging from the new science of landscape ecology.

Such an approach is particularly called for in response to the major challenges facing the rural environment, including new recreational pressures, the upheaval in agriculture and the effects of pollution and climate change. Clearly, the Trust has little or no control over the determining forces behind these developments but it must respond to the consequences and formulate adaptive strategies. In doing so, there may well be lessons of wider reference.

Take, for example, the possibility of rising sea levels due to climate change. With its hundreds of miles of coastline, the Trust is literally on the frontline. It is therefore particularly well placed to experiment with a move away from a highly engineered approach of coastal defence towards a more natural approach of coastal management that involves working with, rather than against, physiographic processes (see p.80). This so-called managed retreat, by creating habitats that will absorb environmental change, has the added bonus of restoring lost natural features such as salt-marshes.

New recreational pressures also require novel management approaches. The

Trust has developed considerable expertise in the repair and maintenance of footpaths, the development of alternative surfaces such as stone pitching and boardwalks to combat erosion,and the recladding of eroded surfaces. Whereas these problems arise simply from the sheer pressure of numbers, the Trust's approach to other activities that are particularly destructive or obtrusive – such as the driving of off-road vehicles, motorised watersports, war games and ghyll and stream scrambling – is severely to restrict or exclude them from its properties. But for other increasingly popular activities, including orienteering, hang-gliding, white-water canoeing, all-terrain biking, fell running, rock climbing and paragliding, the approach must be one of identifying suitable sites, the provision of wardening services and liaison with representative organisations and commercial providers to establish licensing schemes or codes of conduct.

Perhaps the greatest management challenge that the Trust faces is in relation to the upheaval in agriculture. Official efforts to reduce overproduction and to liberalise agricultural markets have allowed a reappraisal of the high input/high output approach to farming vigorously pursued throughout the post-war period. This has lead to the removal of some of the incentives and pressures to intensify production and the acceptance of social and environmental goals for agricultural policy. In the main, the scope for pursuing landscape conservation and amenity objectives has been greatly increased and the pressures on the countryside decreased. While therefore the changes should be good news for conservation, the upheaval they threaten in traditional farming practices and the need to develop alternative arrangements demand an innovative stance from a body like the Trust, which could then indicate how farming might adapt.

Already under the set-aside scheme, large areas of arable land are being taken out of agricultural production. More is likely to follow and what was intended to be a temporary expedient may well become a permanent feature of production management. If planned carefully and from a sufficiently long-term perspective, this removal of land from farming could do a great deal to reinstate much of the wildlife, landscape and amenity interest of the lowlands and to protect water quality from agricultural pollution. The Trust is perhaps the only organisation with the scale of ownership and resources, and the range of expertise, to demonstrate what could be achieved over an extensive area. In these ecologically and scenically impoverished areas the approach required is one with an emphasis on landscape restoration and habitat re-creation, including the re-establishment of lowland heath and species-rich grassland, the creation of wetlands and the regeneration of woodland. This would represent a major departure for the Trust from its preoccupation with preserving and maintaining the pristine.

However, the retreat of agriculture will also create major difficulties for existing management systems. Much nature conservation and landscape management is about securing grazing regimes which maintain open ground, keep habitats open, allow flowering and seeding and still provide a livelihood for the grazier. Both undergrazing and overgrazing can have serious adverse effects on the landscape, public access and natural history of particular habitats, including upland and lowland heaths and chalk and limestone grasslands. While pressures of overgrazing are likely to diminish, reduction in the numbers and changes in the geographical distribution of grazing animals may well exacerbate the Trust's difficulties in finding stock to maintain the conservation interest of marginal agricultural land. There may be a case, especially in certain upland areas whose ecology and landscape have been impoverished through a combination of overgrazing and agricultural improvement, for the managed retreat of farming activities and the reinstatement of the full ecological profile of natural vegetation types from the valley bottoms to the hill tops. Here again, only a large landowner like the Trust could contemplate such a comprehensive experiment.

It is vitally important that the Trust makes its experience and expertise as a land manager widely available, and not only to those similarly responsible for managing land. There is a task of public education and information too. The Trust takes pains to be as unobtrusive as possible in its management operations. But it helps thereby to perpetuate the common misconception that beautiful landscapes and rich habitats are nature's handiwork alone. In its presentation of historic houses, the Trust has begun to show how their running and upkeep typically depended on a small army of servants and gardeners. In contrast, it does relatively little to explain the conservation interest of its properties and the management needed to maintain it. To be sure of winning the resources to continue with its admirable and pioneering work in countryside management, it must do much more to reveal its hidden hand in the landscape and the great deal of thought, skill and hard work done behind the scenes.

The Trust as landlord: responsibilities to rural communities

The Trust is the largest landlord in the countryside. Forty per cent of its land is let, in over a thousand holdings. It also owns over 4,000 houses and cottages, including several entire villages. It has always taken very seriously its responsibilities as a landlord striving to look after its properties 'in the manner as far as possible of the best private owners'.[10] In assuming the mantle of large landowners, it has also shown a strong paternalistic regard for its many tenants.

Inescapably, if not always wittingly, the Trust has become a significant agent in rural development. In realisation of how much it depends on the co-operation of its tenants, it has been anxious to select tenants in sympathy with its wider purposes. Particularly in the uplands it has been quite deliberate in its social engineering, resisting farm amalgamation that would remove smaller family-sized farms, in order to keep sufficient people on the land to maintain the landscape. In areas of concentrated Trust ownership, it has also felt a responsibility towards helping to maintain the local community by giving priority to local families in letting its cottages. Its influence has not always been accepted as benign, however, but has sometimes been seen as restrictive and high-handed.

Given the scale and implications of its ownership, the Trust's influence on rural development extends well beyond the properties it owns and is of concern to more people than its tenants. Many communities, particularly on the coast and in the uplands, are greatly affected by the Trust's presence, either because of the visitors it attracts to the area or because of its impact on the local economy or through the restrictions it imposes on development. This demands of the Trust not only considerable sensitivity in its dealings with local communities but also a more progressive outlook towards their needs for housing, jobs and services than it has shown in the past. A restrictive attitude will simply turn such communities into the preserve of the well-heeled, whose lack of dependence on local services and employment will further undermine the rural economy. In turn, that will impinge on the work of the Trust by increasing the difficulties in finding the people locally to carry out the labour intensive tasks of countryside management.

The Trust, however, is well placed to demonstrate how rural areas can benefit socially and economically from positive environmental management that is responsive to the needs and aspirations of rural people. Its potential contribution in this regard is of the utmost significance given the precipitous decline since the 1950s in traditional forms of rural employment which continues unremittingly. Far from seeking to reverse these processes, the Trust should be in the vanguard of a broader transition in the functions of the countryside, generating new economic and employment opportunities.

This transition might be broadly characterised as from a production to a consumption countryside – from one dominated by primary production to one which accommodates other important functions to do with recreation, leisure, residential amenity and conservation. These other functions were neglected during the post-war push for self-sufficiency in food production. They are now receiving new emphasis in the context of surplus production and through recognition of the vital functions that rural areas perform, acting as environmental reservoirs which maintain and renew the quality of natural and genetic resources, and also as living space, providing human refreshment through their cultural, aesthetic and ecological qualities. The crucial issue for policy makers is how to effect this transition by reorienting agricultural and planning policies while ensuring continuity for the farming and rural communities on whom the vibrance of the countryside depends. A particular problem is how to ensure sufficient income for those engaged in the tasks of countryside management, given that there are no markets for landscape and wildlife as there are for food.

The Trust provides a mechanism for overcoming just this problem, of obtaining from those who value and want to visit countryside properties the resources to maintain them. Its main traditional form of generating income from a property has been through farm rents, but its net income from this source has shown a long-term decline. In contrast to historic houses, the Trust cannot and would not charge for access to its open spaces, so it is largely dependent on membership and grant income and other indirect revenue to cover the maintenance costs. As these costs have mounted, it has become more and more adept at finding additional income sources associated with its countryside properties, through such means as the organisation of events such as horse trials, membership recruitment by roving wardens, fund-raising appeals, sponsorship and fees from location filming. Of particular significance has been the growing contribution from its trading arm, National Trust Enterprises, which runs its shops, catering establishments, holiday cottages and mail order service. In 1991, the income from Enterprises exceeded that brought in from agricultural rents, marking for the Trust the decisive shift commercially from the production to the consumption countryside.

How might the Trust help others to make a living from conservation, and thus help ensure a vibrant countryside more generally? Of particular concern to the Trust are its tenant farmers. Many of its smaller hill farms hardly provide a viable family income. In such circumstances, the Trust must assist farm families in finding additional income sources. For example, farmers could be paid for carrying out some of the Trust's estate maintenance tasks such as footpath repair or acting as part-time wardens. The initiative of helping farming families to provide bed and breakfast could be extended to encourage the development of farm tourism or farm shops. Farm diversification has been part of government policy since the mid-1980s, but it has been treated by the MAFF in a perfunctory and individualistic manner that has overlooked the support systems, of advice, training and marketing, needed to help farmers to seek new outlets for their skills and services. The Trust is in a position to help provide such a support system for farmers wanting to diversify into tourism, recreational provision or conservation.

The Trust could also help local communities, for example, by employing more local people at its properties or by developing training schemes related to the Trust's work. More also could be done to sell and promote local produce at the Trust's restaurants and shops. This could develop into regional green marketing schemes promoting local products related to particular landscapes. Green consumerism has emerged as a powerful force amongst the sort of well-off and concerned people who belong to the National Trust. At the same time, there is growing demand for localised and craft products of high quality and identifiable origin. There would seem to be scope, through effective marketing including product development, for these two trends to converge in demands for products and services that help to sustain both the local economy and the local environment.

Conclusions

In many respects the key tension that the National Trust was set up to address – that between private ownership and public benefit in the management and protection of the countryside – is as pressing now as it was a hundred years ago. The specific resolution represented in the creation of the Trust – an élite voluntary organisation, supported by private donation and public subscription, and with its land protected by inalienable status – seemed for many years unique and to some extent set apart from more general developments in the twentieth century, including the collapse of paternalistic landownership, the growth of state planning and the spread of egalitarian values.

Not only has the Trust had to respond to these developments, however, but they in turn have not necessarily resolved the underlying dilemmas of countryside management and protection. Today, as the nation's largest private landowner, the Trust itself undoubtedly faces considerable challenges coping with structural change in agriculture and the rural economy and in seeking to achieve integrated management of its holdings. Increasingly, however, its experience and expertise may be seen to hold more general lessons for the wider countryside and for the environmental movement. Its unique contribution will be to act as a bridge, between various conservation interests, between the urban and the rural, between community development and environmental protection, between present and future generations. This key position demands of it a sensitivity, a responsiveness and a farsightedness which raises specific questions for the Trust itself concerning the flexibility of its organisational structure and the accountability of its constitution.

Notes

1 Hunter, 1884.
2 *National Trust Magazine*, Summer 1990, p.3.
3 Dame Jennifer Jenkins, NT Annual Report 1990, p.3.
4 Lord Chorley, *National Trust Magazine*, Autumn 1993, p.3.
5 Gaze, 1988, p.311.
6 NT Annual Report 1992.
7 Fedden, 1974, p.98.
8 Murphy, 1987, pp.131–2.
9 Angus Stirling, NT Annual Report, p.5.
10 Gaze, 1988, p.186.

VI

Archaeology in Trust

PETER FOWLER

I T SEEMS INCREDIBLE THAT fifty years have passed since the publication of the other chapter in a commemorative book summarising archaeology in the National Trust. The book was, of course, the Batsford half-centennial volume, *The National Trust: A Record of Fifty Years' Achievement*; the Chapter was called 'Ancient Sites'; and the author, then a young man but now long-since Professor, was Grahame Clark – from 1993 Sir Grahame. While it is inevitable that a centennial essay on the same topic should look back to its half-age predecessor, this is more than a reflex or mere act of piety.

It is interesting that Grahame Clarke's chapter is there at all. On the one hand its presence offers a modest rebuff to those who say that for too long the Trust was unaware of its archaeological responsibilities (it was, but did not know how to discharge them); on the other, it indicates an achievement of considerable significance not just in fifty years but in the *first* fifty years. We all tend to be a bit impatient and the modern age in particular wants instant results. In its perspective fifty years is a long time. One of the major common concerns of the Trust and archaeology, however, is that both are not only interested in the long-term but that their basic interests are best-served by thinking and acting long-term.

The archaeological approach involves a past which, far from being rather boringly confined to 'ancient times', comes up to yesterday and is involved with the dynamics of current affairs. The Trust has to live with this and adapt to it, for it is not, and should not try to be, an academic leader in matters archaeological nor even pretend to be an archaeological body. Yet, *inter alia*, the Trust practises archaeology, a subject which, in the proper meaning of the word ('the *study* of artefacts'), is by definition fundamentally an intellectual concept and activity. That is so, however much we dress up our involvement with it in presentation, performance, print and image.

The Trust, therefore, merely as the holder of a large and crucially important repository of primary evidence, is deeply involved in a field of intellectual endeavour. The same is true of other facets of its holdings and activities, in the natural sciences for example, and in art history; yet the Trust itself could never be accused of being an intellectual or academic institution. Whether or not a part of its ethos is positively anti-intellectual, there is clearly more to its significance as property-owner than preserver of pretty views, facilitator of bracing walks and provider of afternoon tea. Archaeology, along with other field sciences like geology, botany and ornithology, sits on this interface between the Trust and its publics, between popular images of the Trust, the Trust's self-perception, and the realities of its scientific responsibilities. Lest that sound too high-faluting let it be added that many an archaeologist, walking in from field-work with fine views over inalienable land, is also only too pleased to sit in a Trust tea-room at the end of a descent to the pleasurably mundane from the high ground of intellectual endeavour.

While by and large, then, the Trust has to respond to learning and understanding about the past, it nevertheless has much to parade in terms of managing that past. Those who adopt the basics of contemporary archaeological thinking, marrying that to the Trust's approach, not only find great sympathy with the acquisition of what some see, by conventional Trust standards, as oddball properties like Mr Straw's '1930s time-warp' home at 7 Blyth Grove, Worksop, and Erno Goldfinger's 'Modern Movement monument' of 1939 at 2 Willow Road, Hampstead; they actually find it difficult to understand what all the fuss is about. Such structures (and their fittings and contents in both these cases) are *a priori* just as much aspects of the archaeology of an age as are unquestioned chunks of archaeology in the Trust's portfolio such as the Hadrian's Wall and Stonehenge estates. That the twentieth-century homes are of a time two thousand years later than the Wall is as irrelevant in this context as the fact that the Wall is two thousand years later than Stonehenge.

Clark wrote his chapter within a much less flexible intellectual model. It was, for the time but not for the author, a characteristically insular one too, at best with an occasional nod towards Europe. The purpose of archaeology was assumed to be humbly to fit its story of early times – before real History began with the Normans and reliable, written evidence like the Domesday Book – into an historical framework canonised by Teutonic methodology and the 'scepter'd isle' school of great 'Victorian' historians (continuing into the mid-twentieth century in the books of writers like Winston Churchill and Arthur Bryant).

Such an approach is, however, no longer sufficient. Merely by assuming responsibility for large tracts of land the Trust has unwittingly acquired a huge amount of archaeology, much of it from the post-Roman centuries. This consists not merely of thousands of discrete sites but whole landscapes from the most recent millennium and a half. These consist of or contain characteristically the earthworks – the banks and ditches, humps and bumps – of pasture field, valley side and moorland edge, the surviving remains of abandoned farms, hamlets, villages, field systems and trackways. This sort of evidence is not, by and large, listed in the succinct *Properties of the National Trust*, partly because it has not yet been properly recorded or even discovered, partly because there is so much of it – we are talking of tens of thousands of items within the Trust's whole estate – and partly because the Trust still has a bit of difficulty in accepting the concept of post-Roman or medieval archaeology. It is, of course, now reasonably comfortable with the idea of 'Industrial Archaeology'. Indeed the Trust has recently celebrated its holding in and contribution to that field during Industrial Heritage Year in 1993 ('The Power and the Glory', Industrial Heritage leaflet, NT 1992). Time, however, is needed for the Trust to recognise that, on the one hand, the great bulk of its estate consists of 'archaeology' – *sensu* the artefacts of former times – and that, on the other, there are likely to be archaeological implications in changing, let alone developing, any part of any property, whether it be a landscape or a building, whether the item's perceived date is prehistoric or post-medieval.

The Trust and archaeology in recent years

Both the Trust and archaeology have come a long way since 1945. A very clear signal of the shift in thinking, and of the changing relationships within the Trust, is provided by an example from industrial archaeology. Very much the same sort of thing could be said about other aspects of the Trust's archaeology, but the quotation is particularly telling because it comes from David Thackray, the Trust's Archaeological Adviser, its senior professional post in the field:

> The great variety of landscapes owned by the National Trust incorporates numerous sites where industrial and commercial activity took place, often drawing on the natural resources of those areas. Many of these sites occur on land acquired for other reasons; fine coastal or inland scenery or the estates of historic houses. Others have been acquired specifically for their importance to the history of technology. Many of the great range of activities encompassed by the term 'industrial heritage' can be found on Trust properties, including examples of extractive industries, mines, quarries and mineral processing, manufacturing industries, agriculture, fishing and the processing of their products, communications and the distribution of goods, trade and commerce. Examples of the houses of both workers and industrialists help further to show the extensive infrastructures associated with industrial activities.
>
> The Trust is surveying its properties to identify the wealth of industrial sites and to help preserve them, not just as sites but in their wider landscape contexts.[2]

A considerable range of concept and practice is encompassed within this statement. It demonstrates the Trust to be in line with current thinking within the archaeological profession, academic and practical, and not just in relation to industrial archaeology. That the quotation is about that sort of archaeology does not limit its significance to that field: almost exactly the same could be said, by changing the odd word, about the Trust and prehistory:

> The great variety of landscapes owned by the National Trust incorporates numerous sites where people lived, worked and died in prehistoric times, invariably drawing on the natural resources of those areas. Many of these sites occur on land acquired for other reasons: fine coastlands under Enterprise Neptune, inland countryside for scenic beauty, the estates of historic houses. Others have been acquired specifically for their importance to the study of prehistory. Many of the great range of activities encompassed by the term 'prehistoric archaeology' can be found on Trust properties, including examples of . . . [exactly the same list as above]. Examples of the living-places and house-sites of people occupying Britain two thousand and more years ago help further to show the extensive infra-structures associated with prehistoric economies.
>
> The Trust is surveying its properties to identify the wealth of prehistoric sites and to help preserve them, not just as sites but in their wider landscape contexts.

In both statements can be seen seven of the key elements forming the basis of Trust policy in relation to archaeology at the centenary. Fundamental is the *recognition* that, almost willy-nilly, the Trust has acquired a large amount of archaeology – as with other resources, such as wildlife habitats – merely by becoming a larger and larger landowner. A part of that recognition involves the perception of the existence of *variety* within this resource, with the implication that variety is, *ipso facto*, a good thing. The real significance, however, lies not just in the recognition itself but in the Trust's acceptance of the *responsibilities* consequent on such recognition. Management, and estate management in particular, has to expand to take in these new responsibilities, and new tasks have to be undertaken. With the archaeological resource, again as with others, the basic need is to establish the existence, location, nature and significance of the elements making up the resource; that is, not merely to list the relatively small number of archaeological sites deliberately bought as such but to initiate *survey*, involving documentary as well as field reconnaissance. The purpose of what is a highly skilled, labour-intensive and expensive operation is specifically managerial; it is based on the principle that, by acquiring information about it, the resource can be *better managed*, though almost inevitably there is a research product too.[3] Following survey, identification and some assessment, however minimal, such management is directed towards *preservation* of the resource, not just as sites but 'in their wider landscape *contexts*.'

Here then are, as seen from inside, the key components of the Trust's approach to its archaeological task: a now-willing recognition that it has a responsibility in a professional and academic field which is, by the 1990s, at least on a par in Trust terms with such properties as woodlands and vernacular architecture. Variety and context are signal characteristics of the archaeological resource, the location and nature of which have to be established by survey; providing such information enables management to fulfil better its primary objective of preservation. That, in summary, is the Trust's current *credo* in archaeology, a significant development, a maturing, since Clark was writing fifty years ago; yet, in a good sense, basically the same, more aware and more sophisticated but still aligned with the eternal verities. Archaeologically, as with other irreplaceable resources, the basic verity is that if you lose the site, if you lose the context – that is it: gone. But if you have kept it, then all your options remain open. Among the options omitted from the above *resumés* are access and interpretation, critical aspects which, along with 'context', will be considered later in the discussion about the future.

The increased Trust awareness of and responsibility for archaeology have recently been reflected in organisational change. Far and away the most important has been the creation of full-time, professional archaeological posts, both centrally and regionally. The establishment consists of a professional head (Archaeological Adviser) with a staff of three at Cirencester and nine dispersed in ones and twos around some of the regions. The Cirencester staff are primarily concerned with centrally generated matters like policy, overall standards and data control (the Sites and Monuments Record); they also have a considerable executive task in advising, on the one hand, regions and, on the other headquarters, while their regionally based colleagues are primarily in place for survey purposes. Inevitably, however, they become involved with specific sites and particular operations and, in general, with questions of property management and acquisition; so the Trust target of 'finishing' the archaeological survey of its estate by 2000 becomes increasingly remote. There are good reasons why this should be so anyway.

The whole operation is, quite properly, placed within the Chief Agent's demesne, reporting therefore to the Properties Committee. That Committee created an Archaeology Panel in 1989, its members consisting of the hon. archaeological adviser from each region with two or three invited specialists. It meets only annually but small groups of Panel members carry out a modest programme of visits based on invitations and need, always reporting back to the Properties Committee but more immediately and practically relating to the Trust's professional archaeological staff and their non-archaeological regional colleagues. Thus, for example, Panel members have looked very critically over recent years, both indoors and in the field, at proposals for the management of Stonehenge and its environs, with a view to advising the Trust in general. It has examined in detail predominantly regional concerns such as the archaeological implications of the Trust's acquisition of a large area of limestone landscape in Upper Wharfedale and the rather different implications of ambitious proposals for a co-operative tourism-led enterprise involving the derelict tin-mining industry, including Trust property, in west Cornwall.

That organisational structure has been grafted on to and then developed inside an institution imbued with the ethos of management.[4] The Trust is, quite properly, especially proud of its estate management, and one of the great achievements of the last decade is the way in which Archaeological Resource Management (ARM) has been fed into and then practised within that tradition without producing either a two-headed monster or too many an upset. As already noted, the Trust has taken aboard an awareness of its archaeology, most of which was acquired unknowingly; simultaneously it has developed an awareness of the fast-developing field of ARM, also known as both 'archaeological heritage management' and 'cultural resource management'.

Whatever its name, there is no doubt that 'management' is the key, and the Trust is very good at that in the sense of adopting a long-term, laid-back approach to the conservation of what is on its properties. The thousands of archaeological sites and landscapes involved have therefore been absorbed into a well-founded and increasingly sophisticated system of land management within a concept of the 'estate' as a whole. 'Estate' here means the whole of the Trust's property, all 580,000 acres of it; and with that scale for scope as well as responsibility, it is fair to say that the Trust, far from merely acceding to fashion and professional precept in such matters, is proudly at the forefront of ARM. Organisationally, philosophically, and in practice, it can be strongly promoted as a model which others would do well to learn from if not actually copy.

The Trust's integrated estate management stems from a centuries-old tradition of the great landowners, now regularised by professional training and standards. There might even be a certain irony in these supposedly democratic days that the best management in the public interest might be virtually identical with that practised privately for the familial élite in the days of yore, which the Trust is at such pains to capture for the present. The capacity of this conservative approach to perform well depends crucially on the presence of three factors: a deep understanding, perhaps even personally a love, of the land; a long-term policy of husbandry (definable perhaps in late twentieth-century terms as conservation-oriented exploitation); and an ever-increasing data-base of what exists on the estate to inform the practicalities of year-to-year stewardship. This certainly applies to archaeology: its nature and extent – 'ubiquity' some land agents would despairingly say – require constant and careful moderation with other interests involved in the running of estates and properties, and clashes are inevitable despite the best of management systems. Indeed, it could be argued that conflicts are a sign that the systems of management are working. The sort of clash in mind is easily exemplified:

> A 200-year old hardwood plantation in a country house park needs, in silvicultural terms, surgical attention and partial replanting. It is, how-

ever, a key visual element in the late eighteenth-century historic park-
land so beloved of the visiting aesthete, though documentary research
shows a differently-shaped plantation to have existed fifty yards east of it
in Repton's original design. Which should be 'restored'? Furthermore,
the lichens on some of the old bark are being used as test-beds in a long-
term study of aerial pollution funded by the Natural Environmental
Research Council, and the Trust's own Biological Survey has identified
the plantation's present semi-derelict condition as the northernmost
known habitat of Dickie's Bladder fern (or whatever). The rookery is
considered to add much to the ambience of the place, and there remains
the question of whether the small folly in the undergrowth was built as a
ruin by the Ninth Earl or, like him, merely became one.[5]

'Not archaeology and not old enough', the critic will say, but of course the
whole complex of competing interests and conflicting cross-currents – an invented but typical scenario – is founded on time and artefacts and their relative
values, not so much to people in the past as to us now. By what criteria is it
judged that a folly is more important than a rookery, that a view is of greater
value than a lichen? Who in fact decides? The optimist would answer that such
are the wrong questions, for estate management is not, for the most part, concerned with the black and white issues but with accommodating as far as
possible the continuation of those parts of the landscape which others judge, and
the owner is persuaded, to be significant. In this example (though the author
has not discussed it with the Chief Agent), the solution might well be, given
that long-termism basic to the Trust's approach, to replant Repton's original
plantation, and encourage rooks and ferns to colonise it over the next 50 years
while the existing plantation dies, the bark experiment is completed, and the
folly is consolidated so that it stands firm and fair when eventually exposed as a
free-standing monument.

Another example is perhaps closer to the vernacular and the reality of much
estate management in less mannered, but equally sensitive, circumstances:

> . . . a tenant on an upland sheep farm quite reasonably proposes to
> flatten the redundant earth and stone dykes on his rough grazing, re-
> place them with stock-proof barbed-wire fencing to form efficient new
> fields for cattle, and put down a new ley to increase his stocking capa-
> bility, thus making his highly marginal farm economically more viable
> (with a higher rent to the Trust of course). The dykes, however, happen
> to be a particularly good example of late-medieval assarting, incor-
> porating structural elements from a rare type of prehistoric land
> allotment recently recorded by the Trust's Archaeological Survey.
> Associated with it are the hitherto unrecognised but remarkably well-
> preserved remains of a Romano-British settlement on which two of the
> new fences would meet. Clearly, this 'ancient landscape' provides the

context for the well-known Tiddler's Tump, a single Bronze Age burial mound scheduled under the Ancient Monuments Act and therefore 'of national importance'; though it is probably more significant locally as the place where, in the eighteenth century, the vicar, the Rev. Augustus Tiddler, met the squire's daughter on the night of their elopement. The public right of way to the Tump, claimed by some to be a leyline, would have to be diverted around the new fields. In addition, the rubble core of the dykes provides a favoured residence of small mammals on which two tenuously re-established breeding pairs of sparrow-hawks depend for their food supply.[6]

The example is again imaginary, though each of its components is from real life. It depicts a truly complicated situation, though a typical one; but note how much of the complexity comes from detailed and wide-ranging information. Much of the complexity would not exist in ignorance; it is up-to-date data and a sensitivity to a spectrum of legitimate interests that, in a way, creates the management problem in a situation where the 'obvious' answer is to encourage the tenant, as landlords nearly always have, to improve farming productivity and thereby the value of the land. This is especially so in the Trust's case where a senstivity to tenants' needs is long-established and particularly important in the economic circumstances of the 1990s.

As the example illustrates, however, the 'obvious' is not always the best in these conservation-minded days. Furthermore, as the case is also meant to demonstrate, practical matters in estate management now have to be decided in the light of special interests like archaeology, and archeological management has to be modulated in relation to a host of other interests bearing on the same place. In this case, however, the existence of a multi-period ancient landscape, which is the context for individual sites rather than single sites in isolation, gives the archaeological dimension a particular value; this should be respected in working out the detailed plans for the tenant to proceed. He should not, for example, flatten the earthworks in replacing them functionally with barbed-wire fencing, and his new fields should be arranged so as not to affect the elements of the former landscape or the public right of way.

Rather more fundamentally, however, the question has to be asked as to whether archaeology is merely another special interest in the suite of Trust responsibilities? It is recognised as a responsibility, and it is taken seriously – but perhaps as a separate 'thing', a bolt-on to the structure rather than an integral part of it. Is it, then, in the same category as tapestries and furniture, waterfalls and foreshores, things with their own intrinsic merits and attractions, characters and problems? Whatever the anwer now, the argument must be that archae-ology is not a mere component of the Trust's estate but, in a wide sense, should be fundamental to the Trust's thinking in future.

Archaeology in the Trust in the twenty-first century

The standing of archaeology in the Trust is indicated by its presence here with its own chapter, on the same footing as 'The Coast' and 'The Countryside'. This compliment, going a long way to answer the question at the end of the preceding section, is interpreted as meaning that this chapter should represent the time dimension, and in particular the production of artefacts through time, in considering the Trust's future. So there is clearly more to this than considering only 'archaeology' as defined by the lists of 'Roman antiquities' and 'Prehistoric sites' in *The Properties of the National Trust* (1992).

The Trust has, of course, made archaeological mistakes, digging a trench through a site here, ploughing over a site there. This is probably inevitable though by now on a very small scale. It is quite rapidly accepting the realisation that a building is an archaeological site too, and not just a piece of architecture. Proposing changes to a building involves archaeological implications to be assessed and archaeological investigations to be carried out; it has learnt too that archaeological methodology can actually be of direct help in deciding and implementing 'restoration'. The fire at Uppark in 1989 has been the trigger here: without an archaeological approach to first of all the salvage operation, and then to the recording of the old and building the new, the late twentieth-century version of the former house would probably not have been possible. So the argument is, just as archaeology as part of the Trust portfolio came to be recognised and accepted into normal Trust management during the 1970s and '80s, so in the '90s it in its turn is influencing the nature and style of property management itself.

The next step in the argument is that this process should go further, not by making the Trust into an archaeological organisation – that will never do – but by encouraging the Trust to be more archaeological in its thinking and therefore in its policy-making. A more profound understanding of what archaeology is actually about would, so it is argued here, help the Trust in understanding the problems and opportunities with which it is, and will be increasingly, faced. To say so is not of course to plead for more dinky 'Iron Age villages' created on Trust lands or for wildly successful commercial theme parks in historic parks: nothing of the sort. The plea is about something much more fundamental and, curiously, in the last resort not specifically archaeological.

It is partly to do with the consideration of issues in an historical perspective, and particularly in the long-time perspective that becomes second nature to the archaeologically conditioned thinker. It is also partly to do with increasing an awareness that many matters coming before the Trust are not specific to the Trust but both impinge on and have often been deeply considered by others. The Trust, obviously, is deeply involved with the past, with archaeology and history, and doubtless it will be further sensitised to its own history by its centenary. It has often seemed to the writer, however, that the Trust understands very little about history in the sense of history either having been created by processes as much as events or being the result at any one moment of a continuous dialogue between 'them' and 'us', between 'then' and 'now', between evidence and interpretation. Further, because the Trust is deeply and understandably conservative as well as conservation-minded, it seems to the writer (who clearly at this point is moving from being a mere archaeologist observing the Trust to giving options stemming from his participation in the Trust) that it is sometimes less critically aware of what is going on in contemporary life than is good either for its own health or that of its considerable responsibilities and influence.

Three recent examples of matters involving the Trust in the present of different pasts illustrate the generality. Stonehenge, in particular, covers a multitude of sins from the Trust's point of view, such as the 'travellers' and their ill-fated desire for a so-called 'festival'. The topic has been well-covered elsewhere and this is not the place either to review the arguments or open old wounds.[7] Indeed, the point of mentioning it is futuristic rather than retrospective, though it is relevant to remember the argument that the Trust never understood what it was dealing with and therefore never moved solution of the problem beyond confrontation. It is a point not discounted by the counter-argument that the Trust 'won', ie festivals on Trust land were banned and the line preventing their recurrence has been held. The confrontations of the 1980s and early '90s were unpleasant, something the Trust would have wished to avoid – but didn't. That is the point, and it is unfortunately a fairly safe prediction that issues and events similar to 'Stonehenge' will recur.

They will do so specifically over archaeological sites, within the greater matrix of social fragmentation. Archaeology and its sites have not on the whole been regarded in Britain as controversial subjects; what is not generally appreciated in Britain, and especially in England, is that this is unusual. In many other countries, sites and the past are inextricably bound up with public debate and dispute. On the one hand, non-British people tend to be overtly concerned about and become much more excited by the fate of 'their' antiquities – witness the Danes whose archaeology is so palpably a part of their cultural environment; the recent involvement of museums in the political upheavals in Italy; and the attacks on cultural tourists for politico-religious purposes in Egypt. On the other hand, Britons as Britons, and even English as English (but not Britons as Welsh or Scottish – or Cornish for that matter) are much less emotionally and intellectually involved. Some sort of past, preferably cosily nostalgic and safe, and perhaps some sort of archaeology, preferably dramatic and (monetarily) valuable, impinge on awareness and time as extras or leisure, but not as basics; yet that cool attitude may be fragmenting, not so much because concern about sites themselves is necessarily increasing but because sites can become icons and therefore, as at Stonehenge, the *foci* of issues, such as access, civil rights and interpretation.

The way in which the archaeological card was played in 1992-3 at the destruction of Twyford Down by a road-building scheme was probably a straw in the wind: it was played by non-archaeologists in the course of a show-down over much bigger issues than the safety or otherwise of a prehistoric field system. Again, echoing the remark above about the Stonehenge travellers, the Ministry of Transport may have won that particular battle, but clearly it has not won the 'war'. The Trust is bound to become more often involved in such specifics which are really about much wider and deeper issues. Such a development may well be regretted, but the real sadness would be if the Trust merely continued to regret what it regards as incidents instead of recognising the realities of life in an overcrowded island with an increasingly less cohesive society.

Exactly the same sort of suggestions could be adduced from other examples of specifics as parts of issues. Hunting, itself part of the island heritage if not exactly an archaeological site, is one case. It has roots deep in prehistory when it was necessary to catch food, and a 'respectable' history merely as a sport but one nevertheless with a great influence on the creation of both 'typical' English landscape and perceptions of what it should be. Yet already, as the Trust knows only too well to its cost, a completely different issue of animal rights rears its head in succession to the unresolved one of whether or not hunting for pleasure is socially acceptable. Whatever one's personal stand on the hunting issue, it seems increasingly unrealistic, and uncomprehending, of the Trust to take refuge in the pious hope that this is a one-off piece of unfairness by aliens seeking to impose a single-issue on an innocent body. Doubtless Charles I felt the same. But hunting is not a one-off; different issues will cause similar difficulties for the Trust, and it will become increasingly unrealistic to regard them as unfair through being either single or external to the Trust's primary purposes.

In any case, most single issues are multi-facetted, or at least have complex origins and purposes. One such that is just around the corner in terms of becoming a difficulty is very close to the heartlands of archaeology and the Trust's relations with it. This concerns the superficially non-controversial question of interpreting the past. Even in straightforward terms of historical interpretation, the exercise is by no means easy; in and for a multi-ethnic society it becomes distinctly sensitive. At its simplest, for example, is it enough, the best or inadequate only to state the basic facts about a site? – 'X is a megalithic burial place of the third millennium BC' or 'Y is a twelfth-century Cistercian monastery dissolved in 1538'. And if it is inadequate, down which of several interpretive routes should we go? Should the Trust, indeed, attempt to go down any? Does it need to provide information in Urdu, or interpret an adulterine castle for a fourth generation descendant of Afro-Caribbean immigrants to Birmingham? Should it accept that most of the ethnic minority – 12 per cent of Britain's population – feel unattracted by what the Trust loves most, the countryside, or seek to educate them, or to acquire property which 'means' something to them? There are major issues here, of policy and even of what the Trust will be about in the twenty-first century; they will not go away, nor will they be resolved only by repainting the present signs.

Yet, there is a great tradition to build on, a tradition which, despite all appearances, has always involved innovation. In fact, the Trust has survived and developed because it has changed, slowly perhaps and sometimes too slowly but thereby able to absorb improvement, not just follow fashion. This is particularly true of its estate management, on to which archaeological management has been successfully attached. In general terms of its land management and archaeology, the Trust has basically put its house in order and should be able to maintain it. The major issues for the future, then, are likely to be the externally introduced ones, and it is *they*, primarily intellectual rather than physical, with which the Trust is going to have to deal. A surprising number of them will be archaeological in a general sense, both as a result of the Trust's properties *per se* and also because of its very significant stake in the contemporary 'past business'. Archaeologically that stake, and the responsibility in terms of landownership, is far more significant than that of English Heritage, for example. The statutory and financial responsibilities of the latter are, however, an essential complement to those of the Trust.

Issues involving access, intellectual and cultural as much as physical; science-based conservation (the new élitism?) versus populist leisure amenity; interpretation – what sort of past(s) and for whom? – these and others will arise to test the members and staff of the Trust in mind, conscience, and in management on the ground. Furthermore, the whole question of 'pastness' and its role, and the role of 'past custodians', so easily dismissable now as the theoretical agonisings of the academic fringe, will move up the agenda – we have already been given a foretaste with the totally unexpected but sustained public interest following English Heritage's announcement in late 1993 of its plans for its Properties in Care. Such 'academic' questions as 'Who owns the monuments anyway?', 'Who indeed owns the past?' are now in the public demesne, and they, and similar, will continually be asked of the Trust too. Is the Trust merely a purveyor of nostalgia or should it be reflecting, in its acquisitions, management and interpretation, the filling of some social need? But what if nostalgia is a social need? Are its monuments merely inert artefacts or do they contain some inner truth? But what if, in some fragmented future, truth, as archaeological authenticity or as moral imperative, no longer matters?

A much sharper perception of society, studies of and changes in it, and the implications of both, are probably about to become a necessity, not an option, for the Trust. A deeper understanding of the multiple relationships between the present and its pasts, and of how the past itself works, is also vital. That understanding, perhaps to be acquired only painfully over the next fifty years, will have to bridge peoples ranging from millions of individuals to very large groups, themselves created for a complex of reasons. It would be idle to pretend that archaeology, as an old-style, introverted academic discipline (now nearly extinct), is going to be important to the Trust in future, though its 'ancient sites' will be, and for lots of reasons other than archaeological. Nevertheless, the discipline that it actually is now could be significant for the Trust, if the Trust will but listen and recognise the relevance to its own long-term, holistic approach.

Archaeology is obviously about the long-term, and it too is now, if not holistic, then catholic or interdisciplinary to a quite remarkable degree. The sort of thinking, intellectually, theoretically and practically, that it now embraces is, in one dimension, on the interface between the humanities and the sciences, and, in another, on the pinpoint of time between present and past. That is the model of relevance to the Trust. It would be the supreme irony if the national body created and fostered and loved precisely to care for the nation's past was itself to stumble through a failure to understand what a past was in time, what many pasts are today, whether today be 1995, 2020, or 2045. Maybe the Trust really will address this matter of awareness and perception, both of the past and the contemporary; maybe it will even have to become a little more intellectual.

Notes
1 Lees-Milne, 1945.
2 'The Power and the Glory', 1992, Industrial Heritage leaflet, the National Trust.
3 Well illustrated by the historic landscape surveys in the Lake District.
4 The following paragraphs echo, in part paraphrase, in part expand, the author's passage on the Trust and archaeological management in Fowler, 1992, *The Past in Contemporary Society: Then, Now*, Routledge, pp.99–101.
5 Op. cit., p.100.
6 Op. cit., p.100.
7 Chippindale, C. *et al*, 1990, *Who Owns Stonehenge?*, Batsford.

VII

Buildings

GERALD CADOGAN

As it starts its second century, the National Trust is blessed that its purposes are still those that the founding trinity of Octavia Hill, Sir Robert Hunter and Canon Rawnsley set out in the Articles of Association agreed at the inaugural meeting on 12 December 1894. The articles are worth reading, as is the National Trust Act 1907, which is the first of six National Trust Acts[1] and marks the Trust's coming to maturity at the early age of twelve years old. Two phrases are as relevant now as they were then. The first occurs in both the Act and the Articles: 'the permanent preservation for the benefit of the Nation of lands and tenements (including buildings) of beauty or historic interest'. The second concerns buildings only. The articles specify that they should be 'places of resort for purposes of recreation or instruction', which in the Act becomes, 'for the purposes of public recreation resort or instruction'.

Preservation is tied to public enjoyment and education. The Trust is for the nation. But it is equally clear that it is not *of* the nation. It is to be a private body with members. Although it was sufficiently successful by 1907 that the Act granted it the unusual power of declaring properties inalienable,[2] there was no suggestion that the nation owned them. The Trust was set up as a private steward for public benefit. The founders knew that the clause in the founding declarations showing that it is here for the long term – 'permanent preservation' – would give it the strength of detachment in decisions about its properties, and that responsible private ownership usually ensures the best protection. If a property was inalienable, so much the better.

This arrangement has stood the Trust well during the twentieth century, strengthened by the various legal arrangements and government decisions that have allowed it to accept property at a cost to the Exchequer. The charge has usually been foregone death duties, which were reimbursed to the Inland Revenue from the National Land Fund. This fund was set up in 1946 with Treasury funding as a war memorial, and replaced in 1980 by the National Heritage Memorial Fund which has the additional power to give endowments.

These continuing conditions and purposes have governed its approach to acquisitions. But changing general economic circumstances produce different threats at different times to different parts of the country or groups of buildings. These dangers have compelled the Trust to act, notably for the coast and country houses when both looked doomed. Views of what constitutes history have also changed and affect acquisition and management policies. In the case of country houses this has meant moving on from seeing them simply as art objects to emphasising their value as social testimony, in which the human-affected landscape of an estate is part of a whole together with the country house and its ancillary buildings.

The founders would surely approve if they could see the impressive expertise and tact the Trust applies now to its buildings (although this has not always been the case). The demands upon staff and volunteers constantly expand, as new ways appear to investigate properties – whether archaeological surveys, tree counts, inventories of stuffed animals or working out where garden paths used to run by tracing the stumps of the yew trees that lined them – and new ways to maintain them and present them. The Trust must marry new technology in its management to old craft skills and be ready, when necessary, to prefer a slow solution that ensures long-lived quality to the quicker solution that the pressure of time and money first suggests.

It is harder now to find the one-time 'dead hand' of Ghastly Good Taste in the Trust's buildings (when rooms in country houses were painted the same peach colour and furnished the same way) – except perhaps in what is for sale in the successful and popular Trust shops. Recent acquisitions demonstrate that the possibilities, and attendant complexities, of promoting 'the permanent preservation, for the benefit of the nation, of lands and tenements (including buildings)' are much more varied.

The language of the Act and Articles of Association is sparse but, viewed on the timescale of permanence (meaning at least 200 or 300 years from now), there is no need to say more. The challenge could not be more enticing.

Historic interest was the first criterion for taking on buildings, and popular benefit the second. An early attempt to save a building by Hill and Hunter was a failure but it reveals the principles on which the Trust was founded. Sayes Court near Deptford had been the house of John Evelyn, the seventeenth-century diarist, where he made a fine garden (and found a young carver called Grinling Gibbons). In 1884 W. J. Evelyn offered it, then in a sorry state, to Hill as an important garden and open space for London. She and Hunter tried to vest it in a trust to be incorporated under the Companies Act. It did not work, but the experience was a formative influence in setting up the National Trust.[3]

The Trust's first two buildings, Alfriston Clergy House in Sussex and Long Crendon Courthouse in Buckinghamshire, could not boast associations with important people but, as vernacular buildings, they were part of ordinary people's history, which ideally suited the founders' populism. Both had had a long life in their communities and stood for the strength and tradition of yeoman (middle-class) England, and both faced collapse or demolition. And so it continues today that the Trust's first question about a building is 'What is its merit?', and the second, 'How serious is the risk?'

In those early years country houses did not appear to be at risk. Despite occasional bankruptcies and fires, the country house system – a big house set among pleasure grounds and surrounded by income-producing farmland – was flourishing. People of means were still building them from the profits of industry and commerce, such as Julius Drewe's Castle Drogo in Devon, paid for with the profits from a chain of grocers. So the acquisition in 1907 of Barrington Court in Somerset, an Elizabethan house being used as a cider store, was unique for 30 years. Rawnsley was attracted by 'the huge open garrets, with little recesses for cubicles to accommodate the servants', which gave 'a good insight into Elizabethan ways'[4] – an attitude which rings well in today's Trust.

Taking ordinary buildings to make them sound without introducing major changes followed the artisans' ideology of the Society for the Protection of Ancient Buildings (SPAB), which William Morris had founded in 1877 on the 'anti-scrape' platform of 'Repair, not restore'. Restoration had been the soulless fate of many churches in the nineteenth century as doctrinaire views (of which period of the Middle Ages marked the essence of British ecclesiastical architecture and/or liturgical performance) took them back, often in pastiche, to a dead time to which it was thought that they should belong. Such attitudes had led to wholesale remodelling of churches and cathedrals throughout the country. The reaction came with SPAB whose mission remains to treat buildings as living entities that continuously change. If they happen to need preservation, they should be preserved as they are now since that is itself an important stage in their life story. The same pragmatism governed the early Trust in taking the buildings in Alfriston and Long Crendon, and is still at work, as visitors to the recently acquired Calke Abbey or Mr Straw's House in Worksop can see.

Pragmatism – such a British characteristic – has been evident also in those acquisitions where the Trust has had the role of reacting to need as the last resort. Occasionally, having perceived the need, it plays a pro-active, anticipatory role, as with Canons Ashby or Enterprise Neptune. Barrington Court was a need of this sort, which met opposition on the grounds that the lack of an endowment would make it a continuing drain on funds. When that proved to be the case, it deterred the acquisition of other country houses, but the Trust did campaign for houses to be helped through tax reliefs for their owners.

By the 1930s, times had changed and, after years of attrition, some estates faced collapse from death duties and the recession in farming, prompting Lord Lothian to devise the Country Houses Scheme (see pp.20–1). The National Trust Act 1937 does not mention the phrase 'country house' but did establish the scheme in law by extending the general purposes of the Trust to include, for the first time, buildings of architectural importance and their chattels and contents. Lothian's speech to the 1934 annual general meeting had already identified the country house as 'a treasure of quiet beauty which is not only specially characteristic but quite unrivalled in any other land'.[5]

The view that country houses were a uniquely British contribution to civilisation set the tone for the succeeding decades. No other culture, the argument went, has managed to blend so sophisticated a combination of architecture, art, landscape gardening, farming and local administration, and have the persons in charge residing for much of the year in the houses which were the heart of the system. (The argument is not correct. Both the second millennium BC Minoans of Crete and the Romans had buildings of similar purpose and quality, whose mixture of farming, fine art and architecture and local administration anticipates the country houses centuries later – as one can see at the Trust's Roman villa at Chedworth in Gloucestershire. And the best starting point for studying country house theory is the sixteenth-century work and writings of Andrea Palladio.)

Missing from Lothian's speech – but not from Palladio – is the idea of the country house as the hub of a working system that involved the whole estate and its surrounding communities. It may be that Lothian took this for granted, but it could be indicative of an attitude in the Trust that put too much emphasis on the house as an art object, albeit in a landscape, rather than as a socio-economic entity, and led to the 'dead hand' criticisms. How different had been Rawnsley's reaction to Barrington Court, and how removed from today's presentation of country houses as the heart of a large system.

The Trust should be proud that it did take so many country houses, especially after the Second World War when heavy death duties were compounded by unprecedented tax on high incomes at 19s 6d (97.5p) in the pound, and many houses went to institutions – as had happened even before the war at Stowe and Bryanston (which was built only in 1890 and had a short life fulfilling its original functions).

The war accelerated the houses' decline. Evacuees, hospitals, schools and servicemen took their toll, and it was hard afterwards to find the money to repair the buildings or people to staff them. Owners also foresaw an uncertain future under a Labour government which some saw as antipathetic to the landed capitalism of the country estate – this led surprisingly many of them, or their executors or trustees, to take the roof off or demolish their houses (which had already happened to the Trust's Clumber Park in Nottinghamshire in 1938). The owners arranged to live somewhere smaller or, like Lord Marchmain in *Brideshead Revisited* by Evelyn Waugh, went abroad, mostly to escape income tax and socialism.

Far fewer houses would have come to the Trust in this period had it not been for Hugh Dalton who created the National Land Fund in 1946, to reimburse the Inland Revenue for death duties lost on houses passed to the Trust. He saw the Trust 'as a typically British "example of Practical Socialism in action"'[6]. The need for the Trust's rescuing embrace, often with the help of the National

Heritage Memorial Fund, the successor to the Land Fund, has continued up until Chastleton in Oxfordshire in 1991. Buildings acquired in the 1980s with NHMF aid are a distinguished list: Belton House in Lincolnshire, Calke Abbey and Kedleston Hall in Derbyshire, the garden monuments at Stowe in Buckinghamshire, and Studley Royal in Yorkshire. In Northern Ireland, the NHMF paid for refacing Castle Coole in Co. Fermanagh.

Other sorts of buildings that the Trust has assembled make a diverse list, ranging from the prehistoric stone circle at Avebury in Wiltshire and various Roman remains to twentieth-century houses. They include castles and towers, mills, town and village buildings (continuing the Alfriston/Long Crendon tradition) and homes of famous people, where artists and writers predominate, such as Thomas Bewick's Cherryburn in Northumberland which the Trust has recently taken over from a local preservation scheme.

In Wales the Trust has focused on Welsh life and military and industrial history through castles, a gold mine, and small houses in town and country of which the gem is Plas yn Rhiw in the Lleyn peninsula (Gwynedd). Large country houses are generally scarce, except near the English border where the Trust has Chirk Castle and Erddig in Clwyd and Powis Castle in Powys, and near the sea where it has Llanerchaeron in Dyfed, and Penrhyn Castle and Plas Newydd in Gwynedd.

In Northern Ireland, by contrast, where the framework of society was different, it has some magnificent houses and gardens (such as Florence Court in Co. Fermanagh, and Mount Stewart House and Rowallane garden in Co. Down). It has also two splendid documents of Irish life, a High Victorian pub in Belfast (the Crown, open only during licensing hours) and the imaginative recent acquisition of Patterson's Spade Mill, which worked commercially until 1990 making spades mainly for cutting peat – and now makes them again for the Trust to use or sell.

In England the recent acquisitions of Mr Straw's House and Erno Goldfinger's house in Hampstead (2 Willow Road, NW3), both with their contents, would suggest that the Trust has turned away from acquiring yet more country houses. A prize rarity, the almost unaltered Elizabethan manor house at Chastleton, is exceptional. Any further country houses in England will have to be likewise in great need, of similar architectural or historical importance, and fundable from outside sources.

Visitors enjoy Mr Straw's House (7 Blyth Grove, Worksop, Nottinghamshire) because house and contents are part of so many people's experience, at least in memory, as if one was dropping in on one's grandparents for tea. It was partly chance that it came to the Trust who would never have knocked on the door if William Straw had not left the Trust (of which he was not a member, but he was a strong believer in educational self-improvement) almost £1m plus the house's contents. When Simon Murray, the East Midlands Historic Buildings Representative, arrived, he realised that here was a house that modern times had passed by, as was the case at Calke Abbey – and also at Chastleton. Murray proposed using the money to buy and endow the house and the semi-detached house next door and follow the example of Calke Abbey's conservation in leaving the house and its collections as far as possible as they were. In both cases the result is to immortalise the owners: the Straws, who were seed merchants, and the Harpur Crewes of Calke with their mania for stuffed animals and shooting trophies.

No. 2 Willow Road, a Modernist house will also be left unchanged, complete with the Goldfingers' art collection, which includes the work of Hans Arp, Max Ernst and Henry Moore. Yet again chance brought this opportunity, although the Trust's reputation for tactful preservation of buildings must have been an important factor. And The Homewood in Esher in Surrey (also Modernist), which architect Patrick Gwynne designed for himself with its furniture in the 1930s and has lived in ever since but will be leaving to the Trust, will be handled in the same way. This approach focuses on the life that has gone on in a house.

Another interesting recent purchase is Orford Ness, a wild shingle bank and marsh on the Suffolk coast which has been acquired primarily for its natural history and being part of England's coastline. But it is also of great interest for modern history as radar, which proved crucial in the Second World War, was first tested here. Later the site was used as a testing ground in the nuclear weapons programme. Some of the boffins' buildings survive.

But these twentieth-century buildings that still contain the trappings of their former life and usage remain oddities among the Trust's holdings. The Trust would benefit from owning more, although obtaining them will, doubtless, still involve chance. On the other hand, it would be naive to think that the Trust will never take on another country house.

The Trust has also acquired many farms and cottages, or they have come as part of the estate of a country house, along with stables, lodges, garden buildings and even whole villages. Trust villages now total 60, and the Trust has 37 pubs. The reason for acquiring these vernacular buildings is that the landscape, buildings and traditional way of life are all intertwined – especially for Trust holdings in the Lake District or Cornwall – and each is incomprehensible without the other. The Trust's vernacular buildings survey can assess their merit – from pigsties to dovecotes – and determine what work is needed to bring them up to the Trust's standards of maintenance. As this conservation costs millions of pounds (which are not immediately to hand), realising it is a slow business. But the survey can also look for appropriate new uses for the buildings. An exciting project of this type has been the Home Farm at Wimpole Hall in Cambridgeshire which, even though Sir John Soane designed its great barn, was derelict. The Trust has brought the farm back to life, stocking it with unusual breeds, and last year 16,500 children visited Wimpole on organised visits.

The Trust rents out many of its ordinary buildings, a small percentage of them for holiday lets when they are not needed or suitable for permanent occupation. Some have been sold on long leases but, under the Leasehold Reform, Housing and Urban Development Act 1993, Trust leaseholders have no right to obtain the freehold. Although these houses are usually not open for public visits, the Trust is still safeguarding them. It looks hard for sympathetic tenants and can be a tough landlord if they do not care for the property. Occasionally, it sells freehold a few buildings that it did not declare inalienable.

The 1995 *Handbook* lists the buildings that the public meets. Dividing them by what I see as their principal attribute, and adding Chastleton (not yet open) and Orford Ness (not in the 1995 handbook), we have the following table of buildings open to the public:

	ENGLAND	WALES	NORTHERN IRELAND
1 **Country houses** (including manor houses, castles that continued in use as country houses, and Chastleton, Clumber Park, Gibside, Mottisfont, Overbecks and Studley Royal)	121	8	8
2 **Town buildings** (including assembly rooms, markets, pub, school, theatre, and town houses in London and elsewhere)	26	2	1
3 **Village buildings** Also: West Wycombe village	19	1	–
4 **Farm buildings** (including barns, dovecotes, duck decoy, farms and farmhouses, fenman's cottage, stables and Wimpole Home Farm)	19	1	–
5 **Buildings with historical associations**	17	1	–
6 **Mills** (agricultural and drainage)	13	–	–
7 **Castles and towers** (post-Roman) and other military sites (including Orford Ness)	9	1	–
8 **Mills** (industrial), mines, presses and engines	4	2	3
9 **Abbeys and chapels** (pre-Reformation)	8	–	–
10 **Roman**	4	1	–
11 **Chapels and churches** listed separately (post-Reformation, including Studley Royal)	4	–	–
12 **Other:** Lighthouses	2	–	–

Also: A La Ronde feather house, Avebury stone circle, Belfast historic pub, Conway suspension bridge, Fox Talbot Museum, Kinver Edge rock houses, River Wey and Godalming Navigations, Templetown mausoleum, Watersmeet fishing lodge.

Not included are buildings in gardens (including Downhill Castle) or the steam yacht *Gondola*.

These figures are a rough guide. It would be easy to argue about the classification. Is Chartwell in Kent, for instance, primarily a country house (as here) or one with historical associations – a shrine to Churchill? Nor do the figures show that many estate buildings that belong with the country houses (but are not specified separately in the *Handbook*) nor whole villages (like Blickling, Broadclyst, Coleshill, Lacock, Slindon and Studland) that are an important part of the Trust's building stock.

All the same, the table demonstrates a strong slant to country houses and other country buildings, which is not surprising in view of the combination of the Country Houses Scheme and the Trust's other remit for preserving places of natural beauty. But it does suggest that there are desirable alternatives to country houses for the Trust to consider when opportunities for new acquisitions present themselves. I return to this below.

Management and presentation

The demands of managing so many different buildings, and the good fortune of being able to take a long view of its properties (as Oxford and Cambridge colleges can, and the Church of England used to do), have accumulated in the Trust an impressive expertise backed by research. Trust staff, volunteers and contractors are learning constantly more of how the past worked – meaning, how people of all sorts lived – in practical detail, and how to demonstrate that or reproduce it. An example is the restoration of Uppark which has enriched our view of the eighteenth century through the craftsmen's having to relearn the secrets of moulding plaster. Similarly the planting schemes of Stowe that have been found among the Stowe papers (now in California) are vital for re-creating the landscape garden. Equally necessary for deciding how to manage a building is the research that resurrects a complicated architectural history, or discovers unimagined uses that the building once had.

A 'research first' policy demonstrates a proper modesty in the face of the buildings and the evidence about them, and meets the demanding standards of management, as the range of what can be learnt – and achieved – ever increases. It is becoming standard practice to survey for archaeology, gardening, and flora and fauna, and the details of the buildings and their contents, as well as to hunt through the archives. In the future there will be yet more recording demands, which the Trust must meet, to help it to handle the buildings best as living entities, and to teach others what best practice involves. That means learning, for example, which brushes to use on which fabrics when winter-cleaning a house (the Trust does not spring-clean as that is reopening time) and may eventually stretch to re-roofing Cherryburn in Northumberland with heather thatch as it used to have.

As a side-effect of its present concern for best practice in preserving its properties (which may entail restrictions on visitors), and the fact that it has obtained so many country houses in the last half-century (often with their former owners or their descendants staying in part of them), the Trust is accused in the media of being élitist, or of laying a dead hand on its buildings (though not on its landscapes or its field barns), or of both together. If there has been substance in these charges, in 1995 it is hard to find it. Both accusations are confused.

It is not clear what lies underneath the emotive charge of élitism. It is probable that the Trust is labelled élitist because: (1) it is thought to have an undue number of upper class toffs in charge; (2) this promotes an out-of-date model of society, distorted by class, and behaving in unacceptable ways (which would include hunting); (3) it is run too much for the benefit of others of similar background, allowing too easy a life to members of the former owner's family still in residence – which they do not deserve as the house is not theirs. At the back of these charges is probably a resentment of the better off. Another latent resentment may be against things being done well.

Enlightened bourgeoisie began the Trust and they, on the whole, are the people who still run it. There are, of course, aristocrats who sit on the many volunteer advisory committees, but they are there only for their expertise – which, not surprisingly, includes managing estates. To concentrate on the in-essential of background misses the key question of whether they do the necessary work, and how well they do it.

The charge of encouraging an out-of-date, self-serving model of society is also misconceived, with its presumption that donors or their descendants should not be allowed to continue to live in part of their old homes. Rather, they should be encouraged to do so (subject to clauses to allow eviction for criminal or persis-tently unreasonable behaviour). Why? Because today we realise that country houses were not, and are not, just art objects created for the pleasure of a few but rather are part of a complete system of country life, in which these people – the family – are the core.

Their economic power has gone since the Trust is now the owner, but an institution like the Trust simply cannot fulfil their various roles in society. The family is/was as much a fitting as the furniture, cider press or estate cottages. So let them stay, to present the whole picture of the pattern of life. They can continue to perform traditional functions (church, charities, councils, cricket club and magistrates' bench), host the village fête, support appeals, and take their part in the intricate unwritten system of mutual obligations and favours with people of *all* levels of society, which is how the countryside works.

As for the 'dead hand' accusation, that may be an attack on insensitive uniformity which had some validity a generation ago when stereotyped schemes of decoration coloured probably too many Trust houses. Or it may be to suggest that the Trust is making morgues of its buildings by enshrining them as museums, when they should be different. Here the Trust is in a dilemma. It should not aim to mummify buildings but to be flexible in presenting their individual qualities and claims to interest, and imaginative in identifying uses and attractions besides simply inspecting the house. The large numbers of visitors show that it must be doing the right thing in many places. Nevertheless, to some extent it has to 'stop the clock' whenever it takes a building on. It is usually best, or at least the honest course, to conserve the building in its state at that moment, warts and all. Restoring it to some earlier ideal state, which did happen to some Trust buildings, would be both improper and opposed to the William Morris/SPAB ideology of the Trust's founders.

In this vein, the clock stopped at Calke Abbey and Mr Straw's House at the time of acquisition; the Trust decided to retain the grime and tears in the wallpaper, which show how the former owners lived without bothering with regular maintenance. I hope that the Trust will present more buildings in this decisive way that appears without artifice, but it should not become a universal precept. It is easy to imagine buildings with a feeble preceding life, disused stables perhaps or a chocolate box of a Georgian house, that would gain a new breath of life from thorough refurbishment.

The other side to stopping the clock is that the Trust can breathe new life into properties, by holding concerts, art exhibitions and flowers shows, or making the house and its estate a focal point of local community activities, as is happening so well at Gibside outside Gateshead and at Sutton House in Hackney. Revitalising in a different way is the restoration of old garden buildings and orangeries, where it makes sense and the Trust has the money.

A new variant of the 'dead hand' criticism accuses the Trust of giving undue emphasis to life 'downstairs', especially in the kitchen. There is little substance here. Since everybody has to cook and wash up, many visitors understand this part of a big house better than what went on upstairs in the drawing-room. The moral is to keep the downstairs but put more effort into explaining how the main rooms worked upstairs, and how much activity – political, literary, ecclesiastical, academic – they housed besides the social.

The Trust's shops must not allow grounds for 'dead hand' accusations. There is a danger of too much cosy chintz and twee-dom, and an excess of Peter Rabbit (however much Beatrix Potter is a Trust saint). It matters because it may damage the visitor's experience. The shop is usually at the end of the tour and becomes the visitor's last – and lasting – impression. That may distort the pleasure and learning of the visit. The ideal is to have a variety of well-designed goods that present the best of modern British craftsmanship and live up to the excellence expected of the Trust.

Preservation vs access

This long-running debate is incapable of easy resolution. The Trust must achieve both but preservation comes first, as the founding documents and the Trust's title make clear. Otherwise there is nothing to access. Timed tickets and other restrictions are inevitable, as is low-level publicity for fragile buildings and gardens. Some buildings can hold only a few visitors, and at others crowds can ruin the experience. Access, however, remains a (but not the) prime obligation. The founders spelt that out, and it is the main justification for the Trust's favoured treatment from the Treasury.

Education and community involvement

The Trust is starting at last to make proper use for education of its fantastic resources, at all levels from primary school to PhD and carrying on into lifelong learning in the Minerva programme – and residencies for artists to work and teach in Trust buildings. The value of what the Trust's buildings can offer for the new history curricula is enormous, as are the chances for children to learn about the country and how to use it – and to increase their self-reliance – through the National Trust Newcastle Inner City Project which uses the local properties. Similar schemes are running at Sutton House in Hackney, while the touring Young National Trust Theatre is an exciting way to reach into history and the life of the past in places where what is being acted could really have happened. These children are the future members of the Trust. The only constraint on education is money, since the first call on the Trust is to look after its properties. But the statistic of 520,000 children on organised educational visits in 1994 indicates the value of the education programme.

The inner-city projects are part of the educational programme. At Gibside, the Newcastle project offers walks, camping out, and work in the grounds for people of all ages, from housebound pensioners to young mothers and their children. It is proving a rare success as it brings a new and positive view of life to people living in a deprived part of the country. In doing this, it is turning the usual pattern of conservation on its head. As Gatehead Borough Council realises by making grants to Gibside, the old estate is helping to restore modern Gateshead and Newcastle by giving point to people's lives. The Trust's use of the various government youth employment schemes, which are ideal for estate work and usually as valuable for the participants as for the Trust, has also been a helpful contribution to society, as have Acorn Camps for young volunteers.

The next century

The Trust must maintain a diversity of approaches, based on research to determine what is special about each building or group of buildings. That does not mean that every country house stable block has to be stocked with horses and carriages but, if some are, that is to the good. At Ormesby Hall in Cleveland the local mounted police use one and at Erddig there is a riding-school. These uses give visitors pleasure and show how the buildings were designed to work (and are better than automatically making them into tea-rooms). The same holds for the Home Farm at Wimpole Hall, or the cottage at Wicken Fen which shows the life of a fenman in the 1930s.

Explaining how daily life worked is a vital task that needs imagination and effort as the pre-motor car world becomes ever more remote. There are still people alive who knew it themselves or have heard from parents and grandparents about walking miles to school, or the drama of crashing the pony trap. But it will all soon be memory.

This is a fine opportunity for the Trust. If it cannot fill the stables with horses, it can at least create displays – including videos or slides – of how the horse was the premier means of transport for centuries. Another display could be about the imposing stables built to house these valuable animals, and another on how many livelihoods depended on them. At Calke Abbey the video shows a craftsman who worked on the restoration – not an actor – explaining how he did it. This is rich, graspable history, which will shortly depart from direct experience.

Such arguments apply to all types of building and all aspects of them. The greatest need for instruction is in architecture itself. Unlike the impressive general level of horticultural knowledge, fairly few visitors have learnt how to scrutinise buildings for function, style, pretension, building sequence and historical value. With the Trust's copious building stock, it is easy to remedy that.

One way would be widespread use of videos or slides with commentary, or to have a brief talk from a volunteer, for an introduction before people start the visit. The aim should be to answer in six minutes, why the place matters, and what should visitors particularly look out for? It should be feasible for visitors to return for a repeat to consolidate their visit, perhaps after they have passed the shop and before they leave the property. Such presentations would also help with crowd control on busy days, and fill the delays of waiting for admission on timed tickets.

These introductions might develop into virtual reality displays or use models and smells in reproduction scenes, like the Yorvik Viking Centre in York – techniques which can all help in enriching people's visits. But there is one essential condition. The reproductions must be utterly separate from the real thing, so that there is no chance of confusing the two and visitors can progress from the amusing electronic lesson to the greater fun of recognising and understanding for themselves the real past. (The Trust should also consider audio-tapes, as used in art exhibitions, for the visitors as they go round the building.)

At an advanced level, CD-ROM will help those who want more knowledge. Topics could include architectural history (reconstructing the development of buildings, park and gardens), the history and deeds of the family, the role of the building in the history of society, or detailed explanation of the pictures and furniture. The medium is ideal for introducing comparative material to put buildings in a wide cultural and historic context, demonstrating, for instance, how Penrhyn Castle in North Wales was built out of the profits – and the ghastly conditions and famous strike – of the Penrhyn slate quarry.

Research

Research must be recognised as a top priority, both for the practical purpose of managing properties (as the Trust is already putting in hand through various surveys) and for historical scholarship. The Trust owns some of the country's richest sources of architectural, artistic, cultural and economic history. But until they have been studied, they miss the extra dimension of releasing all their inherent information. Surveys such as the vernacular buildings survey need extending until the Trust has listed all its holdings (whether French fans, Chinese wallpapers, Tudor oak settles, farm waggons, or the contents of its country house libraries) on a database which should be available on Internet, which will allow scholars and the general public to make best use of the Trust's holdings.

Emphasis on scholarly work as an important part of the Trust's best practice presupposes that the Trust becomes more academic. This seems to be exactly what is happening, spurred by the proper desire to make better management decisions; but how much the Trust sees this as an overall evolutionary step, is not clear. Yet this is surely the right way for the Trust to grow, and the fulfilment of the least developed of the three purposes of the 1907 Act ('public recreation resort or instruction'). The result will be that the Trust will become a hybrid institution, which is the implication of keeping such a valuable collection of buildings and contents, while wanting to extract more from them than simply securing them for the nation.

For an academic role to succeed, the Trust must be willing to grant its officers sabbatical leave to pursue specified research and prepare work for publication. Leaves should be flexible in length, while the Trust should pay regular salaries or help with applications for grants, and could approach foundations for the establishment of an in-house scheme of National Trust Research Fellowships. The Trust must also continue to encourage outsiders to research Trust material. It helps the Trust, and there is far too much material for the Trust's officers to handle themselves.

Research is of little value without a vigorous publications programme. To leave the research that has already been done languishing in office files does not fulfil the duty of public instruction. A model might be the British Museum Press, where the sale of general books helps to fund scholarly works. Some publication might be on disc or microfiche rather than as printed books.

Education and community work

The Minerva programme and the various community schemes are a fresh start in expanding the Trust's educational and social activities, which are bound to expand. Other possibilities might include: more use of Trust properties by professional art schools and amateur drawing classes; enlarging the theatre programme for children – who love it; increasing the training for the public in housekeeping and traditional crafts in order to make most use of the Trust's accumulation of practical wisdom. These sorts of ideas and many more are in the Trust's Education Appeal.

Other aspects of the Trust's broader educational work help to achieve the objective of encouraging repeat visits (which are infrequent, according to Trust statistics). Establishing the Trust's Foundation for Art, and making Beningbrough an outstation for the National Portrait Gallery, suggest that changing exhibitions are one way to achieve this, by bringing new life to the buildings, especially by showing modern works in old settings. Besides pictures, there could be exhibitions around the architecture, pictures or furniture of the building, or its former occupants, or the grounds, outbuildings and local community. Saltram already has art exhibitions, and Blickling Hall and Felbrigg Hall have changing displays of books.

Exhibitions need not be large but they must be meaty enough to merit a Michelin-type verdict of *vaut le voyage*. One possibility would be a series of teaching exhibitions around pictures that Turner painted at Petworth, which would use his pictures and sketches, and Petworth papers and other contemporary material. In the background visitors would see the park at Petworth which, thanks to the Trust's campaigning against running a bypass through it and its being an inalienable Trust holding, remains much as Turner painted it: a place of serenity and exquisite beauty.

Other ways to encourage repeat visits are opening different parts on different days, connoisseur's days when parts that are not normally open will be available at an extra charge (which all should pay, including Trust members), holding concerts and paying functions, and even using the chapels of Trust houses for services as they were intended.

Future properties

For future acquisitions, general principles are of more utility than specific suggestions, not least as the last hundred years show how much chance has played in adding to the holdings. Hitherto, the Trust's general policy has been opportunist, taking or refusing buildings offered to it but not usually making the first move to acquire a building. And, after painful experiences of country houses acquired after the war without enough funding for subsequent maintenance, it has become a prerequisite that a property has an endowment (whether from the donor, the NHMF, public appeal or perhaps now the National Lottery).

There is no necessity that this should continue to be the policy. There are strong arguments for a pro-active stance with the Trust setting out to obtain specific buildings, or examples of types of buildings, that are at risk of vanishing. The buildings in use during the apogee of British industry before the First World War come at once to mind; and they and other possibilities are discussed below. But finding the money to obtain such buildings, and endow them so that their maintenance and preservation are not an extra charge on stretched funds, is

price change
due to
new methods

bound to inhibit such a change of policy, if not stop it dead. A yet more urgent factor is that the Trust has the obligation of a huge backlog of repairs to its present properties, which must be a prime charge on funds. And it is generally the case that the higher standards become – and they have risen greatly of late – and the more new methods are discovered, the more costly the maintenance tends to be.

A pro-active policy may be impossible. If so, the Trust will continue to await whatever interesting proposal comes its way. But whether that is the situation in the future, or the Trust finds the money to acquire a wish-list of properties, either way it must have ready criteria to evaluate possible acquisitions.

Acquisitions must continue to be: of national importance; right in their setting; preferably an architectural unity without shoddy accretions like abutting nissen huts (which in today's climate would probably have to be kept as part of the building's history); and in need. The need will probably be so severe that no other conservation body is likely to be able to marshal the resources for the building, except perhaps English Heritage. But the Trust has an advantage over English Heritage in that it is private and independently run, and can make controversial choices that would be difficult for English Heritage, being a semi-government quango of uncertain autonomy. The Trust must continue to encourage local trusts and conservation societies to take buildings, as is also English Heritage policy, notably for its archaeological sites. If local initiatives fail, the Trust must remain ready to be the last resort.

Here are some suggestions for classes of buildings that deserve better representation:

THE TWENTIETH CENTURY

The Goldfinger house and Mr Straw's House are an excellent start because they have come as complete entities, as the Gwynne house also looks likely to do. The Goldfinger house is important for documenting the arrival of Modernism in Britain and, less frequently mentioned, as a monument of the national good fortune in receiving so many clever refugees from the Nazis in the 1930s. The Straw house shows the conservative daily world of a prosperous family of merchants of much the same era, a conservatism that lasted for many people with little alteration from the early 1900s to the 1950s.

But these are only two or three buildings. The Trust should consider gathering more before they have been altered. That is often the worst risk for modern buildings. Occupants feel entitled to alter them in ways that they would never dream of doing to older buildings, even if they are by distinguished architects. They do not carry the inhibiting sanctity of age. English Heritage's drive to list modern buildings is a start in trying to pre-empt unneeded or injudicious changes (as applying for listed building consent gives parties time to think out what really is for the best) but the total listed is still small. The Trust has plenty of scope to help in its way.

An acquisition list might include two characteristic building types of the 1930s, a swimming lido and an Art Deco cinema, preferably one that still has its organ and is part of, or next to, a 1930s shopping development. As for houses, I hope that more donors will give the Trust interesting houses of all sorts, with contents, before alteration. This is urgent, because in a hundred years it will have become an archaeological exercise to work back to the original state of, say, a terrace of village council houses. Their straightforward, unpretentious architecture, often the work of an unknown architect, is now constantly sullied by painting the pebble dash different colours, changing the doors and windows, and adding porches, satellite dishes and roof extensions – which demonstrate the individuality of the private owner (who has been freed from council restraint) and destroy the communal strength of the whole. Terraces of council houses, and a suburban drive in Pinner, are ideal for the Trust. After repair, they could be rented to the sympathetic tenants that the Trust demands.

INDUSTRY

Although it has a prime document of the Industrial Revolution in the cotton mill workers' village at Quarry Bank (preserving the complete system, as on the country estates), the Trust has few industrial buildings. One possibility is a coal mine, but there are several mining museums. In the meantime, the Trust shows the public its Dolaucothi gold mine.

Other possibilities are a traditional brickworks, a pottery or an ironworks (perhaps beside a Wealden hammer pond) if one survives in good enough state to repair. An opportunity that has now gone was William Morris's (Lord Nuffield's) garage in Longwall, Oxford, where his car-making empire – in its time a major part of British industry – started as a small business in the heart of the medieval city. Similar opportunities may recur.

BUILDINGS IN THE COUNTRY

The Trust has no need to take any more windmills and watermills, unless they belong to an estate. And there is probably little need for acquiring further farm buildings for the sake of their architecture, but every reason if they belong to a larger unit of social and historical importance or are part of a scheme for safeguarding a landscape. Cottages or farms which would help a distinctive way of life to survive would also be candidates for acquisition. This is already a Trust policy in the Lake District.

Villages are another part of rural life that is under threat. In a hundred years traditional villages and hamlets may be an extreme rarity. The Trust could add to the villages it has, ensuring that all its villages have a viable, village-centred economy, whether farming, light industry (such as a forge) or handicrafts. As happens already, it would have to decide how much new building to allow. Acquiring surrounding farmland would keep the village in its proper setting. The result should aim to combine natural beauty and historic interest.

I have already suggested village council houses. A nineteenth-century work-house is a brilliant idea under investigation in Dorset – a nice complement to the Trust's Max Gate, Thomas Hardy's house.

URBAN BUILDINGS AND SPACES

Nineteenth-century urban parks and cemeteries are ideal candidates, now often falling into ruin through cuts in council expenditure and vandalised once the lodges are boarded up and the keepers removed (as a recent report from the Victorian Society points out). They are not expensive to run, and vandalism drops as soon as keepers return to the lodges. They are an important part of British urban history. In big industrial cities the Trust could combine these spaces with terraces of unreconstructed workers' cottages.

CHURCHES

Churches are one of England's greatest glories and always need maintenance. The Church of England is increasingly stretched to look after them, and the Churches Conservation Trust (formerly the Redundant Churches Fund), Friends of Friendless Churches and local church trusts do not have the resources to manage all those that are worth keeping. The Trust could consider taking on churches or chapels that are next to a country house it already owns and part of the house ensemble, which would be a small but appropriate contribution towards saving the churches of England. It is already responsible, for instance, for those at Canons Ashby, Gibside and Clumber. The Trust might also consider the places of worship of immigrant communities into this country that are under threat, which will be mainly synagogues and mosques.

Hill, Hunter and Rawnsley founded the National Trust to preserve buildings and landscapes so that all could enjoy them in perpetuity. Its success, their success is obvious. Doubters need only consider what the Trust has preserved, how many members it has and how many visitors. Less obvious, and much more exciting at the start of its second century, is the liveliness of today's Trust in its debate (of which this collection of essays is a small part) on how to maintain its mission and what are the best initiatives for the twenty-first century. Nothing beats a visit to Stowe or Gibside to see the Trust's new directions. Stowe is a research-based project where it is rescuing what was probably the country's greatest landscape garden. At Gibside ('the Stowe of the North') it is bringing life back to what was a piteous wilderness a few years ago, as old Gibside gives new life and vision to the inhabitants of the grimmer parts of Tyneside.

These successes say much about the hard work and imagination of the Trust's staff, and their ability to induce a similar hard-working enthusiasm in the great body of volunteers. I see little sentimentality in today's Trust, but plenty of scope for more hard work, excitement, enrichment and enjoyment in the countless projects and experiences waiting to be offered to visitors.

I have barely touched on money. As Constraint Number One, it looks set always to inhibit schemes. But until now there has usually been a solution. That may not carry on and it may seem overly optimistic but, as the Trust starts its second hundred years with an emphasis on the social documents of the past and the integration of man and nature in the British landscape, it is hard to think of better purposes for grants from the Millennium Fund and the National Lottery. What could be more part of the history of British society than gambling? And what better way to use its profits than in combating philistinism, apathy and the short-term view?

'It will all be there after we are gone', a Trust member remarked. That is why Hill, Hunter and Rawnsley founded the National Trust.

Notes

1 The others are the 1919, 1937, 1939, 1953 and 1971 National Trust Acts.
2 The first schedule of the 1907 Act lists the existing properties that were to become inalienable, which was all except 185 acres of farm land at Barrington Court.
3 Waterson (n.1) tells the story, pp.25–9.
4 Waterson (ibid.), pp.51–2.
5 Quoted by Jenkins and James (n.1), p.79, in a moving account of the Scheme, pp.74–101.
6 Jenkins and James (ibid.), p.136.

VIII

Gardens

ANNA PAVORD

THE FACTS RELATING to the National Trust's incomparable collection of gardens can be quickly established. Each year 162 are open in England, Wales and Northern Ireland. In 1994 8.4 million people visited Trust gardens, which always feature heavily in any list of the Trust's most visited properties. In 1993–4 they took eight places out of the first fifteen. The two most popular, Studley Royal in North Yorkshire, acquired by the Trust in 1983, and Henry Hoare's eighteenth-century masterpiece, Stourhead in Wiltshire, on their own attract more than half a million people each season. In its most recent budget, the Trust allocated about £10 million to its gardens, the lion's share going towards the salaries of its 375 gardeners. More remarkable than the *number* of gardens held is their quality and range, which covers nearly four hundred years of garden making. Taken together, they contain the world's largest and most diverse collection of cultivated plants.

Those are the facts, but however thickly you pile them up, whichever way you order them, they do not answer the central question: what are these gardens for? What motives determine their management, their future appearance, their style? Are the gardens exercises in nostalgia, first cousins to theme parks, re-creating the settings of a vanished way of life for us, as tourists, to wallow in? Or are they museums, chronological chapters in a book of garden history, to be preserved forever in aspic? In an age such as our own, which sees the gardens largely in terms of the plants that they contain, some see Trust gardens as botanical holding pens, providing the widest possible range of growing conditions in which rare plants can thrive.

Those with a beady eye on the Trust's balance sheet may consider its gardens solely on the basis of their earning capacity. Though the philosophy of the founding trio, Hunter, Hill and Rawnsley, was based on protecting and giving access to land, there is no turnstile at the entrance to a long-distance footpath. As the Trust's own figures show, gardens, more than any other type of property, attract visitors who pay, as distinct from members who do not. Gardens are in great demand for fund-raising events – *fêtes-champêtre*, fireworks, concerts, plays

– but careful accounting is needed here to ensure that short-term profit is not at the expense of long-term loss. The extra time that gardeners spend on such events may find its way into the costs, but the long-term wear and tear on the garden will probably not.

Trials and errors

The Trust had been in existence for more than 50 years before it began to consider gardens as assets in their own right, rather than as subsidiary adjuncts to historic houses. Barrington in Somerset, its first country house, had come to it in 1907, Montacute, its second in 1931. A desultory attempt was made to set the Montacute garden on its feet, first from advice given by Vita Sackville-West, passing through on a motor tour with her husband, Harold Nicolson, then according to planting plans provided by Phyllis Reiss of nearby Tintinhull. The first garden that the Trust acquired entirely on its own merits was Hidcote, Lawrence Johnston's Gloucestershire garden. This was in 1947 and it became the responsibility of a new Gardens Committee, formed jointly with the Royal Horticultural Society under the powerful leadership of Lord Aberconway, President of the RHS.

The terms of reference were carefully laid down. The committee was to recommend gardens worthy of acceptance. A new Gardens Fund would provide money for their upkeep and the committee would advise on how it was to be spent. They would 'arrange' for the control and maintenance of Trust gardens, although routine matters could be dealt with by the area agent. Local committees would handle day-to-day problems. The gardens committee would visit when necessary to advise on questions of policy. From the beginning, muddle was built into management. Three different sources of 'advice' were on hand to add to the often strongly held opinions of the owner still in residence and their head gardeners, who might have entirely different agendas in mind.

The painful birth of a policy for gardens is charted in a series of large files in the Trust's archive. The handwritten index of the first volume (1948–63) indicates the matters under discussion: an appeals organiser for the Garden Funds, a broadcast by Vita Sackville-West for the same purpose, an interview with the Chancellor of the Exchequer to talk about tax exemption for historic gardens (an issue still unresolved). The idea of garden tours tailored for American visitors was first mooted, the desirability of an apprentice scheme for gardeners first voiced. The question of labels – green plastic or grey zinc – was debated at length, taking up rather more time than the question of publicity for gardens.

Nowhere in this neat index do questions of taste, design or historic intent appear. The committee members, who included the Earl of Rosse at Nymans and Vita Sackville-West at Sissinghurst (neither yet Trust properties), were primarily plantsmen. The predominant aura of gardening at that time was one of plantsmanship, fuelled by the torrent of new plants that had come into the country over the previous fifty years. The Garden History Society had not yet been born. The committee's concerns were with *gardening*, in the sense of keeping plants well cared for, paths swept, lawn edges trimmed. But not to document. Although it was standard practice to make minute inventories of houses that came into its care, no inventories were made of the Trust's gardens, no plans of planting schemes or lists of key plants drawn up.

Hidcote, the Trust's first garden, had only a short history. It was created entirely within the first 40 years of this century by the American Lawrence Johnston. It was all of a piece. But when Johnston died, the Trust spread his collection of Regency garden furniture round other more 'historic' properties. Two tubs were sent to enhance the forecourt of Charlecote in Warwickshire. In a single year, the Gardens Committee recommended that the paintwork at Hidcote should be a different colour, that the camellia shelter should be demolished (they had already pulled down the other large plant shelter), that cedars at the end of the top lawn should be replaced by ilex, that 'Kanzan' cherries should be removed from the area called Mrs Winthrop's Garden. There seemed to be little awareness of the place as a historic document, a template of early twentieth-century taste, a memorial to its creator. Would a house have been treated in this cavalier way? The plant houses, important elements of the garden in Johnston's day and demolished without any record being made of their dimensions, construction or contents, remain a great loss. The Trust is now more careful to ensure that the values of one generation do not prejudice the possibilities of the next.

Two problems in the conservation of gardens are as prevalent now as they were in the early days of the Trust. One of them will never go away – the natural cycle of growth and decay that affects all living things. Vistas change, trees blow over, hedges bulge, roses sicken. It is not always possible, nor even desirable, to replace like with like. The Trust talks now of planting 'in sympathy with' the aims of the creator of a garden or 'in keeping with' the period in which it was made. Inevitably decisions are influenced by present notions of taste and style, which perhaps is why 'Kanzan' cherries have never found their way back into Mrs Winthrop's Garden at Hidcote. Though all the rage in 1913, when they were first introduced, they are now derided.

The second problem is money – still the primary consideration in the way that the Trust manages its gardens. In 1948, with only 15,000 members, the problem was acute. The Garden Fund was slow to accumulate. Hidcote, which came to the Trust without an endowment and on terms extremely favourable to Johnston, ate up money faster than it could be raised. Without the Queen's Institute for District Nurses and their National Gardens Scheme, the entire venture might have folded, but fortunately the Institute agreed to pay a proportion of its takings from the gardens scheme each year into the Trust's Gardens Fund.

But in the hard years after the Second World War, there were more owners trying to shed gardens than help to prop them up. Typical was the case of Rousham Park in Oxfordshire, described by Christopher Hussey as the *locus classicus* for the eighteenth-century landscape designer William Kent. Its owner, Mr Cottrell-Dormer, did not want to transfer the whole of his property to the Trust but was anxious for the Gardens Committee to take over the management (for which read funding) of the landscape park. On 14 May 1948, as he recorded in his diary, James Lees-Milne motored down to see the place. 'The gardens are very important as the only Kent layout to survive, apart from the mess left by the urban authorities in Chiswick. There are statues, in a distressing condition, a seven-arched portico (praeneste), grottoes, glades, a cascade, bath, pools, temples and straight and serpentine rides. The gardens are miraculously intact after 200 years.' But no miracle produced the money to pay for their upkeep and the Gardens Committee decided that no garden could be taken on without sufficient endowment.

The same answer went to the owners of Bramham Park in Yorkshire, Inkpen Old Rectory in Berkshire and Lilleshall, Shropshire. The National Trust did, however, accept the generous gift of Bodnant in Clwyd, well-endowed by Lord Aberconway, and, in 1953, another plantsman's garden, Nymans in Sussex. Calculations of the necessary endowment were not always accurate. It was not long before loans to Lord and Lady Rosse at Nymans turned to grants. Wakehurst Place in Sussex came to the Trust in 1957 with an endowment of £200,000, but only six years later it was evident that this was £112,000 too little. To the visionaries in the Trust, the money men appeared boring nags, but the nags reminded the aesthetes that even beauty has a price.

Sissinghurst Castle in Kent, perhaps the Trust's most famous garden, came to it after Vita Sackville-West's death. Her diaries suggest that this is not what she herself had in mind. 'Never, never, never,' she wrote on 19 November 1954, when the idea was first mooted. 'Not that hard little metal plate at my door. It is bad enough to have lost my Knole, but they shan't take Sissinghurst from me. They can't make me. *I won't.* They can't make me. I never would.' She bequeathed it to her son Nigel Nicolson, who by his thorough examination of the entrails of his parents' marriage, has done so much to publicise the property. Like most successful gardens, Sissinghurst is the product of a personal (or more exactly, two people's) vision. It has a short history. Though no inventory of plants was compiled at acquisition, it is better documented than most gardens of its kind. It has benefited from a degree of continuity right up to the present time. This is unusual amongst Trust gardens, few of which can display their provenance so clearly and confidently.

The problem of deciding where, as it were, to stop the clock in terms of a garden's restoration is exacerbated by the cheerful vandalism of Britain's garden makers over the last few hundred years. A single garden may have had at least half a dozen major refits. Sometimes a kind of double-bluff is at work, as at

Montacute, where, although the garden pavilions are contemporary with the 1590s house, the garden itself is a late Victorian pastiche of the sixteenth-century style. The terraces at the most stunning of the Trust's gardens, Powis Castle on the Welsh borders, are of the late seventeenth century, but all traces of the elaborate gardens of that period on the flat ground below were swept away in the eighteenth-century remodelling. A Kip engraving of Dyrham Park near Bath, commissioned in 1712 by its proud owner William Blathwayt, Secretary of State of William III, shows the house magnificently accoutred with terraces, canals, intricately patterned parterres, fountains, balustrades, staircases and formal lines of clipped topiary. From a hill in the park, the water ran down a cascade of 224 steps through pools and fountains into a long canal. 'Very considerable Sums have been expended to bring these Gardens to that Perfection which I some Years since saw them in,' wrote Stephen Switzer, the eighteenth-century landscape designer. But they were expensive to maintain and most of the work disappeared in the new craze for landscaping that swept England after Blathwayt's death. However much we regret the loss of this late seventeenth-century garden, the loss is now part of Dyrham's history and development. To replace it would be to create a Disney world in William and Mary mode.

Horticultural correctness

It was some time before the Trust addressed the tricky problem of 'correctness' in gardens, first by way of adjusting the balance between features, then by full-blooded restoration. Adjustments depend on prevailing criteria of worth. In the Trust this has generally meant preferring the eighteenth century to any other. The first tentative steps in rewriting history happened at Stourhead. The garden, made in reaction against the kind of formal layout that William Talman created for Blathwayt at Dyrham, represents the eighteenth-century English view of Arcadia, a 'natural' landscape which is in fact manipulated to the last blade of grass.

'Never do I remember such Claude-like, idyllic beauty here,' wrote James Lees-Milne on 21 May 1947. 'See Stourhead and die. Rhododendrons and azaleas full out. No ponticums, but pink and deep red rhododendrons – not so good – and loveliest of all, the virginal snow white ones, almost too white to be true. Azaleas mostly orange and brimstone.' Brenda Colvin, the eminent landscape designer who died in 1981, started the 'correctness' debate with a letter to *The Times* in 1960, criticising the planting of modern rhododendrons carried out by the sixth baronet, Sir Henry Hoare, in the rhododendron boom years of the 1920s and 'thirties. By 1962, the Gardens Committee had agreed in principle with the recommendation of its Gardens Advisor, Graham Stuart Thomas, that the eighteenth-century nature of the landscape at Stourhead should be restored by removing much of Sir Henry Hoare's twentieth-century planting – the bright rhododendrons. Lord Aberconway, a rhododendron fancier himself, dissented robustly from the decision. Many of the offending plants were shifted deep into the woodland, but Stourhead, of course, remains busier during the rhododendron season than at any other time.

A quotation from Virgil over the door of the Temple of Flora at Stourhead warns visitors not to enter unless they are 'initiated' into the mysteries of the classical world. The English landscape garden is an intellectual game, invented by the essayist Joseph Addison who happened to have had a particularly good day on the Campagna outside Rome during his Italian visit of 1701–3. Addison derided over-gardened gardens, and at Rousham, Nathaniel Kent first showed how England could undergo the unlikely transformation into Italy. The first prototypes, Rousham, Stowe, Stourhead, inspired 'Capability' Brown whose landscapes eventually rolled up to the doors of 350 houses, mostly in the southern, flatter half of England. The Trust has 14 properties where Brown had a hand, and an appreciation of the landscape style has long been a mark of refinement among garden historians. But a straw poll, taken among visitors to Stourhead in April and May, would surely reveal that more had come to enjoy the rhododendrons than ponder on Virgil. This is not an argument for majority rule. It is, rather, confirmation of the sixth baronet's contribution at Stourhead as a valid part of the garden's history.

Leaving aside the question of taste, landscape gardens suit the Trust's purposes very well. Because they are not gardened intensively, the ratio of staff to acres is low. Stourhead's 40 acres are managed by fewer gardeners than work at either Sissinghurst or Hidcote, which are a quarter of the size. Because they are large, landscape gardens can easily absorb visitors. Access is one of the key principles in the Trust's philosophy, preservation of course being the other. But the two cannot always be reconciled. Three thousand people turned up at Sissinghurst on Good Friday 1991. The following year, the National Trust, which had already raised ticket prices at the property, introduced a system of timed tickets, limiting the number of people in the garden at any one time to 400. The problem of over-visiting is not confined to physical damage. There is also the question of mood, of atmosphere, which is an important part of the pleasure of visiting gardens.

In this respect, the Trust is a victim of its own success. It took 86 years for it to gather together its first million members, but that figure has doubled in just nine years since. A burgeoning dissatisfaction with the way things are done in the present may have something to do with this obsession with the past. And with traditional sources of income, such as farm rents, declining, the Trust needs its members to finance its properties. But there are problems. In gardens the question of access is one of the most obvious and the problem is likely to get worse rather than better over the next hundred years. 'Preservation may always permit access' said a wise former chairman of the Trust, 'but without preservation, access becomes forever impossible.' At what stage should the Trust stop building larger car-parks, or increasing the number and prominence of its lavatories? Manipulation by ticket price is a poor solution, and completely at odds with the philanthropic ideals of the founding three. The timed ticket has the desired effect but is frustrating for visitors. Pre-booking turns the garden into theatre, with a subtle shift in the 'audience' expectation of the 'performance'.

Access, in terms of the way that visitors approach a garden, is also important and is not always satisfactorily resolved. It is particularly acute at properties such as Hidcote, where the house is tenanted, or where, as at Sheffield Park in East Sussex, it was never part of the original acquisition, so that visitors now come in by an entrance that bears no relation to the original conception. The spine of the Hidcote garden is the long vista which starts at the cedar lawn (where Johnston entered the garden from the house) and stretches through the red borders to elegant tall gates at the end. Visitors are now brought in side-ways through the yard, originally the marshalling area of the garden, where they swill about, uncertain how best to tackle the place. The central idea of the design has become much more difficult to grasp. It does not help either when the dominant smell hanging around the entrance is curry lunch rather than the perfume of roses. The way we approach a garden should be a subtle preparation for what we are going to find there, the steps as it were, before a cathedral.

Managing our garden heritage

The gradual acceptance within the Trust of gardens as works of art in their own right naturally affected decisions about their treatment. The first steps had been taken at Stourhead. In 1967, at Westbury Court in Gloucestershire, the Trust embarked on its first full restoration. Money was raised by a mixture of stratagems: a grant from the Historic Buildings Council, a gift from an anonymous donor, a public appeal. The late seventeenth-century garden was at least small, only four acres, but completely derelict. It had been laid out in the Dutch manner by Maynard Colchester with canals, clipped evergreens, a tall pavilion, all contained within brick walls. Kip, the aerial photographer of his day, captured it in an engraving, though how much of the owner's wishful thinking came into play here, we do not know. More important for an accurate restoration were Colchester's own account books. In them he recorded the exact number of the plants he used: yews, hollies, fruit trees, including plums for the orchard that surrounded the vegetable garden. During the Trust's restoration, the canals were dredged, their retaining walls rebuilt, the pavilion demolished and re-erected, the yew hedges replanted. Part of the original parterre was re-created in the area west of the T-shaped canal and the small walled garden was planted up with flowers of the period – primroses, auriculas, old tulips, lavender and iris. The restoration encapsulated much of the Trust's future approach to gardens: the historic skeletons, the bones are sacrosanct, the planting an exercise of the imagination (though informed by an understanding of the history, the character and the atmosphere of the site).

It was entirely appropriate that the planting at Westbury should be 'in period', but this is not an approach that should be extended to all Trust gardens. Relatively few are as pure as Westbury in terms of their design and history. Most (as at Powis Castle) have overlays of several centuries. The bold and changing use of modern plants on the seventeenth-century terraces at Powis is a huge delight for visitors. You would not want to place a cold, museum hand on a head gardener as inspired as Jimmy Hancock, who has worked here since the early 1970s.

The restoration at Westbury began just two years after the Garden History Society was formed in 1965 to campaign for a greater public awareness of historic gardens as an important part of our cultural heritage. From the start it was a scholarly, erudite society, interesting itself not only in the history of gardens but in their relation to art, architecture, philosophy. Its scholarly approach perhaps persuaded the Trust to take a more informed line with is own gardens. In retrospect, it does seem odd that it was not until 1979, 30 years after the Gardens Committee had been set up, that the Trust commissioned its first garden survey. Osterley Park, Middlesex, laid out around the Adam house between 1760 and 1780, was the chosen site and the work was done by a surveyor, a botanist and a historian, funded by the Manpower Services Commission. By the time MSC funds ran out ten years later, the Trust had completed surveys of 45 parks and 40 gardens and had also, finally, hired its own Historic Parks and Gardens Surveyor.

In 1990 the Trust began a mammoth survey of its important new acquisition, Stowe in Buckinghamshire. During the eighteenth century all the most famous names of the day – Vanbrugh, Bridgeman, Kent and Brown – worked here and their achievements are superbly documented in a vast archive lodged at the Huntington Institute in California. The National Trust's survey team sifted through three-quarters of a million documents to prepare its survey, the basis of a restoration programme which will cost £15 million. The archive made clear that the Stowe landscape had been envisaged as a series of separate scenes, each with a different character. William Kent was responsible for the Elysian Fields, an open glade decorated with temples and statues, which is the first area that the Trust is tackling during its thoroughgoing restoration. The work is based on research and scholarship, rather than on the more tenuous tenets of 'good taste' that formed the flimsy basis for the earlier rehabilitation of some of its gardens. Compare the careful underpinning of the work at Stowe with the cavalier decisions taken at Hidcote.

The Stowe survey and long-term plan should provide a model for the future, but paying for the necessary research continues to be a problem. There is no funding from the centre to cover the cost. Money has to be scrabbled together *ad hoc*, sometimes from the Trust's regional offices, sometimes by means of government grants such as the Countryside Stewardship scheme. This is a ludicrous situation. The highest standards are, and should be, expected from the Trust. Scholarship in the matter of architecture, furniture, paintings is taken for granted. Infinite trouble is taken to establish the exact nature of a paint finish or the provenance of a picture. Gardens were rather late in being accorded the same attention and this is regrettable, but they must now catch up in terms of research and expertise. The fact that, in Trust terms, they sit uneasily between Land and Art has resulted in a complicated management structure. All departments want to keep a finger in the garden pie. The very popularity of gardens and gardening may also be a problem. The expert in Caravaggio, the scholar of Rubens acquires the status of a witch doctor, the subject being all the more highly valued because of its inaccessibility. But we all think we know about gardens. The subject is not surrounded with the same mystique as art and consequently is not accorded the same status. But to accept the management of a garden without knowing its history is to play blind man's bluff.

Because very little happened at Stowe after 1827 when the family's cash ran out, the template is clear. This is a garden of a particular period, spanning just a hundred years from the early eighteenth to the early nineteenth century. Biddulph Grange, the enchanting garden in Staffordshire made by James Bateman and Edward Cooke, has an equally clear and even shorter history, set firmly in the magnificently eclectic tradition of the second half of the nineteenth century. In terms of restoration, the parameters are clear. But what about the Trust's very first property, Barrington Court, the sixteenth-century Somerset house, presented to them, ruined and without a garden in 1907? The Trust, with no funds to maintain the place, negotiated a 99-year lease with Colonel Lyle and left Barrington's future to him. Lyle called in the architects Forbes and Tate to rehabilitate the house and lay out the bones of a new garden, essentially Edwardian in style. Gertrude Jekyll provided planting plans according to her usual formula: yucca for promontory planting, plenty of lamb's ear and bergenia for edging. She never visited Barrington, but a full set of her plans for the garden has survived. Contemporary photographs and a report written in 1925 make it clear that relatively little of Jekyll's planting was carried out. Mrs Lyle, a keen gardener herself, planned the long flower border that ran under the wall of the squash court. The lily garden was adapted from the original Jekyll plan. Mrs Lyle also changed the roses suggested by Miss Jekyll for the rose garden.

These details emerged as a result of the Trust's survey of Barrington which was completed in 1993. Given the Jekyll mania current at the present time (and with a beady eye on visitor numbers), Barrington could have become a Jekyll shrine. There is little of her work in Trust gardens and that in places with difficult access (Lindisfarne Castle in Northumberland, 100 Cheyne Walk, London). But the survey made clear the importance of the Lyle's contribution at Barrington. The Trust's restoration, starting in the iris garden, will be spread over many years, proceeding at the kind of pace you might expect from a private owner. The white garden, an entirely modern overlay of the old rose garden, designed by the present head gardener, Christine Bain, will stay because it is in the Jekyll/Lyle idiom and is extremely popular with visitors. The restoration philosophy here is pragmatic, different areas of the garden reflecting different influences, but constrained, as all work in all Trust gardens is, by cash.

Right from the early, difficult beginnings, money has remained the chief controlling factor in the way that the Trust manages its gardens. The next most important consideration is the taste of the former owners, then the wider history of the site and its planting. Finally come problems of access and the impact of visitors which will be particularly acute at a new Trust property, Chastleton in Oxfordshire, due to open in 1997. 'Mothballing' is the agreed strategy, but how, in management terms do you mothball a garden? The topiary still needs to be cut, the grass mown. Mothballing is a romantic image, a sepia picture of a golden age, but behind the images of golden afternoons, teams of gardeners were propping up the stage. This liquidity of gardens is a difficulty in an organisation dominated by buildings people. A room can be restored and will stay, to all intents and purposes, as it is put. A garden is always on the move and successful garden management has to embrace this factor. It also has to acknowledge increasing concern for the natural environment. Unimproved gardens are often wonderful places for wildlife, which is blithely unconcerned by the historic correctness of certain plants in certain settings. Then there is the difficult question of organic gardening principles. Will the use of pesticides become a *cause célèbre* in the same way as hunting?

Management of the Trust's gardens depends on a careful balance between the local and the national. At the most local level is the skill and expertise of the gardeners involved in a particular garden. Financial control is exercised by a managing agent working at a regional level. Research, surveys, cataloguing is instigated from the centre, and the gardens team working at national level bring a fresh eye to gardens on their regular forays to advise on (or criticise) the gardens in their care. For the system to work, the team at the centre has to maintain good relationships with the people working at local level. At either level, continuity is the most important key to a garden's success.

Management philosophy can be summed up thus: gardens are living, organic, developing examples of past fashions, styles and gardening activities. Change and development in gardens is inevitable and also beneficial, since a garden is a live being, not a dead museum piece. Any change, however, must be informed by research and historical precedent. Original fabric should be preserved wherever this is practicable. Generally, the Trust favours a policy of non-disturbance rather than 'digging' in the archaeological sense, although digs at Biddulph were useful in revealing the original lines of features such as the long-forgotten dahlia walk. In the management of its gardens, the Trust guides the process of change (which is inevitable) along lines dictated by historical precedent (where this is known), or 'the spirit of the place' where it is not.

English Heritage, for instance, would put the preservation of historical evidence at the top of its garden agenda. Its gardens are managed to provide evidence and documentation of the fabric of history. If, for instance, they were in control of the 300 or so gardens listed now on the Register of Historic Parks and Gardens, they would be loath to allow any further development in those gardens. It is an approach that arises out of English Heritage's primary concern with earthworks and other ancient monuments. Where restoration does take place, English Heritage's aim is to ensure that the historic design is experienced accurately by visitors. The restoration must at all costs not deceive.

The decisions that the National Trust makes about the conservation of its gardens take place within the framework of the gardens' history, but the process of management itself is a key factor. John Sales, head of the small team of garden advisers, uses a theatrical analogy to point up the difference between the two organisations. 'English Heritage's experience, interests and involvement is with preserving the stage, the scenery and the props, while the National Trust is concerned with the whole production, the plot, the score, the performers, the performance and, not least, the practical and financial problems of staging it.' Back to money.

The Gardens Fund, launched so optimistically in the earliest days of the Gardens Committee, never provided the hoped-for sums, but the pot still exists, filled largely by annual contributions from the National Gardens Scheme – £250,000 in 1994. This provides the icing on the cake. In 1993 the Fund provided £1,500 for research into the debilitating disease, powdery mildew, affecting several rhododendron collections in the Trust's care. A further £11,000 went towards replacing the brick paths through the Mulberry Garden at Bateman's, Rudyard Kipling's house in Sussex, £9,000 towards restoring the maze at Glendurgan in Cornwall, £20,000 towards restoring the vinery in the walled garden at Calke Abbey in Derbyshire. But there are always more projects than there is cash to spend on them.

Although the early Gardens Committee was only partially successful in its efforts, it served to bring the whole question of gardens into focus at the Trust. Several important initiatives were taken, some of which have still not been resolved. On 23 June 1960, the Committee considered a confidential memorandum drawn up by the Secretary recommending financial assistance from the government for the upkeep of gardens of national importance. A few years later, the Trust's Chairman Lord Crawford and Lord Wemyss (of the National Trust for Scotland) discussed with the Chief Secretary to the Treasury the possible exemption from death duties of important country houses and their gardens. The government, they reported, were sympathetic to the notion of help for gardens. The Garden History Society later adopted the same argument, but no money (apart from the emergency funds released for replanting after the Great Storm) or exemptions have yet been forthcoming. However, we have at last a register which lists the country's most important gardens, county by county.

The Committee was also prescient in recommending an apprenticeship scheme for gardeners. There is nothing in England to match the National Trust for Scotland's gardening school at Threave, Dumfries & Galloway. The need for good gardeners is self-evident, and as far back as 1957, the Trust's first Gardens Adviser, Graham Stuart Thomas, was pressing for a Trust training scheme. Eventually, money for training up to three apprentices a year was found from the Gardens Fund, a system which still continues. Four trainees have been funded by the Stanley Smith Horticultural Trust and now a new three-year training scheme for gardeners has just been set up by the Trust working with the Training and Enterprise Councils. About twelve young gardeners are being trained under this scheme each year. It is important that the Trust should involve itself in this kind of training because its gardens, in growing contrast to private gardens, require skills that are not taught at horticultural colleges.

When the gardens that the Trust now owns were in private hands, gardeners trained on the job under the critical eye of the head gardener. The progression from bothy boy through various stages of journeyman to the peak of the profession was long, but eminently practical. A good head gardener, by ensuring that all his staff had as wide an experience as possible of a range of gardening tasks, imparted skills that can never be taught from a book. By taking some responsibility for training the gardeners of the future, the Trust helps to ensure the survival of its gardens and of the techniques (which to modern gardeners will seem increasingly arcane) necessary to look after them. The Trust is also pioneering a scheme to offer National Vocational Qualifications in amenity horticulture to all its gardening staff.

Gardens, more than any other category of the Trust's properties, depend on regular and consistent maintenance by people in sympathy with the Trust's aims. Staff who have been brought up, as it were, within the system are more likely to understand and respect the Trust ethos. Labour accounts for 70 per cent of the cost of running gardens, which are massively more labour intensive (though less capital intensive) than houses. Modern labour-saving techniques and machinery mean that most gardens can run on less staff than when they were in private hands, but there is a point at which labour-saving techniques begin to affect the way the garden is presented. Avoiding tall plants in herbaceous borders, 'staking' by means of horizontal stretched wide-mesh netting, using herbicides on paths and terraces where no plants can then self-seed, all these things cumulatively have an effect on a garden. Staff, too, work less hours and have longer holidays than they used to. Health and safety legislation means more staff absences on compulsory training courses. Special events and increased opening hours in gardens cause wear and tear and extra labour on the gardeners' part. The two storms in October 1987 and January 1990 also created a huge amount of extra work. Money rather than need dictates the number of gardening staff at the properties for which the Trust is wholly responsible (Bodnant, still managed by Lord Aberconway, has 16 gardeners). This sometimes leads to a compromise in standards. Inadequately endowed properties of course are particularly at risk – Biddulph and the landscape gardens at Stowe being perhaps the most obvious examples. The problem of understaffing affects the present appearance and the future development of almost a third of the Trust's gardens, and this is a problem that must be addressed if the gardens are to continue to delight Trust members a hundred years hence. The best way of keeping gardens alive and lively is by employing gardeners with the same attributes. The Trust's future in this, even more than other areas, will depend on a wise investment in people.

A platform for the future

Though an owner's choice of plants for his garden is no less indicative of his taste than his choice of pictures, china or furnishings, the Trust was slow to begin any systematic inventory of the plants held in its gardens. The contents of houses were minutely catalogued, down to the last teaspoon, but this interest in possessions stopped until recently at the garden door. In an organisation that holds the largest and most diverse collection of plants in the world, this was an extraordinary situation. It was not until 1976 that the Trust set up a co-operative venture, the Woody Plant Catalogue, with the Royal Botanic Garden at Kew and the Thomas Phillips Price Trust, to catalogue its holdings. The inventory at present covers trees rather than shrubs or more ephemeral herbaceous plantings in 23 gardens and contains details of 23,000 different plants, the biggest collection (more than three thousand) being held at Mount Stewart in Northern Ireland. The survey also identified some extremely rare trees, a *Meliosma beaniana* at Bodnant, a *Michelia compressa* from Japan at Nymans, the deciduous *Poliothyrsis sinensis* at Lanhydrock in Cornwall and a notable golden larch at Biddulph, dug up as a seedling in China by the plant hunter Robert Fortune in 1854 and sent in a Wardian case on a 12,500 mile journey to Staffordshire. James Bateman planted it in his own miniature China, an area of the garden which he developed complete with Great Wall, look-out tower, joss-house, dragon parterre and temple in a willow pattern setting. The tree is now thought to be the only original introduction of this rare species still alive in Britain. The biggest tree recorded in the Woody Plant Catalogue grows at Knightshayes in Devon, a Turkey oak (*Quercus cerris*) planted around 1735 and now 138 ft tall. It is the tallest and fattest tree of its kind in Britain, a champion, though it was not until cataloguing began that the Trust was aware of its status.

The primary aim of the Woody Plant Catalogue is of course to record the major collections of trees in the Trust's hands, but other advantages accrue. The catalogue, updated annually, monitors the rate of replacement of specimen trees in gardens (around eight per cent a year) and so provides a check on the overall composition of plants within a particular garden. It prevents it wandering too far from the original conception. By comparing collections of plants, the National Trust can ensure that each garden retains its own individual character and that the process of swapping plants does not mean that all Trust gardens have the same mix of plants. The importance of an accurate archive was demonstrated in the sad aftermath of the two storms. Because the Trust could pinpoint accurately what it had lost, emergency propagation programmes could be set up, using materials from fallen trees.

Progress in expanding the catalogue is slow. Only one new garden is added each year but the process of updating existing gardens takes longer as the list grows. Once again, cash is the controlling factor. Not all the Trust's gardens call for such painstaking treatment; of those that do, Wallington in Northumberland is being catalogued in the Centenary year and Anglesey Abbey in Cambridgeshire will be tackled in 1996. There is also the daunting question of listing shrubs. A tiny start has been made in Northern Ireland at Rowallane and Mount Stewart. In view of the vast amount of work still to be done, a taxonomist has been added to the Trust's garden staff. It is surely part of a curious intellectual snobbery that pervades the organisation, rating artefacts above living things, supposing built structures to be more worthy of attention (and funding) than gardens and landscapes. This is not an attitude that would have been understood in the eighteenth century.

We have seen that, until the Trust acquired Hidcote, gardens were treated as appendages to houses rather than as works of art in their own right. This randomness has left gaps in terms of the way that Trust gardens tell the story of garden history in this country. The acquisition of Biddulph, a superb garden made in the High Victorian manner, plugged one important gap, but there are others. There is nothing to represent the landscape movement of the 1930s, the work of Christopher Tunnard and his contemporaries, though this may change if the Trust decides to take on The Homewood near Esher in Surrey, designed with a contemporary garden by Patrick Gwynne in 1937–8. This is not to say that, in terms of its gardens, it should have an aggressive acquisitions policy. For parts of the Trust, such as Enterprise Neptune, this is entirely appropriate, indeed necessary, but there are other ways to ensure a future for gardens. The Trust can do useful work here as a pressure group, influencing legislation which will make it easier for private owners themselves to maintain important gardens in good order.

There is, however, one gaping, obvious hole in the Trust's holdings. It has rose gardens and herb gardens. It has water gardens and enough herbaceous borders to line every motorway in the country. It has topiary, rock gardens, conservatories, orangeries and grottoes, but nowhere does there exist that lynchpin of the English country house, a full, working kitchen garden complete with vine houses, hot beds, forcing pits and compost bins. Unfortunately the walled areas of former kitchen gardens have been prime sites for car-parks and the level of maintenance involved in a kitchen garden has hitherto discouraged the Trust from launching into a full-scale restoration. Fruit and vegetables are grown to some extent in more than 30 of its gardens, but there is no property where traditional buildings and equipment are being preserved, nowhere for visitors to see at first hand how a traditional kitchen garden works. The skills and practices acquired in growing fruit and vegetables in the traditional way are disappearing along with the last generation of gardeners brought up in this tradition. Preserving a walled garden means more than restoring its built structures. Skills too need to be preserved and the Trust's work should encompass this duty. Nobody else can provide the continuity that such a project demands. The popularity of a walled kitchen garden, as far as visitors are concerned, is not in question. The viewing figures of the BBC television series *The Victorian Kitchen Garden* attest to that. At least three properties have the necessary attributes: Clumber Park in Nottinghamshire, where once 28 gardeners worked in the seven-acre kitchen garden; Attingham Park in Shropshire, where a good kitchen garden existed into the 1950s; and Tatton Park in Cheshire which has the best collection of kitchen garden buildings, including conservatories, greenhouses, frames and pits. Tatton Park is the current favourite but the cost, taking into account the repair of buildings and an endowment sufficient to fund four or five gardeners, is likely to be not less than £3 million.

This is a project for the future, but no one who has sat in the sun on the terraces at Powis Castle, gazing out over the tumbling terraces to the immaculate borders below, or strolled on a misty September morning by the lake at Stourhead, or ambled through the enchanting town garden of Peckover House in Wisbech can fail to give thanks for the extraordinary commitment of the National Trust. To Graham Stuart Thomas, the Trust's first Gardens Adviser, to John Sales who succeeded him and to the Trust's 375 gardeners, this essay is respectfully dedicated.

IX

The Next
One Hundred Years

HOWARD NEWBY

T HE CENTENARY OF THE National Trust is justly a cause for celebration
and congratulation. The mere existence of the Trust is an extraordinary
achievement, one which results not only from the vision of its founders,
but from the hard work of its staff and volunteers and the commitment of its
millions of members. The previous chapters of this book have demonstrated
clearly that the Trust does more than merely exist, however. It continues to
flourish and grow across a wide range of responsibilities, a uniquely British innovation which, one hundred years later, has seen no diminution in the respect
and affection with which it is held. As the previous chapters have also demonstrated, the Trust has made a demonstrable, even tangible, impact upon our
landscapes, our country houses, our coastline and, by example, the countryside
at large. There are no signs that this impact is diminishing.

Nevertheless, the turn of a century, like the turn of a year, is a time for looking
forward as well as for looking back. No organisation, in a fast-changing modern
world, can afford to be complacent. Trying to stand still simply results in going backwards. Thus, while the Trust can be proud of its achievements, it will
continue to flourish only if it can rise to the challenges which lie ahead. This
chapter is therefore forward-looking, even speculative. It seeks to indicate the
ways in which the Trust's philosophy will need to develop in order to meet the
challenges of the future.

This necessity is one of which the Trust is well aware. For example, as part of
its centenary activities it has launched a Countryside Policy Review in order to
articulate an up-to-date interpretation of the Trust's purposes in the countryside and to consider the best way forward in terms of both policy and
management. Such a review, while it is not intended to be all-embracing, is
certainly timely. It also indicates the necessity of the Trust developing a
strategic approach to key issues which will affect its future. The Trust will
continue to flourish over the next 100 years if it anticipates change, rather than

merely responds to it. Change here refers not only to what one might call the 'external' forces impinging upon the Trust and its activities, but also the more 'internal' factors, such as the changing attitudes and values of Trust members and even the organisation of the Trust itself. The only certain factor about the future is its uncertainty. The Trust cannot predict the future, but the Trust will need to continue to develop a sensitivity to external trends so that it may more effectively control the agenda for change.

This concluding chapter indicates the scope of the policy challenge which the Trust is likely to face over the next decade or so. The changes are likely to be very far-reaching, as the breadth of the key issues outlined in subsequent sections demonstrates. This chapter argues that the Trust will have a key role in educating and informing both its members and the wider public over the policy issues which it faces. But this, in turn, while in keeping with the founders' vision of the Trust, is likely to raise a series of organisational and representational issues.

Trusting the people and peopling the Trust

The Trust's strength is its members. Its members, in turn, need to be informed about the challenges facing the Trust if the Trust is to avoid being a reactive organisation and more one which defines and shapes its own future. But, between the broad brush policy challenges described in the other chapters of this book and the needs of individuals referred to in the previous chapter, there stands the Trust as an organisation. Wise leadership, sound management and robust decision-making processes will be necessary to weld together the vast potential of the membership into a force for positive change in implementing the values which the Trust holds dear. The Trust is already a highly decentralised organisation and this is undoubtedly the best – probably the only – way to structure an organisation of this kind. However, the Trust will also need to ensure that such a devolved organisation continues to have the flexibility and capacity to move quickly when required. This will require the development of a strong strategic framework within which such devolution may take place. As the Trust has grown in size and scope, so, inevitably, has there been a much greater diversity of people, views and interests incorporated into the broad church which is now the National Trust. Most members are entirely 'passive' in their role – essentially they have purchased a season ticket to the Trust's properties and seek no more by way of active involvement. Whilst not entirely apathetic, the membership does not expect, for the most part, to take a lead: that role falls on the Trust's officers. Thus, the Trust will continue to need a strong sense of what it is trying to achieve and where it is going, around which its members can rally.

As David Cannadine's chapter showed, there is a fine balance to be maintained between strong leadership and the perceived preferences of the member-

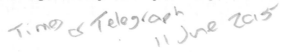

Time of Telegraph 11 June 2015

ship, when a small minority articulates them – the majority uses membership as a season ticket and plays no active part in Trust affairs. There have been periods in the Trust's history when a largely quiescent membership made it easier for certain key individuals to seek to use the Trust for the pursuit of their own values and ambitions. As was demonstrated by the debate over deer-hunting on Trust land, this has sometimes led to resentment over the decision-making structures of the Trust, largely through a misunderstanding of the duties of Council and the rights of members. As the Oliver Report made clear, Council is under no fiduciary obligation to implement members' resolutions if it considers them to be injurious to the Trust's interests.

The difficulty of identifying a consensus across a range of issues among 2.2 million members, let alone the wider public on whose behalf the Trust sees itself to be acting, is only one anxiety sometimes expressed about the size of the Trust's operations. Some fear that the Trust is over-commercialising; others mourn the loss of 'intimacy' that characterised the Trust of old. It is impossible to escape tensions over commercial pressures and management imperatives in a charitable organisation dependent upon voluntary help. Yet management of the Trust is highly devolved, the role of Council being to offer a strategic vision of the way the Trust should fulfil its responsibilities, often in response to changing economic and social circumstances.

This is part of a broader dilemma facing the Trust. Many people join, and become active in, the Trust *because* it is perceived as being committed to resisting change. For many the Trust, through its properties, embodies precisely that antithesis to the uncertainties of the modern world which many amongst older generations crave. Many of the Trust's members do not willingly seek to engage with change because they have joined the Trust in order to escape from it. This presents the Trust, given its devolved structure, with considerable problems of representation and leadership. How far, for example, should the Trust seek to educate its own members and the visitors to its own properties with the greater understanding of the forces of change which are at work in the environmental movement, the countryside, or society more generally? And how far should the Trust actually seek to create a more informed body of opinion concerning the future direction of change?

Ironically, questions like these were in the forefront of the minds of the founders of the Trust. The preservation of property was not entered into for its own sake, but in order to benefit visitors and provide them with an aesthetically, morally and therefore educationally uplifting, experience. Education has, however, not been given the prominence in the Trust's affairs which its founders prescribed until very recently. Indeed, it could be argued that in certain respects the Trust's activities stand in the way of providing a proper under-standing of the forces of change. It is all too possible, for example, for many visitors to the Trust's country properties to come away with a quite false impression of the reality of the English country estate and the countryside beyond.

Here a delicate path has to be trod between giving many members and visitors what they want – to be 'market-led', in the present jargon – and educating and informing them of what lies behind what they see.

In some respects the preservation of the past is precisely what the Trust seeks to achieve. The preservation of the past is, after all, one of the Trust's major selling points. Understandable conservationist motives then combine with mild commercial interest to present the visitor with an image of the past as though this were 'real', whilst the reality of the present beyond the Trust's boundaries is rendered somehow 'unreal'. For example, the countryside is frequently *defined* as a kind of living museum; anything which does not conform to this is perceived as not 'real' countryside. The Trust, it is sometimes argued, inadvertently re-inforces an image of the countryside which is backward looking and, literally, unrealistic, whilst doing little to develop a full understanding amongst its visitors and members of the forces of change which are overtaking the real countryside. Insofar as this contains an element of validity, it produces a tendency for change, when it does occur, to take the Trust and its membership unawares. However, the aesthetic, the ecological and the artefactual cannot exist in a cocoon, insulated from the economic, the social and the environmental factors contributing to change in contemporary England. Most visitors to most National Trust properties could be forgiven, however, for not appreciating this.

The Trust, in other words, exists as a great untapped resource for educating its members into a greater understanding of change, principally in the country-side – though by no means confined to this. Certainly the Trust has made some steps in this direction, so perhaps the word 'untapped' is a little unfair. For example, the Trust is increasingly active in persuading schools to take out Education Group Membership which enables school parties to gain free ad-mission to National Trust properties. However, the Trust's educational pro-gramme began as recently as 1987. While it is being developed to encourage those children who would not normally visit a Trust property – for example, inner city school children – these may constitute precisely a category which many Trust members believe they are protecting their properties *from*. Some ambivalence towards extending these kinds of activities can therefore be dis-cerned. Yet there is a huge potential which can only be to the long-term benefit of the Trust. Nor does this potential exist only among schoolchildren. It can also be extended to other young people, to young mothers and single parent families, and to the inhabitants of inner-city areas. Since 1988 the Trust has been work-ing hard to expand its inner-city activities, following a successful pioneering project in Newcastle. The idea is not new. It rekindles some of the beliefs of, for example, Octavia Hill, who realised the importance of preserving areas of the countryside for the benefit of people living in the industrialised cities. It is there-fore wholly appropriate that the Trust's main centenary project – Minerva – is aimed at strengthening this aspect of the Trust's activities so that its resources can be employed for life-time learning.

153

Perhaps what is now needed is for the Trust to reinforce its emerging policy that this kind of work is part of its core activity and not simply a fringe part of its remit. In this sense, its education role needs to be taken out of the realm of the school system and into the heartland of the Trust's mainstream activities. This will involve a greater commitment to the kind of interpretative activity pioneered by the Countryside Commission and will help to inform the millions who visit Trust properties annually without turning them away by being over didactic. In the long-term, after all, the Trust will only be as strong, and as influential, as its membership allows.

It would be naive to suggest, however, that to proceed along this road would not present the Trust with some fiercesome dilemmas of organisation and representation. As has been pointed out on a number of occasions the terms 'National' and 'Trust' provide two powerful icons to which a wide, and very differing, membership can be drawn. Who, for example, defines 'the nation' in this context? It has not always been clear that 'the nation' and 'the public' are to be regarded as the same thing. Indeed, as a number of chapters earlier in this book have made clear, the concept of 'the nation' has been imbued with a more spiritual meaning which has, at various times, lifted it above conceptions of 'the public'. How far, therefore, can the Trust trust the public?

Rightly or wrongly the Trust has traditionally been involved with – indeed, prided itself on – a series of elite values (see David Cannadine's chapter above). What is preserved is, inevitably, a highly selective process. The Trust's traditional emphasis on landed upper-class property and artefacts has therefore not been merely the outcome of opportunism. In a cultural as well as a physical sense these have been deemed more *worthy* of preservation, in part because they embody a scale of values which puts greater weight on, say, a country house rather than a row of Victorian terraced houses. The 'heritage' which has been preserved has therefore been predominantly drawn from a tiny segment of English society. In the past this hardly needed to be justified: it was taken for granted that a heritage drawn from this source would represent the supreme accomplishments of English cultural history. *but not now*

But in the modern world the nature of this elitism can no longer be taken for granted. It is frequently stated that we live in a less deferential age. The Trust will thus inevitably come under pressure to defend the nature of its elitism. It cannot take for granted that the aesthetic judgements of either the landed upper-classes or the historical *cognoscenti* are automatically shared and accepted by a wider public. In these days the only elitism which is widely acceptable is an elitism of quality, a commitment to preserving the best of whatever its strategic priorities ordain. Of course the Trust cannot preserve everything of quality – and it will always wish to take account of the activities of other, specialist organisations in the 'heritage industry'. But it can ill afford even to hint at a broader form of social elitism which could damage its wider public legitimacy. In terms of a commitment to quality the Trust should be proud of its elitism. It need have no connotations of status or snobbish values, but should proclaim its performance and skills in preserving those aspects of our past which the public most highly value.

Agricultural adjustment

Earlier chapters by Philip Lowe, Adrian Phillips and David Cope have, in their various ways, outlined the changing role of the National Trust in the conservation of the English countryside. There is, therefore, no need to repeat their various analyses in detail here, other than to place them in the wider context of the management of change which this chapter addresses. And change is overtaking the countryside in a potentially bewildering fashion. A combination of economic, social and technological change is rapidly bringing to a close whatever post-war continuities and public policy have shaped our countryside. As a result, certain perceived assumptions about the nature and character of our rural economy in society are facing re-examination and discontinuity. Radical change is therefore in the air – most notably in the case of agricultural policy, but by no means limited to this. We still remain unclear and unsure about the kind of countryside we wish to create in the twenty-first century and beyond.

The Trust has a responsibility – some might say a duty – to involve itself in the debates about the future of our countryside. This lies behind the establishment of its Countryside Policy Review. It is uniquely placed to define, articulate and even implement a vision which is exemplary, very much in the tradition of the Victorian model landowner. The Trust is not a campaigning organisation, but it can, with some legitimacy, assume the mantle of leadership in redefining public policy towards the countryside as we move into the next century.

Why is this necessary? One hardly needs to stress how important the countryside is regarded by a large and arguably increasing segment of the population. It does, without doubt, hold a special place in our affections. Any threat to our 'rural heritage' – its beauty, its landscape, its ancient villages, its wildlife – leads to an understandable outcry. It is little wonder that 'preservation' and 'conservation' have emerged as the watch-words of public debates in recent years. Once the countryside is viewed as the repository of all that we cherish and hold dear, it is not surprising that many of us wish fiercely to guard and protect it. The growth in Trust membership in many ways epitomises the process.

To understand why this is so it is necessary to examine two factors. The first concerns matters of perception – why do we find it difficult to come to terms with the reality of the countryside rather than endow it with a sentimental, and often nostalgic, image? The second is a matter of policy analysis – how far have the public policies developed to regulate the countryside, especially in the immediate post-war era, been overtaken by events? Each of these questions in its own way presents challenges to the Trust as it develops its policies for the future.

Public debate about the future of the countryside has been somewhat constrained by prevailing cultural perspectives. The first, which is deeply embedded in British, or at least English, culture, is anti-urbanism. Our love of the countryside is in part an expression of our failure to come to terms with the realities of urban life. Since the Industrial Revolution the British have signally failed to develop an urban civilisation which is at once sophisticated and humane. We have always rejected it, fleeing instead to seek our solace in the allegedly recuperative powers of the countryside, where it is possible to be at one with nature. One only needs to contrast this perception with that which prevails in, say, most Mediterranean countries, to see how culturally specific it is. The urbane Italian, for example, would look with incredulity at the English tendency to beatify the countryside. Yet it is a cultural perspective which the Trust often reflects and gently exploits – see the contents of the Trust's shops, for example.

The second cultural perspective is, arguably, a more recent development. It derives in part from an atavistic fear of starvation, given understandable focus by the experience of older generations in two world wars. In modern parlance it is translated into the notion of 'food security'. The countryside is here equated with the production of food, and in the production of food every acre counts. Even the mildest suggestion that the area of land under cultivation might be reduced, or the volume of food production be deliberately diminished, is met with dubious historical analogies dating from the 1930s, vague references to the activities of submarines in the Western Approaches and an airy assertion that a ubiquitous agriculture is undeniably a Good Thing.

These cultural predispositions are not only of academic interest. They have been embodied in specific pieces of legislation which have provided the framework for our rural economy and society since the mid-twentieth century. Both our system of agricultural support and our framework of planning legislation owe much to these developments and they both provide much of the context within which the Trust operates. Essential to both farming and planning policy, they have remained unchanged since 1947. They have not been policies which have turned out to be abject failures – on the contrary, one could make out a case that they have been extraordinarily successful. But they were born out of a very different rural economy and society that was reconstructing itself from the traumas of agriculture depression and war time conditions. One need hardly underline the fact that the countryside of today is very different from the countryside of the 1940s, that indeed what is often referred to as the 'traditional rural way of life' has been comprehensively transformed during the intervening period.

Rural England is not now an *agricultural* society, nor is it an agricultural economy. Even in the most rural of areas agriculture and related industries rarely account for more than 15 per cent or so of the employed population, and in most rural areas it is a good deal less than this. Only in terms of land use is rural England still agriculture England. In all other senses – economically, occupationally, socially, culturally – rural England has been comprehensively urbanised. It follows from this that the assumptions which lay behind the post-war establishment of public policy for the countryside are of declining relevance today. There is no longer a natural tendency for economic activity to gravitate to the towns, nor is the rural economy to be regarded as an inherently agri-culture economy. Most of the present rural population has little connection with farming, either economically or culturally. The social fabric of the countryside has been transformed, with a former agriculture population being replaced by an ex-urban, professional and managerial population which often lives in the countryside but works in the town. Meanwhile technological developments in the farming industry have rendered vast tracts of farm land 'surplus' to the needs of food production.

The Trust, as the owner of over half a million acres of land, is not immune to these changes, even though, in certain respects, it might wish to resist them. As Philip Lowe makes clear in his earlier chapter, the public policies which have guided agriculture have done so in ways which have profoundly altered both the structure of the agriculture industry and the day-to-day nature of life and work in the countryside. The encouragement of fewer, larger and more capital-intensive farms has resulted eventually in the catalogue of social and economic changes which are frequently associated with the post-war transformation of the countryside: the mechanisation of agriculture, the changing social composition of rural villages and the widespread changes in the rural landscape and other environmental aspects of the countryside. These changes have not been hap-hazard, nor are they the result of some immutable natural law, but the result of policy decisions quite consciously pursued. A large and complex network of institutions has been erected in the public sector in order to effect the trans-formation that post-war agricultural policy ordained. The consequences have been far-reaching indeed – a move which is traditionally being described as being 'from agriculture to agribusiness'.

The Trust, whose farms cannot exist in isolation from modern economics and modern technologies, has not been, and cannot be, immune from these changes. The Trust has, indeed, pioneered a number of attempts to mitigate the full im-pact of technological change in agriculture on the rural landscape and ecology. For example, it pioneered innovative land management schemes in the Lake District which would combine viable farming with public access and landscape conservation. Many of the tenancy agreements on Trust properties reflect these broader aims and objectives. Yet it is impossible for the Trust to fly in the face of modern agricultural economics. The impact of any further round of radical agricultural change on the Trust properties would therefore be considerable. It is then a question of how far such radical change seems likely.

Certainly there are those who would speculate on an imminent radical reform of European farm policy, not least as the result of recent GATT negotiations and because the burden of the European taxpayer and consumer is becoming progressively insupportable. To the familiar litany of overproduction and high cost it is now possible to add the economic irrationalities of set-aside. There is a growing recognition that the current set of policies is inherently unstable and that a closer alignment with world prices is inevitable. Current policy discussions centre around whether this will come through a controlled and phased period of change or whether the change will be more abrupt (as in New Zealand).

Such considerations can appear remote from the need to manage individual Trust properties. They certainly appear remote to most visitors, one suspects. But this is in part the point. The Trust has had to move upstream into the realm of influencing future policy so that its interests can be well represented in whatever changes emerge.

In part this is an organisational problem for the Trust. How far, for example, does it wish to take itself upstream of its responsibility for managing its properties and enter into the realms of influencing farming policy? This would involve the Trust becoming more active in the affairs of the European Union and in attempting to ensure that its influence in Brussels and Strasbourg is no less negligible than that in Westminster and Whitehall. Much of this represents largely uncharted territory for the National Trust. In part, however, the issue is also one of leadership and vision. How far will the Trust wish to define an appropriate set of policy objectives for agriculture which can take us into the twenty-first century and beyond? On this the debate has scarcely begun. Certainly the key issue will not be so much how to preserve the countryside for one particular function (such as agriculture) but, rather, how to determine an appropriate balance between the sometimes competing priorities of, say, agriculture, forestry, conservation, recreation and rural economic development. Clearly the balance will vary according to local circumstances and needs. Nevertheless, public policy should provide a framework which encourages such diversity, rather than seeking to limit it. Similarly, the precise spacial and economic consequences of any adjustment remain unclear, but they are likely to fall unequally on, say, upland and lowland farms and on small and large holdings. The Trust certainly has the authority and experience to help develop a national vision of what kind of farming is appropriate for the nation in the future. There is a genuine opportunity here for the Trust to take a lead in fashioning a public debate which has yet scarcely begun, but is becoming increasingly urgent.

Balanced communities

A number of chapters in this book have not only touched upon the Trust's complex responsibilities towards the physical fabric of its properties, but also upon the Trust's social responsibilities. The Trust is not only a considerable employer in its own right, but in many parts of the country it has inherited or acquired considerable local responsibility for those who live and work on, or adjacent to, its houses and estates. Not only has post-war agriculture policy substantially changed the everyday life of farming, but the social fabric of the countryside has equally been transformed. While post-war planning policy has – whatever the vicissitudes – successfully resisted the worst excesses of urban encroachment into the countryside, rural society has nevertheless been transformed from within by a series of social, economic and cultural factors over which no planning legislation could possibly have any control. Planning in rural areas has always been based upon a gut feeling that the English countryside needed to be protected rather than planned in any positive sense. The custody of the countryside, it has conventionally been believed, could safely be left in the hands of farmers and landowners; all that was required was to contain the spread of urban sprawl. However, the very factors which have transformed our agriculture have also overturned other aspects of the 'traditional rural way of life'. Former agriculture villages have been turned into community settlements, with only a few rural areas, isolated by bad roads and non-existent railways, lying beyond reasonable travel to work times, but these have often been gobbled up by the equally ferocious demand for holiday homes and weekend cottages. Rural Britain that was once an agricultural Britain has now been turned into a middle-class urban Britain.

These changes have brought into the heartlands of rural England a population who might be thought of as the natural constituency of the National Trust. Most 'incomers' to the countryside care deeply about its landscape and its wild life. Indeed, from the point of view of many farmers and other indigenous members of the rural populations they care almost too much. It is not necessarily a countryside which many of those who traditionally lived and worked there would recognise. It probably owes more to the imagery, referrred to earlier in this chapter, of an idyllic British countryside of the past, but it is also one which this new rural population has sought to implement when faced with sometimes less than agreeable reality. It is not surprising, therefore, that many of the newcomers to the countryside have been in the vanguard of the conservation movement. Politically in the ascendancy, they have supported the 'no growth' or 'low growth' policies for rural areas to become so typical of rural planning – especially in the south of England. They have also contributed to the peculiar myopia of the environmental lobby over social issues in the countryside. They have proved to be particularly adept at exploiting a rural planning system which, though originally designed to limit urban sprawl, has become a means of resisting *any* change 'in their backyard'.

In those areas where the National Trust is a significant landowner (such as the Lake District) a symbiosis has arisen which has threatened to reinforce the social imbalance already introduced by the factors outlined above. Both the Trust and the incoming population have shared a profoundly preservationist sentiment. And while few might quibble with this in areas of particularly high scenic value, there has, nevertheless, accumulated over a time a range of problems which have, necessarily, led some observers to question what is meant by 'conservation' in this context. Should, for example, the 'conservation' of living and working communities be placed alongside the conservation of the physical fabric and ecology as the objectives of the Trust's endeavours? Certainly it is difficult to sustain the view that conservation of the physical landscape of, say, the Lake District has contributed to the conservation of its *social* fabric. Strict conservation of the landscape has simply placed a premium on the price of housing in such areas which have had severe social consequences; similarly, in the context of a declining agricultural labour force, alternative sources of employment have often been channelled away from such areas. The phrase 'living museum' is not strictly accurate to describe such trends, but it does nevertheless summarise a concern about the true meaning of conservation and represents an issue around which locals and newcomers tend to polarise.

The future economic base of rural areas, and future employment growth, lies at the heart of the distinction between conservation and preservation. In the future there is little chance of a significant expansion of employment opportunities in agriculture, or, for that matter, forestry. Modern technologies – particularly information and communications technologies – have, however, removed a number of the traditional barriers to economic development which have characterised rural areas in the past. Probably for the first time since the Industrial Revolution, rural areas are in a position to compete for the benefits of new technology on an equal footing with towns and cities. Indeed rural areas have demonstrated in recent years a number of advantages when it comes to competing for successful development of this kind, particularly amongst small and medium-sized enterprises.

There is, of course, no *necessary* conflict between conservation and development. Indeed, as David Cope's chapter outlined, the term 'sustainable development' has, following the Brundtland Report, been widely used in order to sketch out the way ahead. But a commitment to sustainable development would not be the same thing as a commitment to preservation. Sustainable development embraces change but does so in a way which is environmentally sustainable in the long term. Certainly, what sustains a village community in the long term is not preservation in the strict sense. The Trust may find an increasing need to set out its vision of sustainable rural communities in a manner which extends beyond its traditional concerns, especially in areas like the Lake District, where the Trust is a major landowner.

Two issues stand out as requiring urgent attention: housing and transport. If there is a desire to see a countryside which retains its social and economic diversity, then balanced housing provision would be essential. Housing is not only an essential human need in its own right, but it also acts as a series of social filters. The social composition of a rural community will be highly influenced by the nature of the housing stock available. There is no need to labour here the extent to which changes in the rural housing market, including the lack of suitable accommodation for rent, has seriously unbalanced many rural communities in recent years. Despite the laudable activities of the Rural Housing Trust, the scale of the problem is such that it cannot be solved without some bold and imaginative new initiatives. These might include, especially in the south of England, the construction of new settlements rather than continuation of the existing policy to construct small incremental additions to existing villages. While this would take the Trust away from its traditional role, there is much that it could do both by way of influencing policy and by taking a lead as a large and influential landowner. Small-scale initiatives undertaken in villages like Luccombe (on Exmoor) and Studland (in Dorset) need to be extended much further.

In many respects transport presents a series of more intractable problems for the Trust. It cannot be expected single-handedly to solve the transport problems which impinge upon the upkeep of its properties, for visitors and local residents alike. The Trust is highly dependent upon the motor car to supply the vast majority of the visitors to its properties. This alone can create difficulties for those who do not have access to a car. For the increase in car ownership and use threatens the quality of life – and visitor experience – on the Trust's most popular properties. The Trust thus faces a dilemma – should it actively campaign for a reduction in car dependence (a natural conservationist sentiment) but thereby risk the consequences as far as numbers of paying customers is concerned? The answer probably lies in some form of active traffic management in those areas most at risk from overcrowded roads, rather as the Countryside Commission has undertaken in areas like the Goyt Valley and Ladybower in the Peak District. This might involve some combination of temporary road closure, park-and-ride schemes, subsidised local public transport and even tolls. The precise solutions will vary from place to place, but, as yet the Trust appears to lack a strategic policy which would encourage such local initiatives. The Trust is unlikely to be a major force in transport policy in rural areas, but here, as elsewhere, it can quietly lead by example at the local level.

It might also take a lead with its own members. The public at large still sees the countryside in terms of landscapes and wildlife habitats and rarely as a set of working communities. This means that public pressures on planning policy continue to be suffused with the notion of a countryside which is *inherently* under threat – in other words, that *any* change would constitute a net loss, rather than a gain, for the quality of life. Powerful local coalitions therefore exist in many rural areas to keep out *any* kind of development including that which is necessary to maintain the vitality of the rural economy. Thus, the idea, if not the formal designation of Green Belts has spread out across vast areas of rural England.

As a result entrenched local attitudes threaten to strangle many initiatives at birth. The Trust could usefully take a lead in recognising that 'appropriate' development in rural areas no longer constitutes blacksmiths and basket weaving. High-tech industrial development is not environmentally intrusive nor is it locationally specific. The Trust might take a lead, through demonstrator projects, and by other means to show how it is possible to capture the benefits of modern industrial development and improve the welfare of the indigenous rural population in a manner which is compatible with its traditional values and aims.

Managing change

The various chapters in this book have demonstrated how something so apparently straightforward as preserving the nation's heritage rapidly broadens out into a series of issues and dilemmas which will face the Trust with many challenges over its next century. The Trust is now of a size and strength which will enable it to have real influence upstream of its activities in the world of policy formulation and decision-making. These will continue to provide challenges for the Trust, as a landowner, as an employer, as an environmental lobby, as an organisation with key social responsibilities in certain localities and as a representative of a body of opinion which seeks to guide the outcomes of these and other issues. As the Trust is primarily a preservation organisation, there is a proper presumption against change. However, the Trust is in no position to isolate itself from externally induced changes. Agriculture policy is now made in Brussels and many Trust tenant farmers depend on grants and subsidies to make a living. National and local policies on planning and transport constrain the management of some properties and threatens others, their effectiveness can reduce the need for Trust ownership by protecting the countryside from unsightly development. Government financial land management schemes are in line with many of the Trust's objectives and are playing an increasing role in the taxpayers' support for the countryside. These examples show that the Trust must be aware of, and attempt to influence, public policy.

Together this chapter and the previous chapters of this book have given a fleeting glimpse of the scale of the challenge which faces the Trust. One nevertheless remains confident that the Trust will be in robust good health in 100 years' time. I therefore leave three messages for my successor to take up in the next centenary volume.

First is the continuing necessity to remind ourselves that the Trust was created by people for people to benefit from and *not* to protect property *for its own sake*. The founders were quite clear that protection was to be a means, not an end. The Trust constantly needs to reconcile its duty to protect while developing benefit for the widest possible group of people and continually to adapt and readapt this reconciliation within an ever-changing modern context. The Trust must constantly look *outwards* rather than inwards. It is all too easy for any organisation of its scope and importance to become involuted, inward-looking and impermeable. The Trust must continue to look outwards to embrace all parts of society and to shape its own destiny rather than be shaped by external events.

Secondly – and in pursuit of the above – the Trust must continue to be self-critical. It should encourage debate, not be suspicious of it. It must adhere to the value of continual self-improvement, the very values of the Victorian model landowners on whom, in many ways, its founders based their activities.

Thirdly, and perhaps most importantly, the Trust should always remember why it exists. It must, in other words, constantly focus upon its core values and purposes and not be too distracted by the very many tempting opportunities which, from time to time, come its way but which run the risk of being so diverting as to dissipate its strengths. The Trust has flourished for 100 years because it has been sufficiently successful in adhering to its core values most of the time. It is those values which have attracted its ever increasing membership. The Trust can draw its authority from its membership, but it also draws its authority from the fact that everything it does is undertaken with the highest possible quality. Provided the Trust trusts its members and continues to adhere to its principles of quality, then its authority, far from diminishing, will continue to expand and flourish over the next 100 years. Let us all hope so.

Bibliography

Adams, John, 1993, 'Vogon economics and the hyperspace bypass', *New Scientist*, 14 September, p.44–5.

Bock, Edwin A., 1970, 'Governmental problems arising from the use and abuse of the Future – the last colonialism', *Temporal Dimensions of Development Administration*, ed. Dwight Waldo, Duke University Press, Durham, North Carolina, pp.264–97.

Cope, David, 1992, 'Sustainability in One Country (Region, etc.)', *UK CEED Bulletin*, 40, July–August, UK Centre for Economic and Environmental Development, Cambridge, England, pp.8–9.

Cope, David, 1993, 'Responsibility to and responsibility *for* the future', *UK CEED Bulletin*, 41, January–February, UK Centre for Economic and Environmental Development, Cambridge, England, pp.14–15.

Countryside Commission, 1991, *Caring for the Countryside, a policy agenda for England in the nineties*, Countryside Commission Publications, Manchester.

Countryside Commission, 1993, *Position Statement, Sustainability and the English Countryside*, CCP 432, December, Cheltenham.

Darwin, Charles Galton, 1953, *The Next Million Years*, Hart-Davis, London.

Department of the Environment, 1993, *Countryside Survey, 1990*, Department of the Environment, London, November.

Dower, Michael, 1994, 'The Future of England's Countryside', Land Decade Lecture, Royal Society of Arts, 19 January. Published in *RSA Journal, cxlii*, 5449, May 1994, pp.35–48.

English Nature, 1993a, *Strategy for the sustainable use of England's estuaries*, Peterborough.

BIBLIOGRAPHY

English Nature, 1993b, *Natural Areas; setting nature conservation objectives, a consultation paper*, Peterborough.

Fedden, Robin, 1968. *The Continuing Purpose*, Longman.

Fedden, Robin, 1974, *The National Trust, past and present*, Cape, p.39.

Gaze, John, 1988, *Figures in a Landscape, a history of the National Trust*, Barrie & Jenkins.

Gummer, John, 1993, foreword to Department of the Environment, 1993, *UK Strategy for Sustainable Development, consultation paper*, London, July.

HM Government, 1989, *Sustaining our Common Future, a progress report by the UK Government on implementing sustainable development*, HMSO, London.

HM Government, 1994, *Sustainable Development, the UK Strategy*, Cm. 2426, HMSO, London.

Jenkins, Jennifer and James, Patrick, 1994, *From Acorn to Oak Tree: The Growth of the National Trust 1885–1994*, Macmillan, London.

Laslett, Peter, 1972, The Conversation between the Generations, in, *The Proper Study, Royal Institute of Philosophy Lectures, volume 4, 1969–70*, ed. G. N. A. Vessey, London.

Laslett, Peter, 1991, The Duties of the Third Age: should they form a National Trust for the future?, *Royal Society of Arts Journal*, May, pp.386–92.

Laslett, Peter and Fishkin, James, (eds), 1992, *Justice between Age Groups and Generations*, Yale University Press, New Haven, especially ch. 1 'Is there a generational contract'?

Lees-Milne, James, (ed.), 1945, *The National Trust, a Record of Fifty Years' Achievement*, Batsford, London.

Lowe, Philip and Goyder, Jane, 1983, *Environmental Groups in Politics*, George Allen and Unwin, London.

MacEwan, A. and MacEwan, M., 1982, *National Parks: Conservation or Cosmetics*, George Allen & Unwin.

Murphy, G., 1987, *Founders of the National Trust*, Christopher Helm.

Nicolson, Marjorie Hope, 1959, *Mountain Gloom and Mountain Glory*, Cornell University Press, Ithaca, NY.

NRPB (National Radiological Protection Board), 1991, *Radiological protection objectives for the land based disposal of solid radioactive wastes, consultative document*, NRPB-N279, Chilton, Oxon.

Pearce, David (and 12 other authors), 1993, *Blueprint 3, measuring sustainable development*, Earthscan, London.

Pezzey, John, 1992, Sustainability, an interdisciplinary guide, *Environmental Values*, 1, pp.321–62.

Rich, Lawrence, 1990, *Enterprise Neptune, saving the British coastline*, National Trust, London, (unpaginated).

Waterson, Merlin, 1994, *The National Trust: The First Hundred Years*, National Trust and BBC Books.

WCED (World Commission on Environment and Development), 1987, *Our Common Future*, Oxford University Press, Oxford, p.8.

Acknowledgements

David Cannadine

I am most grateful to Samantha Wyndham, the National Trust's Centenary Research Assistant, for her prompt and expert help, without which this essay could not have been written. I must also thank Margaret Willes and Merlin Waterson for their advice and encouragement. In fairness to them, I should add that the views expressed in this essay are entirely my own, and that no attempt has been made by anyone at the National Trust to influence them.

Adrian Phillips

My thanks are due to John Harvey, Iain Wilson, John Workman and the agents and Trust staff in the Gower, the Sherborne estate and the Lake District for their assistance in preparing this chapter.

David R. Cope

I am grateful to Janet Harley, the Trust's archivist, Iain Wilson, the Trust's Policy Research Co-ordinator, Rob Jarman and David Russell of the Trust's offices at Cirencester, Rick Minter of the Countryside Commission and to Justine Harbinson and Jonathan Selwyn of UK CEED for assistance in preparing this chapter. Roger Chorley, Partha Dasgupta, Andrew Johnson, Peter Laslett, Susan Owens, John Pezzey and Steve Thompson (Ottawa) have been willing (?) participants in discussions over the years which have helped, at least in *my* mind, to clarify some of the concepts discussed. The usual disclaimers apply.

I must also state my gratitude to the National Trust for the opportunities, as a boy, to enjoy the open spaces of the Surrey heaths and hills under their care and, later, for the influence of many such places, but in particular Bodiam and Corfe Castles, Studland Bay, Ballard Down and Golden Cap. The news that the Trust, through Enterprise Neptune, had secured the stretch of Dorset coast which includes Dancing Ledge was a particular pleasure, since it was here my adolescent and enduring fascination with fossils was first kindled.

Gerald Cadogan

I am grateful to the Trust for inviting me to contribute to this collection of essays. As the urgent invitation came during the winter, I have not been able to visit or re-visit as many properties as I should have liked. I have, however, had helpful conversations with Mark Barrington-Ward, Martin Drury, Tiffany Hunt, Tricia Lankester, Peter Nixon, Sir John Riddell, Bt, David Sekers, Lady Emma Tennant (who kindly read a draft and made many improvements) and Margaret Willes, and thank them warmly. I have drawn on their ideas freely but opinions and suggestions are my responsibility.

Index